WHAT IS THIS THING CALLED HAPPINESS?

According to an ancient and still popular view—sometimes known as 'eudaimonism'—a person's well-being, or quality of life, is ultimately determined by his or her level of happiness. According to this view, the happier a person is, the better off he or she is. The doctrine is controversial in part because the nature of happiness is controversial. In *What Is This Thing Called Happiness?* Fred Feldman presents a study of the nature and value of happiness. Part One contains critical discussions of the main philosophical and psychological theories of happiness. Feldman presents arguments designed to show that each of these theories is problematic. Part Two contains his presentation and defense of his own theory of happiness, which is a form of attitudinal hedonism. On this view, a person's level of happiness may be identified with the extent to which he or she takes pleasure in things. Feldman shows that if we understand happiness as he proposes, it becomes reasonable to suppose that a person's well-being is determined by his or her level of happiness. This view has important implications not only for moral philosophy, but also for the emerging field of hedonic psychology. Part Three contains discussions of some interactions between the proposed theory of happiness and empirical research into happiness.

Fred Feldman is Professor of Philosophy at the University of Massachusetts at Amherst.

What is This Thing Called Happiness?

Fred Feldman

OXFORD
UNIVERSITY PRESS

OXFORD
UNIVERSITY PRESS

Great Clarendon Street, Oxford OX2 6DP

Oxford University Press is a department of the University of Oxford.
It furthers the University's objective of excellence in research, scholarship,
and education by publishing worldwide in

Oxford New York

Auckland Cape Town Dar es Salaam Hong Kong Karachi
Kuala Lumpur Madrid Melbourne Mexico City Nairobi
New Delhi Shanghai Taipei Toronto

With offices in

Argentina Austria Brazil Chile Czech Republic France Greece
Guatemala Hungary Italy Japan Poland Portugal Singapore
South Korea Switzerland Thailand Turkey Ukraine Vietnam

Oxford is a registered trade mark of Oxford University Press
in the UK and in certain other countries

Published in the United States
by Oxford University Press Inc., New York

© Fred Feldman 2010

British Library Cataloguing in Publication Data

Data available

Library of Congress Control Number: 2009942570

Typeset by Laserwords Private Limited, Chennai, India
Printed in Great Britain
on acid-free paper by
MPG Books Group, Bodmin and King's Lynn, Norfolk

ISBN 978–0–19–957117–8 (Hbk)
ISBN 978–0–19–964593–0 (Pbk)

1 3 5 7 9 10 8 6 4 2

ACKNOWLEDGMENTS

Several years ago, more or less out of the blue, I received an email from Dale Miller, who was then the book review editor of *Utilitas*. Dale wanted to know if I would be interested in reviewing the Kahneman, Diener, and Schwarz anthology *Well-Being: The Foundations of Hedonic Psychology*. My immediate reaction was to write back to Dale and to tell him "Thanks, but no thanks." But I happened to notice a quotation attached at the bottom of his email. I read the quotation:

And, though quibbling about self-interest and motives, and objects of desire, and the greatest happiness of the greatest number, is but a poor employment for a grown man, it certainly hurts the health less than hard drinking, and is immeasurably more humane than cock-fighting.

(T. B. Macaulay)

I had never seen that before; I thought it was tremendously amusing. So I reconsidered Dale's invitation. I wrote back and said I would take a look at the Well-Being book. After looking at the book, I decided that I would accept the invitation to review it for *Utilitas*. The book contains a large collection of papers on happiness and welfare. The papers were written by psychologists, economists, sociologists and others. Many of the topics discussed in the book intersect with philosophical topics about happiness and welfare—topics about which I have been interested for many years. Subsequently, I gave some talks on some things I found especially interesting in the book. Then I decided to offer a graduate seminar on happiness. After the seminar, I worked up other papers. And in the end I decided that I would like to try my hand at writing a book about happiness, well-being, and interactions between psychological and philosophical research on happiness. The result of that decision is the book now in your hands.

So my first thanks go to Dale Miller. He's the one who opened the door for me. I am especially glad that he attached the amusing quotation from Macaulay at the bottom of his email. Had he not attached that quotation, this book would never have been written.

Several friends generously read and commented upon drafts of the whole manuscript. I am very grateful to all of them for their efforts on my behalf. Each of them gave helpful critical comments, though in some cases they may be disappointed to see that I did not revise the manuscript as they suggested. I am especially grateful to my old friends Michael Zimmerman and Noah Lemos. Each read the whole book; each gave extensive thoughtful criticism; each offered valuable encouragement. Owen McLeod read and discussed virtually every word of every draft of the book. He gave very valuable and extensive comments; in addition, he was a constant source of encouragement and support. My debt to him on this and other projects is enormous. Brad Skow attended my seminar on happiness several years ago when he was (alas, *briefly*) my colleague here at UMass. Recently Brad took the trouble to read and provide comments on a near final draft of the whole book. I am very grateful to him for his help, support, and encouragement. Perhaps in time I will find it possible to forgive him for moving to MIT.

Chris Heathwood, Jason Raibley, Dan Doviak, Justin Klocksiem and Ben Bradley read and commented on long sections of the book. In each case, these friends provided insightful and valuable criticism. I am also grateful to Gustaf Arrhenius for critical help at an earlier stage of the project.

In Chapter 4 I discuss the form of preferentism defended by Wayne Davis. Davis's presentation and defense of this view is outstandingly clear and persuasive. I criticized Davis's view in a paper that was published in an electronic festschrift for Wlodek Rabinowicz. I am grateful to Davis for helpful and enlightening correspondence on this topic.

In Chapter 5 of this book I criticize whole life satisfaction theories of happiness. Wayne Sumner, who is probably the most important philosophical defender of this sort of view, was kind enough to invite me up to Toronto to meet with his seminar and to give a talk at his department. I presented some early drafts of material that appears in Chapter 5 of this book. I thank Sumner for his hospitality, courtesy, and generous criticism. I also want to thank Jennifer Hawkins who provided quite a lot of very helpful insight into the workings of views like Sumner's. My discussion of whole life satisfactionism is much improved as a result of her suggestions.

In Chapter 6 I present my own theory of happiness—Attitudinal Hedonism. I presented some of this material as the Gail Stine Memorial Lecture at Wayne State University in 2006. I am very grateful to Bruce Russell and others at Wayne State for their kind invitation and their incisive and persistent criticism of my ideas. I gave related talks at Edmonton in 2006 and at Arizona State University in 2007. In each case I received helpful criticism from people I met. Peter de Marneffe and Sandra Woien raised a number of insightful objections and suggestions.

I was invited to give a talk at Calgary in 2006. Again, I presented a paper including ideas that eventually found their way into Chapter 5. I am grateful to my friend Ish Haji and others for probing questions and suggestions. Some material that now appears in Chapter 13 was presented as the Leonard Lecture at the University of Utah at Reno in 2007. I thank Ken Lucey for his hospitality and attention to my work on that occasion.

In Chapter 13 I discuss a question about the relevance of empirical research to philosophical conclusions. I presented an early version of some of these ideas as a keynote address at the SPAWN conference at Syracuse University in the summer of 2006. On that occasion I met Dan Haybron. I was familiar with quite a lot of his work on happiness and I enjoyed a helpful and enlightening conversation with him there. I thank Haybron for his attention to my work—especially since he has been at work on his own book *The Pursuit of Unhappiness* at the same time. A later paper on empirical–philosophical interactions was presented as the keynote address at the first Rocky Mountain Ethics Conference at the University of Colorado in the summer of 2008. On that occasion I received extensive, insightful, and very helpful comments from Alastair Norcross, Chris Heathwood, and several others.

I am also grateful to all the students who attended my seminar on happiness in the spring of 2006. I recall many helpful discussions with Dan Doviak, Jeremy Cushing, Meghan Masto, Scott Hill, Alex Sarch, Justin Klocksiem, and others. I suspect that I am overlooking someone here; I hope that if I have failed to mention someone who deserves to be mentioned, he or she will forgive me. I am grateful to everyone who participated.

Work on this book was supported by a generous fellowship from the National Endowment for the Humanities. I am tremendously grateful to the NEH for this support, without which it would have been nearly impossible to complete the book. I am also grateful to Phil Bricker (my department head) and Joel Martin (the dean of my college) and others at the University of Massachusetts for providing support during my tenure as an NEH fellow. My heartfelt thanks also to Shelly Kagan and Ernie Sosa for supporting my NEH application. I am also grateful to Dan Doviak for technical assistance in connection with the NEH fellowship.

Quite a lot of the material that appears here as Chapter 5 was published in *Theoria* in 2008 as 'Whole Life Satisfaction Concepts of Happiness.' I thank the editors of *Theoria* for permission to use that material here. Most of Chapter 4 appeared as 'Happiness and Subjective Desire Satisfaction: Wayne Davis's Theory of Happiness' in *Hommage a Wlodek: Philosophical Papers Dedicated to Wlodek Rabinowicz*, ed. T. Ronnow-Rasmussen, B. Petersson, J. Josefsson and D. Egonsson, 2007. That festschrift was published on line at www.fil.lu.se/hommageawlodek. My thanks to Toni Ronnow-Rasmussen and his co-editors for permission to reprint it here.

Although I have never been very enthusiastic about interdisciplinary collaboration, I originally hoped that some of my arguments would be of interest to researchers in hedonic psychology, economics, sociology and other related fields. This seemed fitting, since I was offering commentary and suggestions concerning the conceptual foundations of some of their work. I recognized from the outset that my own work would benefit from discussion with these empirical researchers. Accordingly, I wrote to quite a few of these people. I gave some background about myself and my project. I asked if they would be willing to discuss certain details of their work. In most cases I received no reply. In several cases I received short, brusque replies in which my intended correspondents made it clear that they had no interest in engaging in any correspondence with me. One indicated that she doubted that a philosopher would have the mathematical skills required to understand her work.

My attempts at interdisciplinary cooperation were modestly successful in the case of one distinguished colleague. Bernard van Praag, known as one of the founders of the "Leyden School" of economics, responded to my first letter in a remarkably courteous, frank, and helpful way. He indicated that he had little background in philosophy but tried to give some insight into his methodology. After a brief exchange of emails, he stopped responding to my letters. I am very grateful to van Praag for his helpful letters. He, among the non-philosophers I tried to engage, stands out as the only one who was willing to consider my questions.

I am also grateful to Sana Sheikh and Aline Sayer (both associated with the UMass Psychology Department) for their efforts to answer some questions about the interpretation of some statistics.

Peter Momtchiloff, Catherine Berry, Louise Sprake, and others at Oxford University Press deserve special mention here. Peter was invariably helpful and encouraging right from the start. Working with him and his colleagues at OUP has been an honor and a pleasure. I also thank Andrew Hawkey and Marcia Carlson for their assistance.

I want also to thank my neighbors Wally and Cornelia Reid for their thoughtful and generous hospitality. I consider myself very fortunate to have such wonderful neighbors as the Reids. Finally, I want to express my deepest gratitude to Elizabeth and Lois. I am grateful to Elizabeth for a steady stream of cheerful and encouraging emails and phone calls; also for her insight into the technicalities of some systems of psychotherapy. I am, as always, grateful to Lois for providing a peaceful environment in which I could work.

CONTENTS

PART III: IMPLICATIONS FOR THE EMPIRICAL STUDY OF HAPPINESS

DETAILED CONTENTS

CHAPTER 1

Some Puzzles about Happiness

1.1 *The Smile-Shaped Curve of Happiness*

A pair of economists recently published a paper in which they claimed that in general, whether in Europe or in North America, people start off being fairly happy in childhood, and then become less happy until they reach a minimum level of happiness when in their forties. They then gradually become happier again as they get older. As a result, the typical life-cycle happiness curve takes the shape of a U, or perhaps the shape of a smile.[1] That is an interesting and surprising result. It might have important implications for public policy, or for the evaluation of medical treatments. It might help to ease the worries of some unhappy middle-aged people.

The claims of these economists conflict with claims made by other psychologists, economists, and other researchers. Others have claimed that (again in general, and in the typical case) happiness steadily increases through life, so that instead of being represented by a U-shaped curve, happiness should be represented by an upward sloping line.[2] And surprisingly enough, yet other economists, after reviewing some of the same data sets that were used by the pair of economists mentioned above, came to the conclusion that happiness through life should be represented by an *inverted U-shaped curve*![3]

---

[1] Blanchflower and Oswald (2007). Their abstract contains this statement: 'Ceteris paribus, well-being reaches a minimum, on both sides of the Atlantic, in people's mid to late 40s.'

[2] See, for example, Yang Yang (2008). Yang's discussion is subtle and complex. She is evidently aware of a wide variety of complicating factors. Yet in broad outlines she seems to endorse the idea that (after age 18) people in the US tend to get steadily happier. In a news article on the University of Chicago website, her conclusion was reported as follows: 'Americans grow happier as they grow older, according to a University of Chicago study that is one of the most thorough examinations of happiness ever done in America.' See also Argyle (1999: 354–5).

[3] Easterlin (2006). Easterlin's abstract begins with these words: 'In the United States happiness rises slightly, on average, from ages 18 to midlife, and declines slowly thereafter.'

A curious observer might wonder about the evidence upon which the economists base their conclusion. How are they able to tell how happy people are at these various stages of their lives? The answer is that there are organizations whose mission is to gather data on happiness. These organizations have constructed detailed test instruments. They have armies of trained questioners. The questioners have been going out into the field to administer their instruments for many years and to huge numbers of respondents. The organizations have gathered, compiled, and published their results. The economists (or any other interested persons) can then study the data. They can use statistical methods to extract conclusions.

In the case of the U-shaped happiness curve, the economists in question used a couple of these data sets. For their information about patterns of happiness in Europe, they used data gathered and published by Eurobarometer. This is an organization supported by the European Union. Their mission is to gather all sorts of social and economic data concerning the countries of the EU. They publish comprehensive reports on a regular basis as well as "flash reports" on matters of immediate concern.

Among other things, Eurobarometer asks respondents to answer a question about "whole life satisfaction." Specifically (in the English language version of the questionnaire), the item is this:

Q1: On the whole, are you very satisfied, fairly satisfied, not very satisfied, or not at all satisfied with the life that you lead?

After studying and interpreting data on the answers that respondents gave on these questionnaires, the economists were able to conclude that the typical European has a life-cycle happiness curve that looks like a smile.[4]

One might be uneasy about the interpretation of the data. How can we be sure that a person's level of happiness varies in lock-step with "satisfaction with the life he or she leads"? Isn't it possible that some people are satisfied with the life they are leading even though they are not very happy? Couldn't there be a respondent who says, 'I am fully satisfied with *the life I am leading*; but I am very concerned about *the lives that others are leading*. The victims of genocide in Africa, for example, are leading terrible lives. I think about these people all the time. My concern for their misery makes me unhappy in spite of the fact that my own life is going quite well.' Such a person claims

---

[4] Yang's research was based on data from the General Social Survey of the National Opinion Research Center.

to be satisfied with the life he or she is leading and so would be counted as happy by the economists, yet the person also claims to be unhappy.

Suppose a respondent understands the question about life satisfaction to be asking whether he is *content* with the life he is leading. He thinks the questioner is asking him whether he has any complaints about his life—whether he thinks he is being short-changed. Suppose this respondent considers all the ways in which lives can be ruined—poverty, disease, oppression, accidents, and so on. Suppose he sees that he has managed to avoid all these disasters. He thinks he has no grounds for complaint. He thinks it would be disgraceful, under the circumstances, for him to complain. He says he is satisfied with his life. His response might be sincere. It's not just that he prefers not to complain; in fact, he feels that he has no basis for complaint. But at the same time this respondent might not actually be *happy*. He might never be in a cheerful mood; he might never actually *enjoy* anything; he might never have a smile on his face. His friends might consider him to be a pretty gloomy person.

Isn't it also possible that some people are very happy even though they are not completely satisfied with the lives they are leading? Couldn't there be a respondent who says, 'I am happy. I am always in good spirits. I have a lot of money, a big house, and a fast car. But I am a striver. I always want more, more, more. I want to have more money, a bigger house, a faster car. I think I would become complacent if I ever allowed myself to be satisfied with what I've got. And I think complacency would mark the end of my achievements. So I never allow myself to feel satisfied.' This person would be counted as unhappy (because he claims that he is not satisfied with the life he is leading), yet he considers himself to be very happy.

I mentioned that other researchers have concluded that happiness steadily increases through life. How did they come to their conclusion? In fact, some of them made use of different data sets. Some of these other data sets are based on responses to different questionnaires. The other questionnaires may not contain the Eurobarometer question about life satisfaction. One of these questionnaires contains a question roughly equivalent to this:

Q2: If you had the opportunity to live your life over, would you want to change many things in your life, or some things, or nothing at all?

If the respondent says that he would not want to change anything, he is understood to be saying that he is happy, whereas if he says he would want to change many things, he is understood to be unhappy.

But, again, there is reason to worry about the interpretation of the question. Couldn't there be a person who is quite happy even though she would not want to live her life over again without any change? Isn't it easy to imagine an elderly person who would say, 'I was happy. It was a good life. But if I had it to do over again, I would not want to live the same life. That would be boring. I would not enjoy it so much the second time around. So I would want to try something different. Perhaps I would want to do something more adventurous; perhaps I would want to live in a different part of the world; perhaps I would want to engage in projects that I in fact never pursued in my actual life.' If such a response is possible, it shows that a person could be happy even though she would want to change a lot of things if she had the chance to live her life over again.

The opposite reaction is also possible. I think there might be a person who says that he had overlooked or misunderstood many of the best opportunities that had come his way. He might say this: 'If I had it to do over again, I would want to live pretty much the same life as the life I actually lived. I would not want to change much. But if given the chance, I would pay attention to all the good things that came my way. This time I would not allow myself to be swallowed by melancholy and sadness. I would not permit myself to sink into depression as in fact I did in the life I actually led.' Such a person was in fact not happy but, if given the opportunity, would want to live the same (or *nearly the same*) life over again.

A thoughtful subject might be perplexed by the question. He might want more information about what is involved in "living your life over again." Does it mean living *precisely the same life* over again, right down to the most specific actions and thoughts? In that case, the person living the life would have no way of knowing that it was the second time around. If, in your actual life, you never thought 'here we go again,' then in the re-lived life you would never think 'here we go again.' You would think whatever thoughts you thought the first time around. It's hard to see why anyone would think that those who want to live their lives over again are any happier than those who want to try something different.

On the other hand, 'living your life over again' might just mean being born again, and having another chance to grow up. This could come with full recognition that it was in fact a "second chance" and with intact memories of the previous life. A person might be interested in living such a life because now, with insight gained from experience, he might resolve to do things differently. Especially if a person has been very unhappy, this might seem like a wonderful opportunity.

My point here is simple: 'If given the chance to live your life over again, would you want to change much?' is an obscure and deeply puzzling question. Different subjects could interpret it in different ways. It is very hard to see what would justify saying that answers to this question give us insight into levels of happiness.

There are further questions. We have seen that some conclusions about happiness are based on data about whole life satisfaction. Apparently conflicting conclusions about happiness are based on data about the desire to live one's life over again unchanged. But one could certainly wonder whether *being satisfied with one's life* is the same thing as *wanting to live it over again unchanged*. And if these are different (as the divergent test results suggest), then it cannot be the case that both of them are the same thing as happiness. Happiness can't be the same as two distinct things. Which one, if either, can properly be identified with happiness?

These thoughts give rise to even more fundamental questions about happiness. What could justify the assumption that a person's level of happiness at a time is equivalent to his or her level of satisfaction with the life he or she is leading? Is happiness the same thing as life satisfaction? What could justify the notion that happy people would want to live their lives over again pretty much unchanged? Is happiness the same thing as desiring to live the same life again? Or is happiness something else, but something that varies together with life satisfaction or the desire to live the same life again? And, if happiness varies with one of these things, how could we demonstrate that these variables are linked in this way? Wouldn't that require that we have some independent way to measure levels of happiness, so that we could then check to see if levels of happiness in fact do vary together with levels of life satisfaction? And (most fundamentally) doesn't all of this at bottom require that we have some idea of what happiness actually is?

1.2 *Troubles about Happiness*

'Does the typical person's happiness through life take the shape of a smile?' 'Are people happier when they are more satisfied with their lives?' 'If a person is happy, would he want to live his life over again pretty much unchanged?' These are undoubtedly important questions.

To the philosopher, other questions are even more important. These are the deeper questions: 'What is happiness?', 'Is there a way to measure how happy a person is at a time?', 'Does happiness invariably make a person better off?' These are questions about the nature and value of happiness. This book is an attempt to grapple with deeper questions such as these.

It might seem that we should turn directly to these intriguing philosophical questions about the nature and value of happiness. However, before we proceed, I want to point out some troubling sources of misunderstanding.

1. One of the greatest sources of misunderstanding in the happiness literature is the fact that two seriously different sorts of enquiry are confused *under the title 'the attempt to determine what happiness is'*. On the one hand, there is a question about the most promising *causes* of happiness. At the beginning of his book about happiness, Michael Eysenck has a section entitled 'What is Happiness?'.[5] In this context, he says that in an earlier era philosophers used to claim that 'durable satisfaction and happiness could be achieved only by pursuing a moral and religious existence.'[6] He goes on to mention that Locke and Bentham argued that 'happiness is based on the number of pleasures in one's life.'[7] He tells us that his young daughter had said that happiness is love.[8] He claims that Zeno maintained that the surest route to happiness involves getting rid of desires that cannot easily be satisfied, while Aristotle said that 'the main way of increasing happiness is to retain all of one's desires, but to put more effort into satisfying them.'[9]

Although I realize that some people talk this way, the title of the section ('What is Happiness?') seems to me to be profoundly misleading. Eysenck is not citing views about "what happiness is." He is citing views about what is likely to cause happiness, or to increase happiness; or views about what happiness is "based upon" or how we can achieve happiness.

The attempt to determine what happiness is (as I use the terminology) is not an enquiry into the causes of happiness. Rather, it is an attempt to figure out the nature of happiness—what are the essential features of the state that people are in when they have finally managed

---

[5] Michael Eysenck, *Happiness: Facts and Myths* (1990).   [6] Eysenck (1990: 3).
[7] Ibid.   [8] Ibid. 4.
[9] Ibid. Eysenck does not identify the place where Aristotle says this.

to get happy? A good answer to this question might come in the form of a definition or philosophical analysis of the concept of happiness. Thus—just to give some examples for purposes of illustration—an answer might look like one of these:

D1: x is happy at t =df. x is feeling more pleasure than pain at t.
D2: x is happy at t =df. x is satisfied with his life as a whole at t.
D3: x is happy at t =df. more than half of the desires that x has at t are being fulfilled.
D4: x is happy at t =df. x is in a bright, cheerful, upbeat, "positive" mental state at t.

Each of these definitions purports to give an account of the nature of happiness. It does this by making a claim about the meaning of the word 'happy.' None of them says anything about likely causes of happiness.

Maybe there is no suitable other phrase in English that means precisely what 'x is happy' means. In that case it would be difficult to give a helpful definition of happiness. We would have to find some other way to give an account of the nature of happiness. Perhaps we could identify it by appeal to its functional role—its standard causes and effects. We might be able to say that happiness is precisely that mental state that is typically caused by such-and-such stimuli, and typically results in such-and-such responses. This would not give an account of the nature of happiness, but it would at least help us to focus on the subject of our concern. Perhaps when we reflect directly on that very state, we will be able to discern its nature. Other options might be possible. But the fundamental point would remain: our aim would be to discover the nature of happiness rather than to give suggestions about ways to increase it.

If we believed in a strict division of labor on these matters, we could say that we have two distinct projects that call for two distinct workforces. One of these projects is the attempt to discover the causes of happiness. This calls for empirical research of the sort normally done by psychologists. The results of the research might be surprising and interesting. It might have considerable practical value. Any conclusions reached would be at best contingent facts about what happens to cause happiness. I think it is misleading to describe any of this as an enquiry into the "nature of happiness." People who pursue this research are not trying to find out "what happiness is."

The other project is the attempt to discover what happiness is; that is, the attempt to give an account of the nature of the state that is necessarily distinctive of all and only happy people (or other happy creatures, if there are any). This job calls for conceptual analysis—or possibly conceptual revision or construction. These are jobs traditionally done by philosophers.

It seems to me that the philosophical project has priority over the empirical project. Suppose an empirical researcher wants to find out what causes happiness, or what is the underlying neurophysiological basis of happiness. Insofar as the concept of happiness is obscure, it will be difficult for her to work up experiments that will test hypotheses about the causes or bases of happiness. Suppose she forges ahead anyway and finds that neurophysiological state X is reliably associated with some psychological state that she takes to be happiness. One crucial problem is that there will be some uncertainty about whether the psychological state that is associated with neurophysiological state X is really *happiness*, or whether it is something else that sometimes or often coincides with happiness. Maybe the researcher has found the cause of "positive affect" or "satisfied desires" or "pleasure." If these things are distinct from happiness, she has not found the underlying basis of happiness.

It appears to me, then, that before anyone can undertake empirical research into the cause of happiness, or the underlying neurophysiological basis of happiness, or the measurement of happiness, there must be some shared understanding of the nature of happiness. The researcher must have a clear idea about what happiness is before she can set about trying to figure out what causes it. In this way, the philosophical project has priority over the empirical project. I will return to this topic later.

In any case, it may be useful to ask the reader to note this well: *my aim here is to enquire into the nature of happiness; the goal is not to discover what is likely to cause or increase happiness.*

2. Even if we recognize that our aim is to elucidate the nature of happiness rather than its typical causes, there are further sources of misunderstanding. One of these is an alleged ambiguity. Sometimes when we say that a person is happy we are simply describing his mental state. We are saying (if D1 is correct) merely that he is feeling more pleasure than pain. If we use the word 'happy' in this way, our statement (by itself) does not imply that the person is in a *good* state, or that he is *better off* than he would have been if he had been less happy. Those evaluative conclusions do not follow directly from the statement that he is happy.

Many philosophers claim that the word 'happy' has another use. According to them, the word is also used in a fundamentally evaluative sense. When used in this sense, the statement that a certain person is happy means that that person has 'positive welfare,' or 'is doing well.'

Let us (just for present purposes) mark this difference by using two different terms for these two different senses of 'happy.' Let us use the term 'happy(D)' to indicate that we are using 'happy' in its descriptive sense. To say that a person is happy(D) is just to describe him—to say that he is experiencing some (not yet specified) psychological state. Let us use the term 'happy(V)' to indicate that we are using 'happy' in its evaluative sense. To say that a person is happy(V) is to say that he is doing well, having positive welfare, having some positive amount of prudential value.[10]

'Happy(D)' and 'happy(V)' are not synonyms. This can be seen easily enough. Consider these two statements:

1. A person is happy(V) if and only if he is happy(D).
2. A person is happy(V) if and only if he is happy(V).

Statement (1) is a controversial claim in axiology. It purports to give necessary and sufficient conditions for positive welfare. According to (1), you will have a positive level of welfare if and only if you are in a certain mental state. In effect, (1) purports to tell us what makes someone's life go well for him; and it says that a certain mental state—happiness(D)—is necessary and sufficient for positive welfare. Although some may quibble about the terminology, it is now commonplace among philosophers to say that statements like (1) express "eudaimonism."[11] This is the thesis that "happiness(D) is the good." Eudaimonism may be true, but it is certainly not true merely as a matter of definition. Thus, (1) is controversial.

Statement (2) is not at all controversial. It is a complete triviality. It just says that your life is going well for you if and only if your life is going well for you. This would be true if eudaimonism were true; but

---

[10] In Easterlin (2005: 29), 'Building a Better Theory of Well-Being,' Richard A. Easterlin starts by saying 'I take the terms "well-being", "utility", "happiness", "life satisfaction", and "welfare" to be interchangeable.' Clearly, no philosopher since the time of G. E. Moore would take the evaluative terms in this list ('welfare,' 'well-being') to be interchangeable with the descriptive terms ('utility,' 'life satisfaction'). My point above is that 'happiness' has been used in both ways. I am trying to point out the distinction between its use as a descriptive term and its use as an evaluative term.

[11] I discuss different uses of the term 'eudaimonism' after Chapter 8, in Appendix D, 'Five Grades of Demonic Possession.'

it would also be true if eudaimonism were false. Indeed, it would be true under virtually all conceivable circumstances.[12] Since (1) and (2) differ in these ways, they are not synonymous statements. And since they are not synonymous statements, and the only difference between them is that (1) contains 'happy(D)' where (2) contains 'happy(V),' we can see that 'happy(D)' and 'happy(V)' must not be synonymous terms.

With this distinction firmly in place, it will be possible to clarify my aim here and thus to avoid a second source of trouble. Thus, I ask the reader to note this well too: *my aim at the outset is to enquire into the nature of happiness(D); only much later will we begin to consider the question whether those who are happy(D) are also happy(V).*

Throughout Part I of this book, I will be discussing theories about the nature of happiness(D). I will have to refer to happiness(D) many times. I will discuss many cases in which I will want to give my views about whether some character is happy(D). I will make claims about the implications of various theories of happiness(D). For utmost clarity, I would have to use the word 'happy(D)' and cognates thousands of times. Thousands of occurrences of the word 'happy(D)' would make the typography look ugly. I prefer to avoid this ugliness. I would rather use the neater word 'happy', but always in such a way that it is synonymous with 'happy(D).' Thus, throughout these chapters, I will use 'happy' and cognates in the descriptive sense. I will never use them in the evaluative sense.[13] Thus I ask the reader to note this as well: *the word 'happy' will be used from here on in this book in its descriptive or "mental state" sense; it is not used in its evaluative sense.*

3. It is by now a commonplace among writers in the happiness literature to say that 'happy' (even when restricted to its mental state sense) is hopelessly vague. Some might go so far as to say that this vagueness in the terminology makes it pointless to try to distinguish among true and false theories about the nature of happiness. One who accepts this view might say that each theory offers an explication of some possible new concept of happiness. It's as if the advocate of the theory were simply stipulating that when he uses the word 'happy,' it

---

[12] If some form of expressivism were true about 'good life,' then perhaps (2) would be some sort of expression of positive emotion; in that case it might lack truth value altogether.

[13] There are a few occasions later on where it can't be avoided. I will try to keep it to a minimum.

will mean just what he says it means. Thus, the advocate of the theory is not claiming to be giving a true account of the nature of happiness. He may think that in light of the vagueness of the terminology, truth is out of the question here.

According to one popular way of viewing the matter, each theory of happiness just calls our attention to one of the many phenomena confusedly going under the name 'happiness' in ordinary language. Advocates of a given theory should be seen as claiming no more than that there is some utility or advantage in focusing on their preferred concept of happiness. Thus, for example, consider someone who says that to be happy is to judge that your life as a whole is going well.[14] We might view this person as doing no more than encouraging us to revise our thinking about happiness. Instead of taking happiness to be a blurry smorgasbord of loosely connected "positive emotions," he is proposing a precisification. He wants us to start afresh with happiness. From now on, he suggests, we should think of happiness in a new way, precisely as he has suggested. We should say that a person is happy if and only if that person judges his life as a whole to be going well. Perhaps the philosopher thinks that if we understand happiness in this revisionist way, we will then be able to endorse a precisified form of eudaimonism. In other words, he may be suggesting that if we use the word 'happy' as he proposes, then it will be correct to say that someone's life is going well if and only if he is happy. Thus, there is a practical advantage to adopting the new stipulation about the meaning of 'happy.' It makes it possible for advocates of a certain axiological view to express that view clearly; it also makes it possible for them to characterize themselves as eudaimonists.

Another philosopher or psychologist might think that so long as we persist in using the word 'happy' as we do in ordinary English, there will be no hope for progress in the measurement of happiness. Measuring happiness will be like measuring intelligence back in the days before the invention of the IQ test—in each case our efforts are stymied at least in part because the terminology is so vague. This philosopher or psychologist thus proposes a different rationale for conceptual revision. He is suggesting that if we use the word 'happy' in the new and precise way that he proposes, then it will be possible to distinguish clearly between people to whom the word does apply and those to whom it does not, and it will be

---

[14] Several theories of this sort are discussed below in Chapter 5 and Appendices A and B.

possible to determine, for each person, precisely how happy he or she is.[15]

So here we have another source of trouble: many contributors to the happiness literature assume that (strictly speaking) there really is no such thing as happiness; that the term 'happy' is just too vague for that; and that at most we can engage in some sort of revisionist construction. They may think that theories of happiness cannot be evaluated for *truth*; at most they can be evaluated for *usefulness* or some other pragmatic value. 'Let us adopt my theory of happiness, for if we do so we will be able to measure (the thing that I call) happiness.'

It is not clear to me that 'happy' is really in such bad semantic shape. Of course, philosophers and psychologists use the word in many different ways. However, I am inclined to think that when ordinary people, unperverted by semantical revisionism, use the word to indicate a mental state, there is a single mental state that they mean to indicate.[16] But of course this is something that needs to be investigated. It cannot be assumed. My point here is that we should not assume that theories of happiness cannot be evaluated for truth, or that there really is no such thing as happiness. My view is that we should assume that 'happy' is innocent until proven guilty. Let us beware of this.

1.3 *Why Worry about Happiness?*

The concept of happiness (understood as some sort of mental state) is important and worthy of careful study. There are several reasons for thinking this.

a. Some philosophers think that the good life for a person is the happy life. They think that "happiness is The Good." A superficial reading of some passages in Aristotle strongly suggests this view. Speaking of 'the highest of all goods achievable by action,' Aristotle says that 'the general run of men and people of superior refinement say that it is happiness, and identify living well and doing well with being happy.'[17]

---

[15] Further discussion of this line of thought can be found after Chapter 5, in Appendix B, where I discuss the idea that happiness can be identified with whatever is being measured by the happiness tests.

[16] Later in the book, in Chapter 6, I give an account of the phenomenon I have in mind here.

[17] *NE* I.4. Of course, the translation is very controversial. Many commentators would say that the choice of 'happy' here misrepresents Aristotle's point.

He goes on to say that this is all just 'a platitude, and a clearer account [of the nature of happiness] is still desired.'[18] This has been taken to be an early statement of the view I called 'eudaimonism'—the view that happiness is ultimately what makes a person's life go well for that person.

Wayne Sumner defends a modified version of this view in *Welfare, Happiness, and Ethics.*[19] He does not say that a person's welfare level is straightforwardly determined by his happiness level. He says that a person's welfare level is determined by his 'authentic, autonomous happiness level.' (Sumner's conception of happiness is discussed in much greater detail later in Chapter 5.)

Some empirical researchers seem to take it as obvious that what makes a person's life go well for that person is happiness. Thus, for example, when he concludes his discussion of "objective happiness" and its measurement, Daniel Kahneman optimistically predicts that 'A combination of methods will eventually be available to characterize the objective well-being of individuals and groups . . . and to provide a criterion for the evaluation of economic and social policy.'[20] It seems clear that Kahneman's work presupposes that happiness (or his preferred "objective happiness") is The Good. Were this not the case, it would be hard to see why the measurement of well-being would be so directly connected to the measurement of objective happiness; it would be impossible to see why objective happiness would provide a criterion for the evaluation of economic and social policy.

b. A closely related view concerns prudential rationality. According to a popular view, the prudentially rational action for a person is the one that maximizes his or her own (expected) happiness level. Insofar as we are interested in prudential rationality, we have reason to be interested in the nature of happiness.

c. Another closely related view concerns moral obligation. Mill said:

The creed which accepts as the foundation of morals, Utility, or the Greatest Happiness Principle, holds that actions are right in proportion as they tend to promote happiness, wrong as they tend to produce the reverse of happiness. By happiness is intended pleasure, and the absence of pain; by unhappiness, pain, and the privation of pleasure.[21]

---

[18] Aristotle *NE* I.6.   [19] Sumner (1996).
[20] Kahneman (1999: 22).   [21] Mill (1957: 10).

In this, Mill was following Bentham, and saying something that many utilitarians have said. On this view, moral rightness is explained by appeal to the concept of happiness. In more modern formulations, the claim would be that an action is morally right if and only if it maximizes the happiness of all those who would be affected by it. (In the second sentence of the quoted passage Mill seems to give an account of the nature of happiness. It seems to be the hedonic theory of happiness. It is the subject of Chapter 2.)

d. Even philosophers who have not been utilitarians have claimed that happiness is somehow or other related to moral rightness. Some might say that eternal happiness in heaven is the reward for morally right behavior here on earth.

e. Happiness might be important for the understanding of human behavior. It's at least conceivable that in our voluntary behavior we strive to make ourselves happier. If so, it might be possible to explain some behavior by showing how the agent thought that doing it would make him happier.

f. Bentham and others have suggested that "the general happiness" figures in the justification of legislation. It's appropriate to pass a law (on this view) if that will help to enhance the happiness of the citizenry. In a passage I have already cited, Kahneman seems to express his acceptance of a closely related idea.

g. Some have said that we have a right to happiness; or at least a right to the pursuit of happiness. You can see evidence of this in the Declaration of Independence where it says that it is self-evident that we have a right to the pursuit of happiness.

h. There is currently a fairly impressive upsurge of interest in "hedonic psychology" or "positive psychology." This is often taken to be the psychological study of happiness (and other "positive" emotions). A lot of this work in psychology is interesting and (in some cases) kind of surprising. People are studying such things as the following. Is happiness an actual psychological phenomenon? If so, what is the best way to measure a person's level of happiness at a moment? How good are people at recognizing or estimating their own current level of happiness? How good are they at estimating their own future happiness? What factors tend to distort a person's estimate of his own happiness? Are happiness levels different from country to country? (The answer to this last question seems to be 'yes.')[22] Or from gender to gender? Or age to age? (As I indicated at the outset, this last question has been answered in several conflicting ways by different researchers.) Or do the happiness levels differ from income level to income level? What about the hedonic treadmill? What about the hedonic paradox? One feature of this work that I find troubling is the fact that some psychologists seem to be content to pursue their research into happiness without first having clarified the nature of the item they mean to be studying. A friend once told me that one of the most prominent advocates of hedonic psychology had adopted the policy of first developing ways of measuring happiness, and only then (if at all) worrying about what happiness is. This seems to indicate a complete perversion of research priorities.

i. Anyway, happiness is interesting and (as we will see) puzzling. We like it but don't have any clear conception of what it is. Many philosophers and others have written about it. The enquiry needs no further justification.

1.4 *What's in This Book*

Part I of this book is devoted to critical discussion of the most important theories about the nature of happiness. I start in Chapter 2 with a discussion of a simple form of hedonism about happiness. Some passages in Mill suggest that he may have accepted this view. It has also been found in Bentham and Sidgwick. According to this view, a person is happy at a time if and only if he is feeling more pleasure than pain at that time; a person's life can be described as happy if and only if the person experienced more pleasure than pain throughout his life. Hedonism about happiness is currently not a popular view. I explain and evaluate some alleged difficulties for the view.

In Chapters 3 and 4, I discuss some views according to which happiness is to be explained by appeal to facts about preferences or desires. I classify all such theories as forms of preferentism. Preferentism comes in many varieties. In his paper on 'Objective Happiness' Daniel Kahneman seems to endorse an unusual theory that has affinities to preferentism. He seems to say that there is really only one desire that counts when it comes to happiness, and this is the desire for your

---

[22] You can find a chart of happiness levels by country on the website: <http://thehappiness show.com/HappiestCountries.htm>.

present experience to continue. If you have this desire, then you are happier. And this seems to be the case whether your desire is satisfied or not. In Chapter 3, I explain and comment upon Kahneman's theory.

According to more typical forms of preferentism, every desire counts. No matter what you want, if you are getting it, then you are happier. This view was very starkly stated a while back by V. J. McGill. It was carefully developed and defended by Wayne Davis. In Chapter 4, after explaining how the theory is supposed to work, I present a series of arguments designed to show that getting what you want is one thing; being happy about it is something else. In other words, I try to show that preferentism (at least in the form discussed here) is false.

Nowadays, the most popular approach to happiness involves saying that to be happy is to be satisfied with your life as a whole. One version of this "Whole Life Satisfaction" theory was formulated by Hastings Rashdall, who said, 'Happiness represents satisfaction with one's existence as a whole.'[23] The classic statement of this view can be found in Wladislaw Tatarkiewicz's monumental work *Analysis of Happiness*. He says 'Happiness is to be satisfied with life as a whole . . .'[24] He specifically adds that this satisfaction must be complete, lasting, 'touching upon the whole of life, and justified.'[25] A remarkable number of recent philosophers and psychologists have adopted this conception of happiness. Careful reflection on their work shows that Whole Life Satisfactionism can be developed in dozens (perhaps *hundreds*) of distinct forms. They are the topic of Chapter 5. I claim that they are all false.

I have to admit that I feel strongly about Whole Life Satisfactionism. I think it is deeply and hopelessly confused. Although I feel confident that the objections raised in Chapter 5 demonstrate that this sort of approach does not work, I feel the need to drive even more nails into the coffin. In Appendix A, I present some further objections to Whole Life Satisfactionism. These are based on some puzzles about time. When advocates of the view speak of satisfaction with one's 'whole life', do they really mean (as Tatarkiewicz actually says) *the whole thing; from beginning to end*? If so, the view is incredible. In Appendix B, I discuss the idea that since the concept of happiness is so obscure, we might as well just say that to be happy is to get a high score on the happiness test. I explain why this suggestion is untenable.

---

[23] Cited in Tatarkiewicz (1976: 8).   [24] Ibid. 9.   [25] Ibid. 8, 12.

In Part II of the book, I turn to the exposition and defense of my own position about the nature and value of happiness. Perhaps surprisingly, my view is a form of hedonism. I claim that happiness can be analyzed by appeal to the concepts of *pleasure* and *pain*. However, my account differs in an essential way from the sensory hedonism discussed in Chapter 2. My view makes use of the concepts of *attitudinal pleasure* and *attitudinal displeasure*, not the concepts of sensory pleasure and pain. I claim, in Chapter 6, that to be happy is to take pleasure in things; or, more precisely, to take on balance more occurrent intrinsic attitudinal pleasure than displeasure in things. The relevant concept of attitudinal pleasure is explained in some detail.

Writers on happiness often assert that 'happy' is ambiguous in ordinary English. In Appendix C, I discuss this idea. I cite some instances in which someone has claimed that 'happy' has three or four senses. I try to explain (following Quine) how difficult it is to prove that a term is ambiguous. Some tests for ambiguity are proposed. Their results in connection with 'happy' are assessed. I conclude by making some suggestions about what the word means as a term of ordinary English.

In Chapter 7, I compare the implications of my theory of happiness to the implications of theories discussed in earlier chapters. I also defend my view against a variety of objections. I say some things in defense of my view that the proposed concept of happiness is not merely a stipulation—it's not merely offered as something we might choose to mean by 'happy.' My view is that the proposed concept of happiness corresponds closely to the concept of happiness already in place as a part of common-sense psychology.

Once we have a sufficiently precise and carefully articulated concept of happiness, then we face the axiological question: is happiness (so construed) The Good? Or part of The Good? Or simply not relevant to individual human welfare? In Chapter 8, I consider the plausibility of a form of eudaimonism that makes essential use of the concept of happiness presented and defended in Chapters 6 and 7. A substantial part of the chapter is devoted to trying to explain the relevant concept of *welfare*.

Some critics might be troubled by my use of the term 'eudaimonism' to refer to the theory that individual welfare tracks ordinary happiness, as I have claimed.[26] In Appendix D, I explain some of the confusion concerning the term 'eudaimonism.' I try to make my own use of the term clear.

---

[26] Thanks to Jason Raibley for impressing the importance of this point on me.

According to eudaimonism, the good life is the happy life; the happier you are, the better your life is going for you. Critics have presented a number of troubling objections to this eudaimonistic thesis. In Chapters 9 and 10, I discuss some of the most important objections. These involve people who are happy but whose happiness seems somehow defective. Thus we have (in Chapter 9) cases involving people who are happy but only because they have been coercively socialized into acceptance of values that are not authentically their own. Are such people living the good life? And we have (in Chapter 10) a case involving a person who is happy in a life of outstanding immorality. Is he living the good life?

A number of philosophers have suggested either that we in fact do have, or that we ought to have, some sort of "authority" over our own happiness. The claim about authority is often linked to the liberal traditional in political philosophy. In Chapter 11, I distinguish among several different sorts of authority. Some are epistemic; others are causal. I try to show that there is no clear sense in which it would be correct to say that we have very much epistemic authority over our own happiness. Likewise, some suggestions about causal authority seem very implausible. But I suggest that if we understand the concept of happiness correctly, we can see that there is some slight chance that a person might be able to exercise a tiny bit of a certain limited kind of causal authority over his own happiness.

In Part III of the book, I extend the discussion into some areas that bear on interactions between empirical research concerning happiness and philosophical inquiry into the same phenomenon.

I have presented and defended an analysis of the concept of happiness. I have argued that this concept of happiness is at least close to what we might call 'the common-sense concept of happiness.' I have also claimed that this concept of happiness figures in an attractive form of eudaimonism. It's not totally crazy to say that happiness—so understood—is The Good. If my claims are right, or even close to being right, then there very well could be some interest in devising a practically useful method for measuring this sort of happiness. I have in mind some sort of test instrument that would enable researchers to determine how happy a person is at a time. Such an instrument would be ideal if it could in addition enable us to make and justify cardinal comparative interpersonal happiness judgments. In other words, if it could enable us to say with some confidence that one person is twice as happy as another. In Chapter 12, I explain why typical test instruments currently in use fail to measure happiness. I go on to sketch a new system of measurement and I discuss the question whether the proposed system would be an improvement over existing systems.

According to popular reports, psychologists and economists in the new Hedonic Psychology movement have done exciting empirical research concerning happiness. One interesting area of research concerns a question about the neurophysiological basis of happiness. Does happiness in the mind correspond to some observable, measurable phenomenon in the brain? In Chapter 13, I discuss some of this research. I focus on questions concerning the relevance of the research to long-standing philosophical questions. Does the empirical research establish that happiness is "real"? Or that interpersonal utility comparisons are possible? Or that happiness is a natural kind and not merely a figment of "folk psychology"? In each case, I explain why I think that the empirical research has no direct relevance to any such question.

The final chapter contains a recapitulation of the main themes of the book.

PART I

SOME THINGS THAT HAPPINESS ISN'T

CHAPTER 2

Sensory Hedonism about Happiness

2.1 *Bentham, Mill, and Sidgwick on Happiness*

The term 'hedonism' can be used to refer to a variety of different views. I suspect that, in its most common use, 'hedonism' refers to the theory that "pleasure is The Good." This is a theory in axiology; it purports to identify the fundamental sources of value. This view is also sometimes known as 'ethical hedonism.' In a different use, 'hedonism' refers to a theory about motivation. This is "psychological hedonism"—the view that people are always ultimately motivated by a desire to get pleasure, or a desire to avoid pain. But the term 'hedonism' can also be used to refer to a theory about the nature of happiness (understood here to be some sort of mental state). This would be the view that the concept of happiness can be fully explained by appeal to the concepts of pleasure and pain. Hedonism about happiness is the topic of this chapter.

Commentators often cite Bentham as an early advocate of hedonism about happiness. It's not entirely clear that this is correct. Bentham's style is notoriously obscure. In some passages he seems willing to use the words 'pleasure,' 'happiness,' 'benefit,' 'advantage,' 'good,' and so on more or less interchangeably.[1] But there are a few places in which he seems to endorse a hedonistic theory of happiness. For example, in Chapter VII, Para. I, he says, 'What happiness consists of we have already seen: enjoyment of pleasures, security from pains.'[2]

Mill is more explicit. In a widely quoted passage near the beginning of Chapter 2 of *Utilitarianism*, Mill seems to be endorsing a form of hedonism about happiness when he says:

The creed which accepts as the foundation of morals, Utility, or the Greatest Happiness Principle, holds that actions are right in proportion as they tend to

---

[1] Bentham (1948: 2). Originally published in 1789.   [2] Ibid. 70.

promote happiness, wrong as they tend to produce the reverse of happiness. *By happiness is intended pleasure, and the absence of pain*; by unhappiness, pain, and the privation of pleasure.[3]

At first glance, it may appear that Mill is offering an answer to our question about the nature of happiness.[4] And it may also appear that the answer he is offering is this:

H1: x is happy =df. x is experiencing pleasure and the absence of pain.

If taken as an account of the nature of happiness, H1 is clearly unacceptable. It should be obvious that the stated condition for happiness is not necessary. A person can be happy even though she is not experiencing pleasure and the absence of pain at that time. Consider the case of Grandma. Suppose that Grandma has a mild case of arthritis. From time to time she feels some pain in her joints. Thus, she does not experience "the absence of pain." (I assume that a person experiences the absence of pain at a time only if she takes note of the fact that she is not experiencing any pain at that time.) Therefore, she does not satisfy the condition stated in Mill's definition. (It is not clear to me that she has "security from pains," and so it is not clear to me whether she satisfies Bentham's criterion.) Surely it would be preposterous for someone to claim, on this basis, that Grandma is not happy. Surely she might be happy even though she sometimes experiences "the presence of pain." Indeed, it seems obvious that she could have been very happy at a certain moment when she was experiencing some pain. Talk of "the absence of pain" should be avoided.

It may appear that this problem is due largely to Mill's sloppy formulation. In his own very similar account of the nature of happiness, Sidgwick is somewhat more careful. He says, 'by "greatest possible Happiness" we understand the greatest attainable surplus of pleasure over pain.'[5] The clear implication here is that to be happy is to have some surplus of pleasure over pain. We will need to take a moment to say something about what such a "surplus" could be.

Let's suppose that whenever a person experiences some sensory pleasure, the pleasure has some phenomenally given sensory intensity.

---

[3] Mill (1957: 10). *Utilitarianism* was originally published in 1863. Emphasis added, FF.

[4] On the other hand, the quoted remark might be nothing more than the introduction of a stipulative abbreviation. Perhaps Mill was not intending to give an account of the nature of happiness. Perhaps he just wanted to save some ink on later pages. Furthermore, we know that later in the book he says a lot of very strange things about happiness, and some of them suggest that upon reflection he would not want to endorse the idea seemingly present here.

[5] Sidgwick (1962: 120–1). *The Methods of Ethics* was first published in 1874.

Intensity here is a measure of how strong, or vivid, or "brilliant" the pleasure is. Let's assume that this intensity can be measured in terms of "hedons." Let's also assume that sensory pain is subject to a similar system of measurement, but that the standard units are "dolors." Let's also assume that one dolor of pain is equal in absolute magnitude though opposite in "sign" to one hedon of pleasure. Now we can say that a person's "hedono-doloric balance" at a time is equal to the number of hedons of pleasure he is then experiencing, minus the number of dolors of pain he is experiencing. I think that when Sidgwick talks of "the surplus of pleasure over pain" he means to be indicating 'hedono-doloric balance.' If so, the core of his account of happiness may be understood in this way:

H2: x is happy to degree n at t =df. x's hedono-doloric balance at t = n.

So, if you want to know how happy Grandma is at any particular time, you need to find out how many hedons of pleasure she is then feeling; you need to subtract from this the number of dolors of pain she is then feeling. The result is her hedono-doloric balance and (if H2 is right) this is her level of happiness for that moment.

By itself, H2 is only the first step in a theory of happiness. Note that H2 does not explain what is involved in simply "being happy." It provides no answer to the question about whether Grandma is happy. It is easy enough to add the missing elements.

We can go on to say that a person is happy at a time if and only if he is happy to some positive degree; and unhappy if and only if happy to a negative degree. In other words, you are happy at a time if and only if you feel more sensory pleasure than pain at that time, and unhappy if and only if you feel more sensory pain than pleasure at that time. If your hedono-doloric balance is zero, then you are neither happy nor unhappy.

Imagine that on a certain occasion Grandma is suffering pretty severe pain from her arthritis. Let's suppose she is feeling 99 dolors of pain. But imagine also that it is a lovely spring day and she is working in her garden. While her knees are giving her pain, the smell of the spring flowers is giving her pleasure. She is feeling 100 hedons of pleasure. In this case she has a positive hedono-doloric balance. The suggested account of happiness then implies that she is happy on that occasion. But the theory also implies that if her arthritis had been one dolor more painful and the smell of the flowers just one hedon less pleasurable, then she would have been unhappy. This may seem undesirable. Some people find it counterintuitive to suppose that such a small shift down the hedono-doloric continuum can move a person from the "definitely happy" range to the "definitely unhappy" range. Maybe it would be better to say that there is a certain minimum positive threshold, such that whenever a person's hedono-doloric balance exceeds that threshold, then the person is happy; and whenever a person's hedono-doloric balance falls below a corresponding minimum negative threshold, then the person is unhappy. When the person's hedono-doloric balance falls between the thresholds, then the person is neither happy nor unhappy.

If we understand hedonism about happiness in this way—making use of thresholds—then we can say that on the day in question Grandma was neither happy nor unhappy. If she had felt quite a bit more pain in her knees, she would have been unhappy. If she had felt quite a bit more pleasure from the flowers, she would have been happy. As it was, she fell into the intermediate zone and could not be described either as happy or as unhappy.[6]

Still, the theory is incomplete. We need to say what makes for happiness during a stretch of time; we need to say what makes for happiness in a domain of life; and we need to say what makes for happiness in life in general. These remaining bits should be pretty obvious: a person's happiness during a stretch of time can be defined as the sum of the person's happiness levels for the various moments during the time. If there are infinitely many such moments, then we can say that happiness during a stretch is the integral of the happiness levels for the moments. Happiness in life as a whole is just happiness for the interval that is the person's whole life. Happiness in a domain of life may be somewhat more difficult to explain. Presumably the hedonist will want to say (roughly) that a person is happy in a domain of life (e.g., his work, his marriage) if and only if events properly associated with that domain give rise to a sufficiently great predominance of pleasure over pain.

The resulting theory is not totally absurd. My own experience leads me to think that I am often happiest when enjoying a lot of pleasure; and of course I am often quite unhappy when I am suffering pain. I assume that others are like me in these respects, and so I think hedonism about happiness is at least worthy of consideration—however brief that consideration may be.

---

[6] Thanks to Brad Skow for pointing out the difference between this "thresholds" view and a different view that would involve a claim invoking "vague boundaries."

2.2 *Haybron on Hedonism about Happiness*

In 'Happiness and Pleasure,'[7] Daniel Haybron discusses and rejects hedonistic theories of happiness much like the one I introduced above in 2.1. He mentions a number of different considerations. One of his arguments against such views is based on the alleged "shallowness" and "fleetingness" of pleasures. Haybron says that hedonistic theories of happiness go wrong because they allow all sorts of pleasures—even the most shallow and fleeting—to count towards happiness:

> Yet such pleasures manifestly play no constitutive role in determining how happy a person is. One's enjoyment of eating crackers, hearing a good song, sexual intercourse, scratching an itch, solving a puzzle, playing football, and so forth need not have the slightest impact on one's level of happiness (though, of course, they may). I enjoy, get pleasure from, a cheeseburger, yet I am patently not happier *thereby*.[8]

Haybron goes on to claim that, even if these pleasures should happen to be especially intense (he cites, as an example, the intense pleasure of an orgasm) or long lasting (as, for example, the long-lasting pleasure one might get from hearing a good song that lasts a long time), these pleasures still might not translate into increases in happiness. Furthermore, the same is true even if the pleasures happen to come in a bunch. A person could experience a lot of sensory pleasures, he says, but at the end of it he might not be any happier.[9] He sums up by identifying what he takes to be the main problem:

> Intuitively, the trouble seems to be that such pleasures don't reach "deeply" enough, so to speak. They just don't *get* to us; they flit through consciousness and that's the end of it. . . . This consideration alone appears to undermine any hedonistic account of [happiness].[10]

Haybron is certainly right when he points out that some episodes of pleasure are fleeting and "shallow." You eat a cracker; it tastes good; you get some mild pleasure from the taste of the cracker. That's the end of the episode. This episode of pleasure has neither long duration

---

[7] *Philosophy and Phenomenological Research* LXII, 3 (May, 2001): 501–28. A revised version of this paper appears as chapter 3 of Haybron (2008b). The line of argument that I discuss here is also presented in the book, though in slightly revised form.   [8] Haybron (2001: 505).
[9] I have adjusted some of the reasoning in the cited passage. Haybron imagines a person who feels an "unrelenting succession of minor irritations." But then, in commenting on the example, he mentions "an aggregation of particular pleasures." I think the confusion is trivial. The argument could be developed either by appeal to a succession of pleasures or by appeal to a succession of pains. I have chosen the former.   [10] Haybron (2001: 506).

nor "depth." Unless the circumstances are really quite odd, a pleasure like this would not have any lasting effect on your state of mind. It would be a fleeting, shallow pleasure. Your level of happiness at the end of the episode might be about the same as your level of happiness at the beginning.

But surely a defender of hedonism about happiness could accept all this and simply point out that sometimes an increase in a person's happiness is fleeting and shallow too. The pleasure of eating a cracker obviously will not have any interesting effect on someone's lifetime happiness. Suppose we have already agreed that Grandma was on the whole a pretty unhappy person. Our view is not likely to be shaken when we discover that there was an additional episode of pleasure beyond the ones we already knew about—she once enjoyed the taste of a cracker. But we might take some small solace in this news. Perhaps we will say that she was just a little bit happier for a short period of time as a result of the fact that she enjoyed a cracker at that time.

Haybron presents another line of argument against hedonism. He claims that episodic pleasures—even if they happen to fall into a pattern—lack a certain dispositional feature. From the fact that you are feeling pleasures during a certain stretch of time, it does not follow that you are disposed to feel more of them in the future. Yet, according to Haybron, something like this dispositionality is an essential feature of happiness. If you are happy at a time, you must be disposed to have more "positive emotions" in the future. So happiness cannot be identified with feelings of pleasure, even lots of them falling into a pattern.

Haybron presents this argument in this passage:

At the root of the problem is the fact that hedonistic happiness consists of nothing but a series of conscious events: to know that someone is happy on this view is only to know that his recent experience has been mostly positive. So construed, ascriptions of happiness are little more than capsule summaries . . . of subjects' conscious episodes . . . Hedonistic happiness is an essentially *episodic* . . . phenomenon. But happiness is obviously not just the having of a certain kind of experience, or even lots of them. It is rather a deeper psychological condition incorporating the more or less stable underlying mental states that *determine*, in part and among other things, the kinds of experiences that will occur. It is a substantially dispositional phenomenon. It tells us not just about subjects' histories, but also about their current condition and propensities for the near future. It is forward looking. . . . Hedonism is thus fundamentally wrong about the kind of mental state that happiness is. It appears to commit something of a category mistake.[11]

---

[11] Haybron (2001: 510).

Although he is in fact making several connected points here, Haybron's main point in this passage seems to be that "dispositionality" is another constitutive element in happiness. In order to be happy at a time, a person must then be disposed to react happily to good news, and to go on feeling "positive" feelings in the future. Merely having a sufficiently positive hedono-doloric balance, obviously, does not have this dispositional feature. Haybron's point seems to be that a person can experience a bunch of pleasurable sensations during a period of time without having any underlying disposition to go on feeling such things in the future. So hedonism about happiness is not true.

It seems to me that Haybron's remarks imply that a certain sort of happiness is impossible. I have in mind something that I will call "fragile happiness." A person will be said to experience fragile happiness at a time iff she is happy at that time, but is also disposed to lose that happiness, or to lapse into unhappiness. If a person has fragile happiness, then that person does not have the sort of deep-seated underlying disposition that Haybron describes. If fragile happiness is possible, and is a genuine form of happiness, then Haybron's objection to hedonism fails. I think it is possible for there to be a person whose happiness is in this way fragile. Let me attempt to describe such a person.[12]

Suppose Grandma formerly suffered from depression. She sought the help of a psychiatrist. The psychiatrist prescribed a controversial drug. The drug seemed to work quite well. Grandma's depression lifted. She began to enjoy some of her hobbies, such as working in the garden, spending time with her grandchildren, and going out to eat in a local franchise restaurant. Suppose that her psychiatrist knows that Grandma could easily relapse into depression. That's because many patients who take that drug suddenly stop taking it without warning. (That's why it's so controversial.) If Grandma stops taking the drug she will no longer enjoy gardening, or hanging out with the children. Thus, though she is currently fairly happy, there is a very good chance that she will not continue to be happy for long. Suppose, in addition, that most of her satisfactions are in this further way fragile: the flowers in her garden could easily be attacked by aphids; and if the flowers should be attacked by aphids, Grandma will be disappointed and will stop taking the drug. Fortunately, though the aphids are starting to multiply in the garden, they have not yet attacked. Grandma is unaware of their presence. The grandchildren often think about going

---

[12] In Hill (2009), Scott Hill discusses Haybron's propensity theory and raises a fundamentally similar objection. I am grateful to Hill for helpful discussion of this point.

to summer camp. They are on the verge of announcing their decision. If the grandchildren should decide to go to summer camp, Grandma will be disappointed. This will also trigger a decision on her part to stop taking her medication. Fortunately, the kids have so far not told her that they will be going to camp. The psychiatrist and Grandma's family are all keeping their fingers crossed. They are hoping that Grandma will not quit taking her medication.

Now focus on a certain week in April during which Grandma enjoyed working in her garden, enjoyed spending time with her grandchildren, and enjoyed going out to dinner on a few occasions. She took her medication as prescribed. The aphids, meanwhile, were just starting to multiply.

Under these circumstances I would want to say that Grandma was moderately happy during the week in April, but I would also want to say that Grandma's happiness was fragile. It was not based on deep dispositional features of her personality. It was based on a chancy drug and some good luck. She did not have an enduring underlying disposition to continue being happy. In fact, on the evidence given, it seems that she was likely to stop being happy sometime soon. Surely there are such people; not every happy person is also disposed to go on being happy. This shows that Haybron is mistaken when he claims that in order to count as happy at all, a person must be disposed to go on feeling happy. Thus, it seems to me that Haybron's remarks about the alleged dispositionality of happiness do not reveal anything seriously wrong with a hedonistic account.

Scattered through Haybron's discussion are some remarks about a connection between happiness and time. Haybron seems to be saying that the hedonistic theory of happiness gets a certain temporal feature of happiness wrong. Here are some passages in which this line of thought seems to emerge:

> to know that someone is happy on this [hedonistic] view is only to know that his *recent experience* has been mostly positive. So construed, ascriptions of happiness are little more than capsule summaries or histories of subjects' conscious episodes. Hedonistic happiness is an essentially . . . *backward-looking* phenomenon . . . . [But happiness] is forward-looking.[13]

> happiness ascriptions possess an interesting and important connection to the present: unqualified true attributions of happiness strongly suggest, and appear to entail, that the subject is happy *now*. They do not merely summarize the subject's *recent psychological history*, but tell us something about the subject's present condition.[14]

---

[13] Haybron (2001: 510); emphasis added, FF.   [14] Ibid. 511.

happiness is not *backward-looking* in the extreme manner that hedonism takes it to be, for ascriptions are firmly anchored in the present. It is doubtful whether hedonism can respect this property of happiness ascriptions at all.[15]

As I understand these remarks, Haybron is objecting to hedonism because, as he sees it, hedonism is in a certain way "backward looking." That is, according to hedonism, when we say that a person is happy *now*, our statement entails that he has recently experienced a series of pleasant experiences. In other words, Haybron is assuming that a hedonistic theory of happiness will incorporate a principle such as this:

H3: Necessarily, if a person, x, is happy at a time, t, then x's hedono-doloric balance during the period leading up to t has been positive.

If this were a component of the hedonistic account of happiness, then Haybron's remarks would make sense. He would be right to say that if hedonism were true, ascriptions of happiness would be "backward-looking" and that they would give us (something sort of like) summaries of the subject's recent psychological history. Furthermore, it would seem that this would yield a strange theory of happiness since, as Haybron says, when we say that a person is happy *now* we do not mean to be giving information about how he has been feeling *recently*. We mean to be talking about how he feels *now*.

I think it is important to note that hedonism about happiness *in the form I have imagined* does not incorporate H3. It does incorporate:

H2: x is happy to degree n at t =df. x's hedono-doloric balance at t = n.

The theory as I have formulated it implies that a person's level of happiness at a time is determined by his hedono-doloric balance *at that time*. A person's happiness during an interval of time is defined as the integral of his happiness levels for the moments during that interval. Thus, when formulated as I have suggested, the theory seems to have precisely the temporal implications that Haybron thinks a theory of happiness should have. An ascription of happiness is not a "backward-looking capsule summary" of recent experience; it is an account of current experience.

Imagine that a person experiences a bunch of fleeting episodes of pleasure during a certain stretch of time, and then they end. The person goes into a hedono-dolorically neutral state. The hedonistic

[15] Ibid. 512.

theory I have proposed implies that the person was happy during the time when he was feeling the fleeting pleasures (assuming that he did not feel any countervailing pains). The theory also implies that the person's happiness level at the end of the sequence will be determined by his hedono-doloric balance at that (post-hedonic) moment. Since we have stipulated that he is no longer feeling any pleasures at that time, the theory implies that he is not happy then. This is apparently consistent with Haybron's intuitions about the case.

It appears, then, that Haybron's temporal argument against hedonism is directed against a somewhat strange-looking and implausible theory of happiness. I know of no one who has ever endorsed such a theory. His remarks seem to be consistent with the somewhat more plausible hedonistic theory of happiness that I have sketched on behalf of Bentham, Mill, and Sidgwick.

2.3 *Why Hedonism is False*

Although none of the arguments so far surveyed has established it, the hedonic theory of happiness is false. A couple of clear examples should suffice to establish this.

First, I will describe a case in which someone is unhappy at a time even though he is feeling more sensory hedons than dolors at that time. Suppose that, after being endlessly bombarded by email advertisements, Wendell has purchased a highly touted orgasm enhancer. Suppose he has paid for, and is expecting a monster 400 hedon orgasm. Suppose when the orgasm comes, it is a pathetic little 12 hedon orgasm. Wendell is disappointed. He thinks he has wasted his money. He is also somewhat embarrassed, since he had been warned that the email advertisements were just scams. However, at the moment of orgasm, his hedono-doloric balance is definitely positive. He feels 12 hedons of sensory pleasure, and no dolors of sensory pain. Yet he is not happy.

Let me describe the case in more detail. During the time in question, Wendell has a sort of pained look on his face. He is not smiling. He says, 'Is that it? Is that all I get? That is pathetic! This orgasm enhancer is a total rip-off!' He thinks about complaining to the outfit from which he purchased the orgasm enhancer; he thinks about writing to the Better Business Bureau; he thinks that he is forever doomed to have unimpressive orgasms. Throughout this time, Wendell is not thinking about any other topic. He's not enjoying the weather, or thinking about his job. He is not feeling any sensory pain; nothing actually *hurts*. He is focused on his disappointment with the orgasm enhancer.

Anyone observing Wendell on this occasion, or hearing about his experience with the orgasm enhancer, or listening to his mutterings, would conclude that Wendell is pretty unhappy. Perhaps not quite suicidal; but definitely unhappy.

H2 goes wrong in the opposite direction too. Suppose Dolores has been suffering from serious chronic pain for a long time. Suppose her doctor informs her of a new pain management drug, which Dolores then takes. Suppose it works. The pain is dramatically reduced. Instead of suffering with constant 400 dolor pain, Dolores is now suffering with pain somewhere in the 12 dolor range. She is very happy about this reduction in pain. Since the pain has been so relentless for such a long time, this is definitely an important matter for her. If asked, she might say that she is surprised, delighted, and in general fairly happy today. Yet she still has a negative hedono-doloric balance. She still feels more dolors of sensory pain than hedons of sensory pleasure.

There are many reasons to think that Dolores is happy in the scenario described.[16] She has a smile on her face; she is asserting that she is delighted with the amazing reduction in pain; she is optimistically looking forward to a better future. She might express her heartfelt thanks to her doctor, saying that the new medicine is truly a miracle drug.

Here is a third example that seems to me to demonstrate in an especially dramatic way that pleasure and happiness are two different things. Imagine a woman who is just about to give birth. Imagine that she has been wanting to have a baby for a long time, and was thrilled when she found that she was pregnant. Imagine furthermore that during the final few weeks of her pregnancy, she began to feel quite uncomfortable. She has reached the point where she wants to give birth to this new baby and begin the project of raising it.

Suppose she is now in the hospital in the final stages of labor. She has decided to try to have the baby without being completely knocked out with drugs. So she is in pain. The doctors and nurses are encouraging her to push. Sweat is running down her face; she is groaning and breathing hard. Then, with a scream of pain, she gives

---

[16] It would be a mistake here to appeal to some other theory of happiness to defend my claim that Dolores is happy on the occasion in question. So I am not doing that. I am just citing a bunch of familiar indicators of happiness—things that we would normally take to be signs of happiness. Later, in Chapter 7, I will return to this case and present a line of thinking designed to explain why I think Dolores is happy at the moment in question.

one last push and the baby emerges. The baby takes its first breath, and is declared to be fine. The mother then collapses in tears of joy and relief.

Suppose afterward her husband asks her to describe her emotional state at the very moment when the baby was born. The new mother then says, 'I think the pain was the worst I have ever felt. I didn't realize it would hurt so much. But at the same time I think that was one of the happiest moments of my life. I was so relieved when I knew that this pregnancy was finally going to be over; I was thrilled when I felt the baby emerge; I was delighted when they told me that the baby was fine.'

This scenario seems to me to be possible. In fact, I think relevantly similar scenarios happen in hospitals every day. Two points are crucial: first, the new mother says that she was in very severe pain at the moment of birth. That's why she was groaning and sweating. Second, the new mother was very happy at that same moment. She was happy because the pregnancy was over; because the baby was being born; because the baby was healthy. This shows in a vivid way that a person can be quite happy even when having a decidedly negative hedono-doloric balance. Hedonism about happiness is clearly false.

These examples remind us that a person can be unhappy at a time even though he is feeling more sensory pleasure than pain at that time; and that a person can be happy at a time even though she is feeling more sensory pain than pleasure at that time. Thus, the examples show that hedonism of the Bentham-Mill-Sidgwick variety is false.

Several comments may be in order here.

i. The three examples I have described show that a person's happiness level at a time cannot be identified with his hedono-doloric balance at that time. Thus, hedonism as a theory about the nature of happiness is false. We cannot explain the nature of happiness merely by saying that to be happy is to be feeling a positive, or sufficiently high, balance of sensory pleasure over pain. Nevertheless, I certainly grant that there might be some sort of contingent, probabilistic connection between happiness and pleasure. It certainly might turn out that there is a loose correlation between high levels of happiness and high hedono-doloric balances. Maybe the cases of Wendell, Dolores, and the new mother are unusual. Maybe most of the time, in typical cases, people are happier when they are experiencing sufficiently positive hedono-doloric balances. This is an empirical question that would have to be settled by appropriate research. Nothing I have said here conflicts with the idea that happiness and pleasure are somehow "associated."[17]

ii. In describing the three cases, I have not made any appeal to any theory of happiness. More specifically, I have not based my judgments about happiness levels on the theory of happiness that I will later introduce in Chapter 6. As I see it, any such appeal to my own theory of happiness would be question-begging and would make the "argument" pointless. Later (in Chapter 7), I will discuss the implications of my own theory for these cases. I will claim (no surprise!) that my theory generates and explains the correct judgments in these cases.

iii. So there is a question about the justification for the claims I have made about Wendell, Dolores, and the new mother. What entitles me to say that Wendell was unhappy, and that Dolores and the new mother were happy, in the situations described? I am just asking the fair-minded reader to reflect on the cases in an unprejudiced way and to assume that the descriptions of the three characters that I have given are accurate. Although of course I have not given an absolutely complete description of any possible cases, I ask you to avoid assuming that I left out something important that bears on happiness. Assume that I have given you the main happiness-relevant features of the cases involving Wendell, Dolores, and the new mother. I know I would say that Wendell was unhappy at the selected moment if the case were as I have described it; I know that I would say that Dolores and the new mother were happy. I merely request that the fair-minded reader reflect on the cases (as so far described) and honestly consider whether my conclusions concerning them seem right.

iv. I am not repeating Haybron's point about shallowness. These examples are designed to bring out a different fact: how happy you are at a time seems to depend upon your attitude toward things that are happening, or things that you are thinking about, at that time; and not merely upon how much pleasure or pain you are feeling at that time.

---

[17] In Sumner (1996: 142), Wayne Sumner mentions a likely connection between sensory pain and unhappiness. He points out that long-term suffering from "intense chronic pain" is likely to make a person's life miserable. It is hard to be happy when you are suffering this sort of pain. But, again, the connection is contingent.

With this, I conclude my discussion of sensory hedonism about happiness. To be happy at a moment, or during an interval, or in a domain of life, or in life as a whole, is not the same as to be enjoying a positive hedono-doloric balance at that moment, or in the interval or domain, or in your life as a whole. Hedonism of the Bentham-Mill-Sidgwick variety about happiness is false.

CHAPTER 3

Kahneman's "Objective Happiness"

3.1 *Kahneman and "Instant Utility"*

Daniel Kahneman's contribution to the revival of interest in happiness has been enormous. He has written a staggering number of papers about happiness and related topics either on his own or in concert with others. His energy and enthusiasm have played a central role in the development of the mostly new field of "positive psychology." A glance at *Well-Being: The Foundations of Hedonic Psychology* should convince any fair-minded reader that Kahneman is one of the most influential of the founding fathers.

Kahneman's own views on happiness have been sketched in a series of papers. The views presented in these papers are not always consistent with each other. Indeed, it sometimes appears that Kahneman toys with several different views within a single paper. Perhaps this explains why some commentators categorize Kahneman as a hedonist about happiness, while others are convinced that he should be categorized as a preferentist.[1] Perhaps all of these interpretations are correct—or at least correct insofar as they represent views that Kahneman has discussed with some enthusiasm in some place.

I want to focus here on some things that Kahneman says in his paper 'Objective Happiness.'[2] I do not mean to suggest that this is

---

[1] In their introduction to *Economics and Happiness* (2005) Luigino Bruni and Pier Luigi Porta identify Kahneman as a hedonist. They go on to characterize hedonism "more precisely" as 'the view that well-being consists of pleasure or happiness' (p. 7). They mention, in this context, that Kahneman co-edited an anthology entitled *Well-Being: The Foundations of Hedonic Psychology* (1999), thus suggesting that the terms 'well-being' and 'hedonism' are essentially equivalent. I think the description of hedonism is misleading, since it conflates what is more properly called hedonism with what I call eudaimonism. Furthermore, as I will show in what follows, Kahneman defends a conception of happiness that is more closely aligned with preferentism than with either hedonism or eudaimonism. In 'Objective Happiness,' he explicitly rejects a hedonistic conception of happiness.

[2] Daniel Kahneman, 'Objective Happiness,' in Kahneman, Diener, and Schwarz, eds (1999).

Kahneman's final view, or that it is the most carefully worked out of his views. I focus on it because it provides a distinctive approach to the question about the nature of happiness. In virtue of Kahneman's prominence in the field and the intuitive attractiveness of some of the things he says, this view deserves to be discussed.

Kahneman says in this paper that he intends to construct a "bottom-up" concept of objective happiness. He means to start with temporally small "atoms of happiness" and then go on to describe mathematical operations on these atoms that will yield measures of a person's objective happiness over an extended period of time, in a domain of life, or even in a life as a whole. The fundamental units of happiness on this view are "instant utilities." Kahneman says that a natural way to make use of the record of a person's instant utilities during a period of time is to 'define the total utility experienced during an interval of time by the temporal integral of instant utility.'[3] If we want to know how happy Helen was in March, we take the temporal integral of her instant utilities for all instants in March. Obviously, the interest and success of such a project depend crucially on the clear identification and characterization of the atoms. What, then, is instant utility?

Kahneman introduces what he calls the "Good/Bad Dimension" (or the "GB Dimension").[4] Although his remarks suggest a variety of possibilities, I am inclined to believe that Kahneman intends that the items to be ranked on this dimension are *instantaneous slices of one person's purely subjective experience*—in other words, such things as "how things are appearing to Helen right now." So we may think that Kahneman is imagining a function that takes a person and a time as inputs, and delivers a number as output. The number represents the person's position on the GB Dimension at the time. Kahneman suggests[5] that Helen could be fitted with a watch-like device with a buzzer. When the buzzer goes off, Helen is to try to record the GB ranking of her current slice of experience. She does this by inputting a number.

Helen has been trained to input the numbers in a certain way. If she feels neither good nor bad; neither pleasure nor pain; neither "positive" nor "negative" at the moment when the buzzer goes off, she is to input zero. If she feels good, she is to input a positive number with higher numbers representing instants at which she feels better. If she feels bad, she is to input a negative number with lower numbers representing instants at which she feels worse. Helen's

---

[3] Kahneman (1999: 5).   [4] Ibid. 3.   [5] Ibid 10.

numbers may have to be "rescaled" so that the numbers have certain further mathematical features. If she feels twice as good at t2 as she did at t1, then the number she inputs at t2 should be twice the number she inputs at t1. If the combination of how good she feels at t2 and how bad she feels at t3 is equal in value to feeling neither good nor bad, then the number she inputs at t3 should be just the negative of the number she inputs t2. I believe that Kahneman intended that the numbers be chosen in such a way as to form a ratio scale with a non-arbitrary zero point, a positive side, and a negative side.

Kahneman describes his measure of happiness as "objective." Philosophers may find this terminology somewhat puzzling. I think it would be more consistent with current philosophical usage to describe Kahneman's intended measure of happiness as entirely "subjective." After all, it is a measure of Helen's own subjective ranking of her own subjective experiences. It's all obviously internal to Helen's psychology. But the contrast Kahneman has in mind seems to be with Helen's after-the-fact evaluation of her previous experience, based entirely on her recollections. One of Kahneman's main points is that a person's after-the-fact evaluations can easily be wrong. Furthermore, he thinks such evaluations can go wrong in systematic ways. Their evaluations are distorted by values at the peaks and ends of pleasant or unpleasant experiences. If we want to know how happy people are, we need to avoid these distortions. So Kahneman thinks we need to have real-time measures of locations on the GB Dimension. Kahneman calls these "objective."

I think Kahneman is obviously right in thinking that after-the-fact evaluations can be wrong. Surely I may wake up thinking that I had a fabulously good time at the party last night when in fact I really didn't enjoy it quite that much. But it seems to me that even a real-time evaluation can go wrong as well. Couldn't a person deceive himself about his present location on the GB dimension? Surely self-deception is possible. What's even more troubling is the possibility of confusion about the GB dimension itself. Maybe Helen thinks she should input a '10' when in fact she should really input a '9.3.' Of course, this all depends crucially upon what the numbers are supposed to represent. And this leads us to the central question: what evaluation is Helen supposed to be making when she selects a number to represent her current position on the GB dimension?

The choice of the name ('Good/Bad'), as well as Kahneman's remarks about "evaluation" suggest that when Helen's buzzer goes off, she is to reflect on her current experience and assign it a score representing how *good or bad* it is. But of course there are many sorts of goodness—moral, aesthetic, hedonic, intellectual . . . In any case, this talk of evaluation is quickly rejected as 'overly intellectual.'[6]

Another set of remarks suggests that the GB score of Helen's momentary experience is determined by its *pleasurableness or painfulness*. Kahneman says 'Being pleased or distressed is an attribute of experience at a particular moment. I will label this attribute *instant utility*, borrowing the term "utility" from Bentham.'[7] He illustrates his view by an example concerning the amount of pain a colonoscopy patient is suffering at each instant during the 25-minute-long procedure. Height on the up-down axis represents "pain intensity." On this interpretation, locations on the GB dimension would apparently indicate intensities of sensory pleasure or pain. Kahneman seems to say that a person's objective happiness is founded upon facts about 'the pleasantness or unpleasantness of particular moments in her life.'[8] He makes a number of other remarks about pleasure and pain. This suggests a sensory hedonistic interpretation of the GB dimension.

The resulting theory of happiness would then be nearly equivalent to sensory hedonism about happiness. It would differ from the theory discussed in Chapter 2 only in this respect: instant utility in that theory represents the subject's *actual* hedono-doloric balance at a moment. That is, it represents the number of hedons the person is then experiencing, minus the number of dolors the person is then experiencing. Kahneman's numbers (if we were to take this hedonic interpretation) would represent the subject's *estimate* of his or her hedono-doloric balance. Obviously, a person could be wrong about this, and as a result Kahneman's theory (on this interpretation) would diverge slightly from the hedonic theory we have already considered.

In any case, Kahneman makes it clear that he does not mean to offer a hedonic theory of happiness. He asks what a concept of instant utility should include and answers 'The hedonic quality of current sensory experience is the first candidate, of course, but it is not sufficient.'[9] The pleasures and pains of anticipation are also to be included, as are "the pleasures of the mind." It must also allow for states of "flow" in which one is so involved in an experience or activity that hedonic value fades into the background of experience.[10] Other factors that bear on instant utility are mood, and the degree to which the current experience has "a promotion focus or a prevention

[6] Kahneman (1999: 3).   [7] Ibid. 4.   [8] Ibid.
[9] Ibid. 6.   [10] Ibid.

focus."[11] These remarks suggest a pluralistic interpretation of the GB dimension.[12]

Pluralism is problematic. Suppose that six or eight different factors play a role in determining Helen's position on the GB dimension. Suppose that in order to determine what number to input on each occasion, Helen has to think about the amounts of pleasure and pain she is then feeling, but also her mood at that time, whether or not she is in a state of flow, and the extent to which she wants to promote her present experience or prevent it from continuing. Then she may be hard pressed to find the right number. She'd have to find a bunch of numbers and then do some arithmetic.

I believe that Kahneman is alluding to this problem when he says[13] that pluralism makes instant utility "intimidating" and "formidable," so he proposes making use of a single factor—the extent to which the person undergoing the momentary experience wants that experience to continue. He says 'Instant utility is best understood as the strength of the disposition to continue or to interrupt the current experience.'[14] Elsewhere he says:

it makes sense to call Helen "objectively happy" [in March] if she spent most of her time in March engaged in activities that she would rather have continued than stopped, little time in situations she wished to escape, and—very important because life is short—not too much time in a neutral state in which she would not care either way. This is the essence of the approach proposed here.[15]

All of this strongly suggests that the GB dimension measures *strength of desire for the present experience to continue*. The more you want your present experience to continue, the higher your instant utility. Objective happiness, in turn, is explained by appeal to instant utility thus defined. As I understand it, this is in fact the view that Kahneman means to defend in 'Objective Happiness.' I will refer to this as the 'preferentist' interpretation.[16]

It should be obvious that the preferentist interpretation gives us a GB ranking of experiences that is genuinely different from the

---

[11] Ibid. 6–7.

[12] Kahneman's position here is somewhat confused. He says that hedonism is insufficient, because it leaves out certain elements. He then mentions some of the missing elements. Surprisingly, several of the elements he then mentions are themselves pleasures and pains—e.g. the pleasures of anticipation and the pleasures of the mind. So hedonism would not have missed these out in the first place.

[13] Kahneman (1999: 7).   [14] Ibid. 4.   [15] Ibid. 7.

[16] This form of preferentism about happiness is not to be confused with standard preferentism about welfare; nor should it be confused with typical forms of preferentism about happiness. Some forms of preferentism about happiness are discussed below in Chapters 4 and 5.

ranking we would have gotten if we had accepted either the axiological interpretation, or the hedonistic interpretation, or the pluralistic interpretation. We can see this if we consider some cases.

1. Suppose Helen feels guilty about some previous sin and strongly prefers to undergo penance. Suppose she is undergoing some uncomfortable penance. Imagine that the penance is in fact moderately painful. Suppose that Helen thinks she needs to suffer for two minutes and suppose that only one minute has gone by. Then, if we make use of the preferentist interpretation of the GB dimension, her experience gets a positive rating—after all, she does want it to continue for another minute. So her instant utility for that moment would be positive. But if we make use of the hedonic interpretation her experience gets a negative rating. After all, the penance is unpleasant. (I am not sure what to say about the pluralist interpretation, since I don't know how to assign weights and I don't know what the relevant factors are supposed to be.) Suppose Helen thinks it is a good thing for her to undergo this penance. Then the moment would get a positive rating on the GB Dimension if we accepted the axiological interpretation.

2. Suppose Helen is smelling an unusual odor. She finds the smell slightly disgusting, but she is curious. She wants to reflect on this smell. If we let *strength of desire to continue* guide her, she will place her current experience high on the GB dimension. If we let *pleasurableness* guide her, she will place it much lower. If we just ask her to tell us *how good it is* she might place it at some other point.

3. Suppose Helen has been told that she will get a substantial financial reward if she can keep her arm submerged in ice-cold water for five minutes. Suppose she has kept her arm submerged for just over four minutes when her buzzer sounds. If Helen thinks that GB rankings are determined by the extent to which she wants her experience to continue, she may be confused: on one hand, she wants it to continue because she wants the money. On the other hand, she wants it to stop because it hurts. This shows that talk about desire is multiply ambiguous. We need to recognize the distinction between (a) a person's *intrinsic* desires for an experience to continue, (b) a person's *extrinsic* desires for it to continue, and (c) the person's *overall* desire for the experience to continue. Perhaps the score on the GB dimension should be understood to represent *strength of **intrinsic** desire for present experience to continue*, where the intrinsic desire represents the person's desire

for the continuation of the experience just for its own sake, and not for any consequences. In what follows, I will assume that Kahneman had something like this in mind. In the present case, then, we can say that while Helen desires to keep her arm in the ice-cold water, this desire is completely extrinsic. Were it not for the money, Helen would never want to subject herself to this painful experience.

3.2 *The Theory of Objective Happiness*

The fundamental elements of Kahneman's theory should be fairly clear in light of what we have already seen. He thinks there is a scale—the GB Dimension—on which we can plot any person's location at any instant. A person's instant utility is his location on this GB dimension. Instant utilities function as the atoms of happiness on Kahneman's theory. A person's instant utility for a given instant is intended to indicate the strength of the person's intrinsic desire for his experience at that instant to continue. If the person wants his present experience to continue, his instant utility is positive. Higher positive numbers indicate greater strength of desire. If he wants his present experience to stop, his instant utility is negative. Lower negative numbers represent stronger desires for cessation.

Kahneman defines a person's objective happiness during an interval as the temporal integral of the person's instant utilities for all the instants during the interval. Roughly, then, the idea is that we determine how objectively happy a person is during a period of time by checking to see the extent to which he wants his experiences to continue during that interval. The greater the extent to which he wants his experiences to continue moment by moment, the more objectively happy he is during the interval.

As I mentioned above in connection with hedonism, we face a choice when we try to move from happiness ratings relativized to numbers (e.g., 'Helen was objectively happy to degree 8 during March') to unrelativized claims about happiness and unhappiness (e.g. 'Helen was happy during March'). On the one hand, we can say that a person is happy during an interval if she has a positive numerical happiness rating for that interval, no matter how close to zero that rating may be.

On the other hand, we might adopt the thresholds approach. In this case we would say that a person does not count as simply "happy" for an interval unless her numerical happiness rating for that interval is sufficiently far above zero. It must exceed some minimum threshold. And a person does not count as simply "unhappy" unless the rating is sufficiently far below zero. That would give us a slightly different concept of objective happiness.

Since Kahneman does not say anything about this matter, and since it seems hardly more than a matter of conceptual housecleaning, I will simply stipulate that we adopt the thresholds approach. The concept of objective happiness thus inherits all the vagueness of the concept of sufficiency. That seems acceptable.

In addition, let us say that a person should be counted as an 'objectively happy person' if and only if he is objectively happy in the interval that is his life as a whole.

I think that Kahneman intended to give a theory that would also account for happiness in 'more inclusive domains of life such as family life or work.'[17] As I understand this, the idea would be that theory should be able to say, for any person, S, and domain of life, D, how objectively happy S is in D. This would enable us to give an account, for example, of what must be the case if Helen is objectively happy in her work, but objectively unhappy in her marriage. Kahneman does not attempt to explain how to do this in 'Objective Happiness' and I cannot see any plausible way to make use of his machinery to do it. I will simply leave it out of the theory.[18]

I think the theory I have here described is at least very similar to the theory Kahneman means to defend in 'Objective Happiness.'

3.3 *The Intended Role of Objective Happiness*

I see no evidence to suggest that Kahneman intended his theory to be taken as an account of the meaning of the word 'happy' in ordinary English. Nor does it appear to me that he was assuming that his concept of objective happiness would be exactly equivalent to any concept of happiness currently in use among philosophers, psychologists, or people walking around in the street.

---

[17] Kahneman (1999: 4).

[18] If the various domains of life were temporally separated so that, for example, Helen could focus on work from 9 to 5, and then on family life from 6 to 10, it would be possible to identify her happiness in a domain as the amount of happiness she enjoyed during the interval in which she was engaged in that domain. But, obviously, the important domains of life are not temporally separated in this way. Helen might be thinking about work during "family time," and she might be thinking about personal problems while at her desk at work.

My impression is that Kahneman may have thought that 'happy' in ordinary English is vague or ambiguous. He may have thought that different people use it in different senses, so that there is no clear way to compare amounts of what one person calls happiness with amounts of what someone else calls happiness. Furthermore, he may have thought that the use of any ordinary concept of happiness would have created problems for the measurement of happiness. Look at it this way: suppose we are fitting Helen with her recording device. Suppose we are explaining the procedure for inputting numbers. Under these circumstances it would not be very helpful to tell her that when the buzzer goes off, she is simply to input the number that represents how "happy" she is. She might have no idea how to select the numbers; furthermore, other subjects might input numbers that represent some other concept of happiness. Comparisons of the numbers would be meaningless.

So, in this context, Kahneman may have wanted to introduce a new concept of happiness. He may have wanted this new concept to be less ambiguous than any of the concepts of happiness already current in ordinary thought. He may have wanted this new concept to be one for which there is a coherent scale of measurement. Furthermore, he may have wanted this new concept to be one that is simple enough so that Helen and other subjects would be able to grasp it quickly and use it successfully when inputting numbers. Perhaps Kahneman's idea was that his concept of objective happiness has these features. If this is the case, then it would be pointless to criticize Kahneman's theory by giving counterexamples. If it's a stipulative definition, it can't be criticized in that way.

But of course there are things that might go wrong even with a stipulative definition of happiness. The new concept introduced in that definition might have some practical problems that make it unsuitable for the job it is intended to perform. It might be unwieldy, or unteachable. In the present case, there is another criterion that is applicable.

The concept of happiness is supposed to measure something of great practical importance; it is supposed to measure "the thing about which we are most concerned;" it is supposed to measure something about which governments ought to be concerned when they evaluate public policies. In other words, although it is intended to be a psychological concept, it is supposed to be a concept of a psychological state that tracks welfare. A person's degree of objective happiness is intended to be equivalent to his degree of welfare. There would be no point in introducing a novel concept of happiness and then urging that subjects be fitted with recording devices to measure amounts of happiness thus defined, unless the proposed concept of happiness is reliably associated with welfare.

There is another factor that deserves to be mentioned. This is the extent to which the newly introduced concept of happiness serves as an explication of some concept of happiness with which we are already familiar. Surely we can hope that Kahneman's concept of objective happiness is a precisification of some ordinary, vague concept of happiness. It would be at best odd if rankings in terms of objective happiness were completely unrelated to pre-theoretical rankings in terms of "happiness." What would be the rationale behind calling the new concept 'objective *happiness*'?

Thus, Kahneman's concept of objective happiness can be evaluated on at least three criteria. (a) Is it practical? Can subjects learn how to apply it? Does it support a robust system of measurement? (b) Is it plausibly associated with welfare? Is it reasonable to suppose that rankings in terms of objective happiness coincide with rankings in terms of well-being, or prudential value? (c) Is it an explication of some familiar concept of commonsense psychology?

3.4 *Problems with Kahneman's Theory*

One central problem with Kahneman's theory concerns the question whether Kahneman has located the real "foundations" of objective happiness. The following example suggests that the foundations are somewhat deeper than instantaneous slices of experience.

Suppose that at some moment Helen is very pleased to be living in California, but very displeased to be stuck in a traffic jam. Suppose that at the same time she is enjoying the music playing on her car radio, but annoyed about the honking of horns nearby. Suppose in addition that she is tired and hungry after a long day of work, but satisfied with the quality of the work she performed during the day. Now suppose her online recording device buzzes, and she is required to indicate the location of "the experience she is having at that instant" on the GB dimension. She is to do this (if my interpretation of Kahneman is correct) by inputting a number that represents the strength of her desire for that experience to continue.

The problem in this case is that it is not clear that there is any such thing as "the experience she is having." She is having hundreds of experiences. She is hearing some sounds and seeing some sights; she is feeling the steering wheel. Perhaps she is smelling the odor of diesel fumes from a truck in front of her. If Helen succeeds in finding some single number that represents her instantaneous level of objective happiness, she will have done this by combining information about a whole bunch of other numbers. Her GB score cannot be an "atom" of happiness. If it exists at all, it is a complex "molecule" of happiness.[19]

Let us introduce a modification that Kahneman hints at, but dismisses. This is the idea that at each instant there are many "atomic" experiences going on. Each of these is an experience whose location on the GB Dimension is not determined by the locations of any of its components. Thus, suppose Helen hears the sound of a honking horn at a certain moment, and also feels the cool breeze coming from her car air conditioner at that moment. Suppose she wants the sound of the horn to stop, and she wants the feeling of coolness to continue. Suppose that in these cases, the ranking of each experience does not depend upon any more fundamental ranking of any parts of that experience. Then each of these experiences would count as one atomic experience that she is then having. (I acknowledge that the concept of an atomic experience is not entirely clear.) For each atomic experience that a subject is undergoing at a time, we can say, there is a number that represents its position on the GB Dimension. Let us make use of Kahneman's central idea here: let us say that the position of an atomic experience on the GB Dimension is determined by the strength of the experiencer's intrinsic desire for the experience to continue. So, in Helen's traffic jam case, there are some atomic experiences she would intrinsically like to continue, and others that she would intrinsically prefer to have cease, and others about which she has no such preference either way.

Where E is an atomic experience, and S is a person, and t a moment of time, and S is having E at t, the *continuation value* of E for S at t $= CV(E,S,t) =$ the strength of S's intrinsic desire at t for E to continue. I assume that when a person wants an experience to continue, then its continuation value is positive. If she wants it to stop, then its continuation value is negative. If she does not care about its continuation, then its continuation value for the person at the time is zero.

Now we can define the instant utility of a moment for a person:

The *instant utility* of a time, t, for a person, S $=$ the sum, for all atomic experiences, E, that S is having at t, of $CV(E,S,t)$.

---

[19] Kahneman (1999) makes some remarks in the section entitled 'Is There One GB Value at a Time?' on pp. 8–9. These remarks indicate that he is aware of this problem. He continues to treat "instant utilities" as the foundational units for purposes of his theory.

Instant utility is a function from a pair consisting of a person and a time, to a number. The function takes us from the person and time to the number that is the position of the moment on the person's GB Dimension at the time. The outputs of the function can be plotted on a graph. We can draw the curve representing Helen's moments during March. We can now find the temporal integral of that function. For any person, S, and interval of time, t1–tn, there is an area under the positive side of the curve and another area above the negative side of the person's curve. The person's objective happiness during the interval is the happy area minus the unhappy area.

The resulting theory is similar to Kahneman's, but not precisely the same. It involves double aggregation. First, it aggregates information about the continuation values of the atomic experiences to find instant utilities. Then it aggregates information about instant utilities to find objective happiness through intervals. Kahneman's theory (as I understood it) takes instant utilities as unanalyzable foundational units and then aggregates only in the second way. However, the proposed theory is like Kahneman's theory in some important ways. It is a "bottom up" conception of objective happiness. That is, it is a conception of happiness according to which a person's happiness during an interval (or in life as a whole) is determined by aggregating information about momentary "atoms" of happiness. Furthermore, the proposed conception of happiness is, like Kahneman's, "objective." It does not depend in any way upon a person's recollection of past levels of happiness; nor does it depend upon his anticipation of future levels of happiness. Nor, importantly, does it depend upon judgments made by external observers. Rather, it is based entirely upon the subject's preferences concerning the continuation of his own current introspectable experiences.

The proposed concept of objective happiness lacks one feature that Kahneman probably takes to be quite important. That is *practical usefulness*. It would be hard to train someone to give the numbers representing amounts of instant utility, since on this theory those numbers are not foundational. They are derived from more fundamental numbers representing continuation values for atomic experiences. Thus, on the proposed account, there are several foundational numbers for each moment, and they need to be summed in order to discover a subject's instant utility for that moment. On Kahneman's theory, there is one number for each moment and it is not derived by any sort of mathematical operation from a bunch of other numbers. It made some sort of sense on Kahneman's original theory to suppose that a person could directly input the relevant number when the buzzer goes off. Perhaps it is thought that each subject can simply "read off" the instant utilities by introspection. But it makes much less sense to suppose that a person could directly access the number on this theory, since in this case the number is the sum of possibly hundreds of other numbers. The momentary global assessment would be difficult to determine. Of course, a person could guess, but she might be wrong. So the theory lacks one of the features that Kahneman was interested in keeping—practical usefulness.

More importantly, perhaps, the concept of objective happiness explicated by this theory seems to me to be of questionable interest. I see no particularly tight connection between anything we would ordinarily call 'happiness' and this concept of objective happiness. Nor do I see any justification for thinking that nations should craft their policies so as to increase levels of objective happiness among citizens. To put it bluntly: objective happiness seems different in important ways from happiness; it seems unconnected to welfare.

The divergence between Kahneman's objective happiness and any sort of pre-analytic ordinary happiness may be seen most clearly if we think about people who thrive on change. Some people prefer always to be "on the go." They get bored easily if things remain unchanged. They are far happier when things are in flux. In some cases, happiness depends essentially upon certain kinds of change in experience.

In order to see this in an extreme case, consider this scenario involving Brett. Suppose that Brett is a competitor in a drag race. Suppose he is enjoying the race immensely. Suppose that, as he quickly accelerates, Brett is happy at each moment to be at precisely the spot he has then reached and to be accelerating just as fast as he is accelerating then. When Brett is $\frac{1}{10}$ of the way down the track, he is happy to be $\frac{1}{10}$ of the way down the track and he is happy to be going 30 mph. He is then having some experiences. These include the visual experience he has when looking at the speedometer and tachometer; also the feeling of the gearshift lever in his hand and of the clutch pedal on his foot. He also has auditory experiences involving the sound of the exhaust of his car. He has no desire to prolong or continue any of these experiences. He wants to be finished with that part of the track quickly, and he wants to be at the $\frac{2}{10}$ mark and going at a higher speed in the next moment. Thus, he wants to have a whole new suite of experiences—the experiences he would be having if he were going faster and were further down the track and in a higher gear. At every moment, he wants the experiences of that particular moment to pass quickly because he wants soon to be accelerating at a higher speed and he wants to be located at a point further down the track.

At the end of the trip, Brett reports that he enjoyed the race. 'I was happy the whole time,' he says. I am satisfied that Brett might be right (though the precise meaning of his remark might be somewhat unclear). But now consider positions on the GB Dimension of the moments during Brett's trip down the drag strip. Consider t8. As I see it, there are some experiences that happen at t8 and that Brett wants to continue or prolong. For example, he is experiencing feelings associated with motion, and he wants them to continue. But there are many other experiences that are happening at t8 that Brett does not want to continue. For example, there are the visual experiences he has of the scene from this particular spot on the track. He definitely does not want those to continue. If they were to continue, that would mean that his car had stopped. There are the visual experiences he has of the speedometer and tachometer. He wants these to change too. He wants one of them to be showing steadily increasing numbers and he wants the other to show changing numbers as he shifts the gears. There is the auditory experience of the sound of the exhaust. He wants that to change as he accelerates and shifts. If Brett focuses his attention on experiences that change as he goes down the track, and ignores ones that remain fixed, then it will turn out that he does not wish to prolong any of the experiences that he is aware of.

Earlier (in Chapter 2) I described the case of a woman giving birth. In that context I discussed the case because it shows that a person can be very happy while enduring intense pain. The same example highlights a problem with Kahneman's theory. Imagine the new mother at the moment when the baby begins to emerge. The pain is very intense but the woman knows that this means that the baby is about to be born. It is "the happiest moment of her life." It would of course be preposterous to interrupt at such a moment, and to ask the woman to input a number representing her position on the GB Dimension. However, there seems to be a fact of the matter. Surely she would not want this moment to be prolonged. Part of her joy arises from her recognition that these almost unbearable pains mark the end of her pregnancy and the beginning of her career as a new mother. She might collapse in despair if the doctors were to tell her that her experiences of this moment are going to continue for another hour.

These examples demonstrate that there is no close conceptual connection between a person's happiness during an interval and the strength of his desire for the continuation of the experiences he is having during that interval. Brett is very happy as he speeds down the track; but he does not want his experiences of any moment to continue. The new mother is happy when the baby is being born, but she does not want her experiences to continue either.

I can imagine that a defender of Kahneman's approach might claim that the scenarios I have described are anomalous. Perhaps it will be thought that most of the time, for most of us, there is a sufficiently close contingent connection between our level of happiness and the strength of our desire for our experiences to continue. I'd like to make three comments about that.

1. If Kahneman (or any defender of this approach) were to fall back to the claim that there is merely a "sufficiently close connection" between happiness and the integral of instant utility, then he would no longer be claiming that to be happy *just is* to be objectively happy. In that case, he would not be claiming that Kahneman's theory gives an account of the nature of happiness. The claim would be far weaker. It would just be the claim that levels of actual happiness are somehow contingently linked to levels of objective happiness. If that's the claim, then the theory does not constitute an answer to the fundamental question I mean to be discussing in this book. For my question here is the question about the nature of happiness; it is not a question about a convenient, loose, contingent method for ranking people for something sort of like happiness.
2. I am inclined to think that the examples I have given are not anomalous. I think there are plenty of people who, like Brett, are temperamentally in favor of change. They like to be bombarded with a constant stream of new and exciting experiences. They find continuation of experience boring. I also think that there are people, like the new mother, who are happy at times when they are having experiences that they want to end soon. For any such people, there is not even a contingent linkage between actual levels of happiness and levels of Kahneman's objective happiness (if calculated in the way I have sketched).
3. In order to determine whether Kahneman's objective happiness loosely tracks actual happiness, we would have to run an experiment. We would have to find some suitable subjects; we would have to train them to input numbers representing instant utilities; we would have to find some independent way of determining how happy these people are for every moment during the experiment; we would then have to check to see if the levels of actual happiness correspond to the levels of objective happiness recorded in their devices.

Obviously, we have no way to run this experiment until we have a way of measuring "actual happiness." This seems to show that there is a philosophical question that should take priority over the empirical question. Perhaps we should first have a fairly clear idea about what happiness is; with that in hand, we may want to proceed to the grittier question of trying to construct a good way to measure it. My hunch is that Kahneman's method involving instant utilities will not be found helpful here. But of course at this stage that's just a hunch, since we have not yet reached any conclusion about what happiness is.

CHAPTER 4

Subjective Local Preferentism about Happiness

4.1 *Forms of Preferentism*

In *The Idea of Happiness*, V. J. McGill presents a classic statement of an important sort of view about happiness. McGill defines happiness as:

A lasting state of affairs in which the most favorable ratio of satisfied desires to desires is realized, with the proviso that the satisfied desires can include satisfactions that are not *preceded* by specific desires for them, but come by surprise.[1]

Although the formulation is a bit convoluted, the idea here is actually straightforward. Suppose a certain person has a variety of desires during a certain stretch of time. Suppose some of these desires are satisfied and others are frustrated. (Keep in mind that in some cases a person starts to want something only when he has already started getting it—these desires are to be counted as well.) McGill means to define the person's level of happiness for this stretch of time as the proportion of his desires during that stretch that are satisfied. If he had 100 desires and 90 of them were satisfied, then his happiness level is 90/100. If only 50 of them had been satisfied, his happiness level would have been 50/100.

The crucial thing to notice about McGill's definition is that he attempts to explain happiness by appeal to the concepts of *desire* and *satisfaction*. The theory is clearly distinct from any sort of hedonism; it makes no appeal to any concept of pleasure. It is also distinct from Kahneman's theory; it does not draw any special attention to the desire for continuation of present experience. Presumably, McGill would say that a person would be made

---

[1] V. J. McGill (1967: 5).

happier if he desired and got a *cessation* of present experience, or if he desired and got something that was independent of his own present experience. Theories such as McGill's may be characterized as forms of "local preferentism about happiness." They are forms of preferentism because they define happiness by appeal to the concept of *desire satisfaction*. They are local because they take account of all desires—even little, temporary desires for things other than one's life as a whole.

Local preferentism about happiness can be developed in a variety of different ways. In some forms, the theory claims that a person is happy if his actual desires are *in fact* satisfied—whether he knows it or not. These may be characterized as forms of *objective preferentism*. In other forms, the theory claims that a person is happy if he *believes* that his desires are satisfied—whether they actually are satisfied or not. These would be forms of *subjective preferentism*. So-called "full information" versions of the theory constitute yet another variation. According to these theories, to determine how happy a person is, consider the desires he would have had if he had been fully informed and thinking clearly. His level of happiness is proportional to the extent to which these hypothetical desires are satisfied.

Wayne Davis presented an especially interesting form of subjective local preferentism about happiness in a series of papers. Perhaps the central paper in this collection is his 1981 paper, 'A Theory of Happiness.'[2] Davis's paper is rich, insightful, creative, wide-ranging, and carefully written. It is in some ways one of the most impressive philosophical essays in the happiness literature. I am dismayed when I consider the fact that many writers who should know better seem to be unaware of Davis's work.[3]

In this chapter, I focus exclusively on Davis's 1981 theory of happiness. In section 4.2, I lay out and briefly comment upon some of the essential conceptual background. In section 4.3, I present the theory together with some friendly amendments. I present a series of objections and difficulties in section 4.4.

---

[2] Wayne Davis, 'A Theory of Happiness' (1981b). Other work by Davis is cited in the bibliography.

[3] This is especially troubling in the case of Kahneman. In Kahneman (1999), Kahneman defends a view that is in many ways similar to the view that Davis presented almost 20 years earlier. Davis's work was published in several leading professional journals, yet Kahneman does not acknowledge Davis's work. Indeed, Kahneman does not mention any of Davis's papers in his bibliography.

4.2 *Conceptual Background*

Davis's theory makes use of three main undefined, or "primitive," concepts. He explicitly claims to define happiness by appeal to these concepts. Thus, Davis's theory is a form of reductivism with respect to happiness. He tries to reduce the concept of happiness to a certain combination of these three concepts.

Let's start with the concept of *belief*. Davis does not define *belief*, but he says a few things that serve to clarify his understanding of the concept. He takes belief to be a propositional attitude relating a person to a proposition at a time. He imagines a ratio scale from −1 to 0 to +1. For any person, S, proposition, P, and time, t, there is a number on this scale that represents how much S believes P at t. If S is absolutely certain of P at t, then S believes P to degree +1 at t. It's important to note that 'certain' here is not an epistemic concept; it is a doxastic concept. You can be certain of something even if you have no evidence for it and are not at all justified in believing it. It's just a maximal degree of belief. You couldn't be more sure of anything than you are of it. If S is absolutely certain that P is false, then S believes P to degree −1. If S is neutral or agnostic about p at t, then he believes it to degree 0.

As Davis uses the term, it would be correct to say that S believes P at t even if S is completely unaware of P at t, or is sleeping or in a coma. As he says,[4] he himself has believed that 2+2 = 4 for decades, even though he has not thought about it for long stretches during that time. So belief, for Davis, is *dispositional belief*. To get occurrent belief, as Davis sees it, you need to add *thought*.

Thought—the second of the three primitive concepts used in the theory—is also a propositional attitude relating a person to a proposition at a time. Davis does not introduce any degrees of thought. If you are thinking P, and at the same time thinking Q, then it would make no sense to say that you are at that moment thinking P *more* than you are thinking Q. Furthermore, thought apparently does not have any "negative" counterpart. This is another respect in which thought is unlike belief, for belief does have a negative counterpart, disbelief. There is no such thing as "dis-thought." If a certain proposition "occurs to someone," or if it "enters his mind," then he is thinking that proposition.[5]

---

[4] Davis (1981b: 113).   [5] Ibid.

Davis defines[6] occurrent belief as dispositional belief plus thought:

D1: S occurrently believes P at t =df. S dispositionally believes P at t
     & S thinks P at t.[7]

The third primitive concept in the theory is the concept of *desire*.[8] It
is also a propositional attitude relating a person to a proposition at a
time. To desire a proposition is simply to want it to be true. There is
a ratio scale on which we can locate every instance in which a person
desires a proposition at a time. This scale is like the belief scale in that
it has a positive side (desire) and a negative side (aversion) and a zero
point. It is unlike the belief scale in that it has neither upper nor lower
limit. No matter how much you want something, you could always
want something more than that.

Davis's project, then, is to define happiness by appeal to belief,
thought, and desire. But before presenting the analysis, Davis takes a
moment to help focus attention on his target—the concept he wants
to analyze. He distinguishes between occurrent and dispositional
happiness.[9] His fundamental aim is to analyze the concept of occurrent happiness. Once he has done that, he will be able to explain dispositional happiness in terms of occurrent. Roughly, and preliminarily,
we can say that you have occurrent happiness if you are enjoying
yourself, being in good spirits, in a good mood, having a happy
moment.

Dispositional happiness is explained in terms of occurrent happiness. Davis says[10] that to be dispositionally happy is to be predominantly occurrently happy; and he also says that dispositional
happiness depends upon what happens over a long period of time;
and he also says that it can end if, for example, you are paralyzed in
an accident. After the accident you may no longer be dispositionally
happy.

I think Davis's discussion of dispositional happiness is misleading.
Perhaps it would have been better if he had used a different name for the
concept upon which he was focusing. The phenomenon that deserves
the name 'dispositional happiness' is distinct from the phenomenon
that deserves the name 'predominant happiness.'

---

[6] Davis (1981b: 113).

[7] It's not clear to me that this definition works as intended. Consider the proposition that
$2+2 = 4$. While you are considering it, or reflecting on it, you might not be particularly
engaged in actively "endorsing" it. You might just be contemplating it. Yet if you, like Davis,
have dispositionally believed this for many decades and still do, then his definition implies
that you were occurrently believing it then. Yet maybe you were not. Maybe you were just
considering it.   [8] Davis (1981b: 112).

[9] Ibid. 111.   [10] Ibid.

In conformity with what I take to be a more standard terminology, we should say that a person is *dispositionally* happy if and only if he is disposed to be occurrently happy; if he would become occurrently happy if he woke up, or if he thought about things, or if some other factor suggested in context were to occur and thereby to "trigger" occurrent happiness. Dispositional happiness (properly so-called) does not depend upon what happens over a long period of time. A person can be dispositionally happy at a moment. The things that Davis says about "dispositional" happiness seem to me to be not true of the phenomenon we would more naturally call 'dispositional happiness.'

On the other hand, these things do seem to be true about a different phenomenon—a phenomenon that we would more naturally call 'predominant happiness.' To say that a person is predominantly happy during a period of time is to say (approximately) that he has been occurrently happy more often than not during that time. Thus, judgments of predominant happiness are summaries of facts about occurrent happiness during intervals. It makes no sense to say that a person is *predominantly* happy *at a moment*.[11] It makes sense only as a summary about a period of time. Furthermore, suppose a person has been predominantly happy during a period of time but then has a serious accident. This period of predominant happiness may then end and it may be followed by a period in which unhappiness predominates. Thus, predominant happiness is probably the phenomenon that "depends upon what happens over a long period of time." I think it was a mistake to use the term 'dispositional happiness' to refer to this phenomenon.[12]

But the concept of dispositional happiness (or predominant happiness) is not the central focus of Davis's efforts in any case. His main goal in the paper is to provide a reductive analysis of the concept of occurrent happiness. He intends to do this by appeal to the concepts of belief, desire, and thinking. The analysis has several components.

---

[11] That is, provided we use the word in this "temporal summary" sense. If we thought that a person could be happy about several different things at a time, and also unhappy about several other things, then we might say that he is predominantly happy at a moment if we meant that he was happy about more things than he was unhappy about. Even in this sense, predominant happiness represents a kind of summary of information about specific episodes of happiness. It is still not a disposition.

[12] Davis has informed me (recent personal correspondence) that at least some philosophers use the terminology in the way he describes.

4.3 *Davis's Theory of Happiness*

The central defined concept in Davis's theory is his concept of *momentary (occurrent) happiness*.[13] A person's level of momentary happiness is intended to be a measure of how occurrently happy he is at that moment. Information about a person's momentary happiness for all the moments during an interval will later be used to define happiness during an interval and in life as a whole. It can also be used in the construction of the concepts of dispositional and predominant happiness. So the analysis of the concept of *momentary happiness* stands at the heart of Davis's theory.

Davis says: 'Take every proposition A is thinking at the moment, multiply the degree to which it is believed [by A then] by the degree to which it is desired [by A then], add up all the products, and the sum is A's degree of happiness [at that moment].'[14] Using 'h' to indicate A's momentary *happiness* level, 'b(P1)' to indicate the strength of A's belief in P1, and 'd(P1)' to indicate the strength of A's desire for P1, Davis states this as a formal definition:[15]

D2: $h = \sum_{i=1}^{n} b(Pi)d(Pi)$, *where P1, . . . , Pn is an enumeration of all thoughts A is thinking.*

I believe the following formulation is equivalent to Davis's:

D2′: A's momentary happiness level at t = the sum, for all propositions P that A is thinking at t, of the products of the degree to which A believes P at t and the degree to which A desires P at t.

Clearly this is intended to be an account of occurrent happiness at a moment, and just as clearly it represents an interesting and attractive idea: to be happy is to be thinking, with respect to a bunch of things, that they are turning out as you want them to turn out. Suppose you want P and Q and R to be the case and you think they are. Then, other things being equal, the more you want these things to be the case, the happier you are; and the more convinced you are that they are the case, the happier you are. These are immediate implications of D2.

Consider the case of Tom, who wants to be healthy, wealthy, and wise. Suppose that at a certain moment he strongly desires each of them (more exactly, he desires each to degree +10). Suppose at the

---

[13] From now on, 'momentary happiness' should be understood to mean momentary *occurrent* happiness.   [14] Davis (1981b: 113).

[15] Thanks to Brad Skow for help in getting this straight.

same time he also very firmly believes that he is healthy, and that he is wealthy, and that he is wise (more exactly, he believes each to degree +1). Suppose, in addition, that at this selected moment Tom does not care about anything else. There is nothing else he wants. He just wants to be healthy, wealthy, and wise, and he thinks he is healthy, wealthy, and wise. Davis's theory implies that Tom is very happy at this moment. More exactly, it implies that his momentary happiness level = +30. (Let us assume that if a person is happy to degree +30 at a moment, then he is *very happy* at that time.)

In a footnote,[16] Davis mentions a possible complication. This turns on the distinction between intrinsic and extrinsic desires. We can distinguish between the case in which you want something, x, but only because you want something else, y, and you think x is a means to y. Were it not for its connection to y, you wouldn't care a fig about x. Opposed to this is the case in which there is no such other more "ultimate" desire. You want x but there is no other thing y such that you want x because you think it is a means to y. Call the first "desire purely as a means" and the second "desire purely as an end." Note that nothing in D2 makes any use of any such distinction. Perhaps it would have been better if this distinction had been employed.

Consider this case. Suppose Tom understands how the starting system on the car works; Alice does not. As Tom turns the key in the ignition, he and Alice both want their trip to begin. Tom is thinking these things:

1. The starter relay is working.
2. The starter motor is working.
3. The choke is working.
4. The ignition system is working.
5. We will soon be on our way.

Assume that Tom wants all of these things to occur, but wants the first four of them only because he wants to be on his way. If these things would not help to get them on their way, none of them would be of any interest to him. Assume that he wants (5) intrinsically.

On the other hand, assume that Alice does not know or care about 1–4. She is not thinking them. She just wants to be on her way. Suppose now the car starts and Tom and Alice are on their way. They are both happy about it. Each has a big grin. Each has an increased heartbeat. Each feels a rush of warmth and satisfaction. Let us assume that Tom's grin, heartbeat, and feelings of satisfaction are equal to

---

[16] Davis (1981b: 113, fn. 9).

Alice's. If we make some innocent assumptions about degrees of belief and desire, we get the result on Davis's theory that Tom is five times happier than Alice. This seems unmotivated.

Suppose in addition that Tom has been taking a logic class. He has been thinking about conjunction. He thinks about these things, which he also wants to be true:

1 & 2
1 & 3
1 & 4
1 & 5
1 & 2 & 3
1 & 2 & 4
1 & 2 & 5

And so on, for about 20 other propositions concerning the starting system in his car. He wants every one of them to be true, is thinking every one of them, and believes every one of them. (Tom has a remarkable capacity for multi-tasking; he can think 30 things at a time.) Alice does not bother with all of this nonsense. She just wants to be on her way and believes that she is about to be on her way. Now Davis's theory implies that Tom is about 30 times happier than Alice. This also seems unmotivated. Davis hints that maybe we should restrict D2 to propositions that are *intrinsically* desired.[17] In other words:

D2m: A's momentary happiness level at t = the sum, for all proposi-
        tions P that A is thinking at t, of the products of the degree to
        which A believes P at t and the degree to which A *intrinsically*
        desires P at t.

If we were to make this modification, the resulting theory would imply that Tom and Alice are equally happy in the example just cited. That's because each of them is described as having only one intrinsic desire. Each of them intrinsically wants to be on their way. Tom has a bunch of other desires that he takes to be satisfied, but each of them is purely extrinsic. He wants those other things only because he wants to be on his way.

Because of its implications for cases such as this, I am inclined to think that the revised version of the definition is preferable.[18] In what

---

[17] Davis has indicated (in personal correspondence) that in fact he would now probably want to sort out this difficulty in a different way.

[18] It should be noted that the introduction of the concept of intrinsic desire carries some costs, too. One can be illustrated by appeal to the example concerning Tom and the starting system.

follows I will assume that D2m is the official definition of momentary happiness.[19]

So far we have an account only of happiness at a moment. We need an account of happiness during an interval and in a life as a whole. Davis gives a sketch of an account of happiness during an interval. He says: 'Happiness can be defined for *intervals* (I was happier in 1978 than I was in 1977) as the *arithmetic mean* of [momentary happiness], the integral of [momentary happiness] divided by the length of the interval.'[20] The idea is this: your happiness during an interval is your average momentary happiness during that interval. Take the integral of momentary happiness during the interval, divide by the length of the interval. That's your happiness during the interval. Your happiness in life as a whole, presumably, would be your happiness during the interval beginning with birth (or conception, or whatever counts as the beginning of life) and ending with death (or whatever counts as the end of life).

There are other procedures that Davis could have used for calculating the amount of happiness enjoyed by an individual during an interval. One example is provided by Kahneman. He lets the integral of momentary happiness during an interval count as happiness during the interval.[21] Davis lets your happiness be the *average* momentary happiness during the interval. Clearly, these are different numbers. Consider these cases: Suppose that in March, Helen is steadily at a happiness level of +10. Suppose that on March 6, Tom was steadily at a happiness level of +11. Then Kahneman would say that Helen was happier in March than Tom was on March 6, while Davis would say the reverse.

This may seem to be a serious difference of opinion on an important topic, but I am inclined to think otherwise. I am inclined to think that Davis has focused on what we might better think of as

Suppose that Tom does indeed want to be on his way but that there is a further explanation: although he is not currently thinking about all the fun he will have at Lake Winnipesaukee, it is nevertheless true that this fact about fun at Lake Winnipesaukee somehow explains why he wants to be on his way. The problem is this: he is not thinking about fun at the lake. Therefore, it plays no role in his happiness according to Davis's theory. The desire to be on his way is the most "ultimate" desire that he is actually thinking about. It seems, then, that this desire must count as intrinsic even though there are other (currently not being thought about) desires that would turn up if Tom were questioned.

[19] Davis goes on to give account of a variety of interesting related concepts such as, for example, the concept of relational happiness, or "happiness about p"; the concept of a "happy thought"; and the concepts of optimism and pessimism. All of this is interesting and would reward careful scrutiny. However, it seems to me that we can profitably discuss Davis's conception of happiness without scrutinizing all of this associated material.

[20] Davis (1981b: 113, fn. 10).   [21] Kahneman (1999: 5).

average happiness during an interval and Kahneman has focused on what we might better think of as *total happiness during an interval*. The fact that the numbers are different does not demonstrate any serious difference of theory; it just shows that if you set out to measure different things, you shouldn't be surprised if you end up with different measurements.

However, it's important to keep in mind that these are genuinely different measurements. This comes out especially clearly in the case of life comparisons. Suppose Tom lives for 50 years, while Helen lives for 100 years. Suppose the numbers are as before. Then Kahneman would say that Helen had the happier life; but Davis would say that Tom had the happier life. We need to be clear about what is being said here. Kahneman's remark concerns the total amount of happiness that Helen enjoyed in her long life as a whole; Davis's remark concerns the average level of happiness that Tom enjoyed in his (much shorter) life. Each measurement is of some interest.

In Chapter 2, I described some cases that illustrate ways in which hedonism goes wrong. It seems to me that Davis's theory is more successful in accounting for our intuitions about these cases. Given natural assumptions about the beliefs and desires of the characters in the scenarios, Davis's theory seems to yield accurate assessments of happiness.

Recall the case of Wendell. He had a positive hedono-doloric balance at the moment of his modest orgasm, but he was unhappy. Davis could readily explain Wendell's unhappiness by pointing out that at the moment in question Wendell was coming to the realization that some of his strongest desires were going to be frustrated. He desperately wanted the orgasm enhancer to work; yet he was then beginning to believe that it would not work. He wanted not to be the victim of an Internet scam; but it was dawning on him that he had been taken. Several other strong desires were at that moment being frustrated. As a result, Davis's theory implies that Wendell was relatively unhappy. This seems correct.

Consider the case involving the new mother. She was in severe pain when she gave birth. Presumably she did not have any intrinsic desire for that pain, and so her recognition of the pain would have tended to make her unhappy. But at the same time she had some very strong desires—to have a baby; for the baby to be healthy; to be finished with the pregnancy. At that pain-filled moment, the new mother was confidently believing all these things to be true. All these desire satisfactions contribute, according to Davis's theory, to the happiness of the new mother. We can suppose that these satisfactions outweigh the frustration associated with the feelings of pain. So the new mother is declared to be happy as she gives birth. Again, the theory gets the case right.

In Chapter 3, I described some cases that cast doubt on Kahneman's approach. Consider the case of Brett at the drag strip. As he zooms down the track, Brett steadily wants his experiences to change. He is definitely not hoping for experiential persistence; he wants dramatic change. Thus, Kahneman's theory (under the interpretation I have proposed) implies that Brett is unhappy. This seems exactly wrong. Davis's theory, on the other hand, seems to generate the correct result. Brett wants to be changing locations; and he believes he is. Brett wants to be accelerating; and he believes that he is. Brett wants the sound of the engine and the appearance of the tachometer to be changing in certain ways; and he believes that they are. Thus, Davis's theory implies that Brett is happy as he zooms down the track. This is consistent with our pre-analytic intuitions about the case.

4.4 *Problems for Davis's Form of Local Preferentism*

In spite of these successes, I am convinced that Davis's theory—and indeed every form of preferentism about happiness—is false. Of course, I recognize that we are often *caused* to be happy when we want something to be true and believe it is true. What I find implausible is the notion that happiness *just is* the combination of believing something and wanting it to be true. I think we can be happy even though we do not believe true the things we want, and I think we can fail to be happy even though we believe true the things that we want. This can happen in a variety of different ways and for a variety of different reasons. Let's consider some ways in which happiness can diverge from desire satisfaction.

Imagine a philosophy graduate student, Susan, who is somewhat pessimistic and despondent.[22] She thinks things will not go her way. She wants to complete a really brilliant dissertation, but she is confident that she won't; she wants to get a job at a major research university, but she is pretty confident she won't. She wants some of her papers to be published in high-prestige philosophy journals but is skeptical about that, too. Suppose that Susan's current psychological state is typical for her. She has always been pessimistic. Even as a child, she was inclined to anticipate that things would not go her way. Furthermore, for a

---

[22] My thanks to Meghan Masto for introducing this example. I have developed it a bit further.

long time she has been unhappy. She has had negative subjective desire satisfaction and has been unhappy. So far, Susan's case is consistent with Davis's view: Susan has negative subjective desire satisfaction and is unhappy, just as the theory says she should be.

But now suppose that Susan begins seeing a new psychological counselor.[23] The counselor first interviews Susan in an effort to determine why she is so unhappy. He suspects that she is unhappy in part because she is so pessimistic. The counselor is interested in Cognitive Behavioral Therapy, and so he first tries to get her to have a more optimistic view of things. He tries to get her to start thinking that her papers will be published in major journals and that she will land a good job.

Unfortunately, the counselor's first efforts fail. In fact, Susan's pessimistic beliefs are solidly entrenched. She cannot give them up. (Perhaps this is due to the fact that she has excellent evidence for these beliefs. They are entirely reasonable, given her modest philosophical abilities.) Susan remains pessimistic and unhappy.

Then the counselor tries a slightly different approach. Instead of trying to alter Susan's beliefs, he tries to alter her desires. He tries to get her to stop wanting to get her papers published in major journals, and to stop wanting to have a job in an excellent department. But these efforts fail as well. In fact, Susan wants these things, and she finds that she cannot give up these desires. They are deeply and permanently entrenched.

Finally, the counselor concludes that CBT is not going to work in Susan's case. He decides to try a completely different approach. Instead of attempting to change Susan's beliefs or desires, he decides to prescribe a drug that is alleged to have a direct impact on mood. According to the manufacturer, this drug will simply brighten Susan's mood. It will make her more cheerful. So he prescribes the mood-altering drug and it works as advertised. Susan feels much better—though she still thinks her work is not very good and she won't get a good job. Although her beliefs and desires persist, Susan becomes much happier.

In the absence of an independent theory of happiness, it is not easy to explain precisely what makes it correct to say that Susan is happier. At best, I can describe the case in greater detail and hope that the reader will share my intuition. Suppose that, after taking the drug, Susan smiles a lot more. Suppose she regains her appetite, and starts sleeping better. Suppose she is less irritable and moody. Suppose that

---

[23] I am grateful to Alex Sarch for constructing the example in this illuminating way.

when asked, she says she is feeling quite a bit better. Suppose time spent on her dissertation is now much more productive and enjoyable. Suppose she says that she is really glad that her counselor finally gave up on CBT and turned to something that works. Suppose she says that she intends to keep taking the new drug.

So here we have a comparison: before she took the drug, Susan had a certain set of beliefs and desires and she was very unhappy. This is all consistent with Davis's theory, since she wanted certain things and believed that she was not going to get them. After she took the drug, Susan had many of the same beliefs and desires but she was no longer so unhappy. In fact, at various moments after taking the drug, she was actually fairly chipper.

I think this example illustrates the fact that the linkage between happiness and subjective desire satisfaction is merely contingent. Before treatment, Susan had negative subjective desire satisfaction (she desired certain things and thought she was not going to get them) and she was unhappy. After treatment she still had negative subjective desire satisfaction, but she was no longer quite so unhappy. Although her beliefs and her desires remained relatively constant, her mood had improved. Of course, for most of us, most of the time, there is a connection between the extent to which we think we are getting what we want and our happiness. Typically, we are happier if we think things are going our way. But this example suggests that the connection is at best loose and contingent. Unhappiness can disappear (or at least decrease significantly) while beliefs and desires remain fairly constant.[24]

Another case is the emotional mirror image of Susan's. Imagine another graduate student—call him 'Glum'—who is disappointed and unhappy. Although he strongly wants all of these things, he thinks he won't produce a good dissertation, won't get any papers published, and won't get a good job. In addition, he is suffering from depression. He is a pretty unhappy guy. He also visits the psychological counselor mentioned above. In his case, however, the counselor's application of Cognitive Behavioral Therapy is somewhat more successful. The counselor gets Glum to take a much more realistic view of his considerable talents. As a result, Glum starts believing that he will get

---

[24] Davis (1981b) discusses a case like Susan's on p. 117. He suggests that when Susan is in a good mood, she will see things "in a rosy light." She will more or less automatically want some things to be the way she takes them to be—for example, the weather, or the flowers she sees. If this is so, Susan's increased happiness is consistent with Davis's theory. But it's not clear to me that Susan would necessarily have occurrent thoughts about such things. As I see it, she might be in a happier mood even though she is not thinking any new and happier thoughts.

some papers published and that he will get a good job. But even when he thinks about these things in this new light, Glum is no happier. His depression remains just as deep as ever.

This example is intended to show in another way that subjective desire satisfaction and happiness do not necessarily march in lock-step. Glum's level of subjective desire satisfaction changed, but his level of happiness remained constant. This suggests that happiness involves something more than, or something different from, merely believing things that you want to be true. As I see it, the missing element is more emotional or affective. In order to be happy, as I see it, one must be pleased about the good things that are happening.

A third example[25] illustrates a slightly different way in which subjective desire satisfaction can fail to have any impact on happiness. Suppose Lois is emotionally neutral—neither happy nor unhappy. Suppose she is taking some children through a museum where they see a dinosaur exhibit. Lois is looking at the skeleton of an apparently ferocious dinosaur in the museum. She hears some other visitors talking. One remarks on how horrible it would be to be eaten by one of those things. Lois thinks about how horrible it would be to be eaten by a dinosaur. Of course she wants not to be eaten by a dinosaur. At the same time, she knows that dinosaurs are extinct and have not eaten anyone in hundreds of years, so she is quite confident that she will not be eaten by a dinosaur. Davis's theory implies that this should constitute an increase in her level of happiness, but it doesn't. Her neutral emotional state persists. She gains no joy from the realization that she is not going to be eaten by a dinosaur. She never felt that she was in danger of being eaten by a dinosaur, and so reflection on the fact that it is not going to happen does not bring any relief.

This example suggests that when you recognize that a certain thing is certainly not going to happen—you take it to be (in some sense) impossible—then your happiness level may not be affected by the fact that you want it to be that way. Many of us believe and want there to be oxygen, and gravity, and sunlight. Yet only some of us gain any joy from these things. Most of us simply take them for granted, just as Lois in the example takes it for granted that she is not going to be eaten by a dinosaur. If you never thought P was possible anyway, knowing that it won't happen doesn't make you happier even if you like it that way. Again, the problem seems to be that Lois does not take any pleasure in the fact that she will not be eaten by dinosaurs.

---

[25] Thanks to Scott Hill for suggesting this example.

That seems to explain why her subjective desire satisfaction yields no happiness.

A fourth case illustrates another way in which it is possible to believe that your desires are being satisfied without getting any happiness as a result. This may be the sort of case that Sidgwick had in mind when he spoke of the "Dead Sea Apple"—which he described as mere 'dust and ashes in the eating.'[26] Here is an illustration: A beer-lover once had some beer in a strange bar. It had a weird and wonderful taste. He really enjoyed it. For many years he wanted to find that beer again, but never found it. He kept looking. He wanted to taste that weird and wonderful taste. After many years of searching, he wandered into a bar in a foreign country. Lo and behold, they had the beer. He wanted to taste that strange taste again and so he ordered a glass. He drank. It tasted the same, but he no longer enjoyed it. It was a disappointment. In fact, he was pretty unhappy about the whole thing. Anyway, he was not happy. But he wanted to taste that old taste, and was certain that he was tasting it. That's all he was thinking about. Davis's theory implies that he was happy; but he was not.

4.5 *A Paradox for Preferentism?*

Another problem for Davis's theory arises from the fact that he places no restrictions on the objects of happiness. Provided that you want something to happen and believe that it is happening, you are supposedly made happier. But some possible objects of belief and desire intrinsically involve *unhappiness*. Something approaching a paradox arises if a person wants and believes in one of these.

To see this in a particularly stark example, suppose that a certain person, S, is neither happy nor unhappy. Maybe he is sound asleep and has no occurrent beliefs. Now suppose we change S at t by adding exactly one desire. Let this be a desire to be unhappy. More exactly, what S wants is:

U: S is unhappy at t.

Let's assume that S desires U at t with a strength of 5.

Suppose S would fully believe U if he believed it at all and would fully disbelieve it if he didn't believe it. That is, he would believe with strength 1 if he believed it, and he would believe it with strength -1 if

---

[26] Sidgwick (1962: 110).

he didn't believe it.[27] Then it seems that there are two main possibilities that we can consider: Either (a) S fully believes that he is unhappy—in other words, S fully thinks U is true, or (b) S fully believes that he is not unhappy—in other words, S fully thinks that U is not true.

Suppose he occurrently believes he is unhappy. Then he is happy to degree +5 according to Davis's theory. (He believes U to degree 1 and wants it to degree 5; $1 \times 5 = +5$. He is not thinking anything else. Therefore the sum of the relevant products is +5.)

Suppose he occurrently believes he is not unhappy. Then he will be unhappy to degree −5 according to Davis's theory. (He believes U to degree −1 and wants it to degree 5; $-1 \times 5 = -5$. He is not thinking anything else. The sum of the products is −5.) Therefore, if he believes he is happy, he is unhappy; and if he believes he is unhappy, then he is happy. This is not exactly a paradox, but it is strange. Whatever this fellow believes about his state of happiness, he is bound to be wrong.[28]

Davis has suggested (in personal correspondence) that the notion that someone could desire to be unhappy is "implausible." He says, 'It is not easy to imagine subjects who actually want to be unhappy.' I disagree. I am inclined to think that I can easily imagine people who want to be unhappy; in fact, I think I know some people who want to be unhappy.[29]

A more complex case arises if we add further stipulations. First, let's assume that the subject is aware of his own mental states in this sense: when he believes something, he recognizes that he believes it.[30] When he desires something, he recognizes that he desires it. Let's also assume that the subject accepts Davis's theory. Assume finally that this subject is smart enough to be able to work out the implications of Davis's theory for simple cases involving his own current beliefs and desires.

Now the situation becomes even more troubling. Suppose as before that S wants to be unhappy. Then suppose he believes that he is not unhappy. Then (since he is aware of his belief and his desire; and he

---

[27] I introduce this assumption merely to simplify the arithmetic. I believe that the main points I intend to make would hold true even for levels of belief between 0 and 1.

[28] Later, in Chapter 11, I will discuss the idea that each person has epistemic authority with respect to her own happiness. The present example shows that if Davis's theory of happiness were true, then the authority thesis would surely be false.

[29] Perhaps it is hard to imagine people who want to have their desires frustrated. That may be right. But it is not so hard to imagine people who want to be unhappy. This consideration by itself may be sufficient to show that happiness cannot be identified with desire satisfaction.

[30] To avoid regress, this stipulation should be restricted to "first-order" beliefs—thus excluding beliefs about beliefs about beliefs . . .

believes in Davis's theory; and can see what follows from this) he will believe that he is unhappy. (Because he will think that he has one main desire and that it is being frustrated and he will see that Davis's theory implies in this case that he is unhappy.) Suppose he believes that he is unhappy. Then (since he is aware of his belief and his desire; and he believes Davis's theory and can quickly see its implications for his own case) he will believe he is happy. (Because he will think he has one main desire and that it is being satisfied.)

Therefore, this self-aware, Davis-theory-believing person who wants to be unhappy is in an odd situation: if he believes that he is happy, then he believes that he is unhappy. If he believes that he is unhappy, then he believes that he is happy. This is not precisely a paradox, but it is a strange doxastic situation.[31]

It might take a fraction of a second for this person to work out the implications of Davis's theory for his own case. If so, there might never be a single instant at which he both believes he is happy and believes he is unhappy. Rather, if at one moment he believes he is happy, then a fraction of a second later he will believe that he is unhappy. Then, another fraction of a second later he will believe that he is happy. This game of emotional ping-pong will go on until something breaks in to interrupt the cycle. One way to interrupt the cycle would be to give up on Davis's theory.[32]

---

[31] Thanks to Chris Heathwood, Ben Bradley, and Brad Skow for helping me to understand the implications of this case more clearly. Thanks also to Wayne Davis for challenging me to get these arguments into a more coherent form.
[32] Thanks to Brad Skow for suggesting this possibility.

CHAPTER 5

————

Whole Life Satisfaction Concepts
of Happiness

5.1 *A Surprising Book Title*

On my desk before me I have a copy of *Happiness Quantified* by Bernard van Praag and Ada Ferrer-i-Carbonell. The authors are economists associated with the "Leyden School" of economics. The Leyden School approach seeks to assess the well-being of groups of people not by looking at statistics concerning the amounts of money or consumer goods those people possess, but rather by trying to determine how happy they are. In the book in question, van Praag and Ferrer-i-Carbonell report in great detail on a huge amount of empirical research bearing on these questions. They summarize results concerning different national groups, gender groups, age groups, income groups; they talk about satisfaction with work, marriage, leisure, health care and many other domains of life. They provide highly detailed graphs and charts displaying the results of very extensive research. They state and discuss statistical methods and formulae. It is a very impressive book.

One surprising fact about this book concerns the connection between the title and the contents. The title strongly suggests that the book will be about the measurement of happiness. Yet the index contains only two references to 'happiness.' The first is a reference to an occurrence on page 162, and even there the word occurs only in an inessential comment. The next occurrence of the term is on page 288, where there is a passing remark about 'the modern literature on satisfaction and happiness.' The index does not give any indication of other occurrences of the term or any cognates. There are, however, several instances in which the authors mention that the word 'happy' appears in some question that was put to research subjects. So, though the title of the book suggests that the book is going to be about the measurement of happiness, I was not able to find any passage in the book where happiness or its measurement is explicitly discussed—that is, I was not able to find a passage where the term 'happiness' was used to refer to the thing whose measurement was being discussed.

Instead, the graphs and tables contain information about the extent to which people in various groups are satisfied with various aspects of their lives. Thus, for example, Table 3.2 reports on the results of research concerning West German workers in 1996. It gives levels of satisfaction with such domains as work, financial situation, health, housing, leisure, and the environment. In the final row of the table we find results for "General Satisfaction." A review of the rest of the tables in the book (cursory, I admit) suggests that they all contain information about levels of satisfaction with domains of life, or life in general, for individuals in various national, age, gender, income, or other groups.

It does not seem to me that this is a case of bait-and-switch. I am not suggesting that the publishers put the wrong title on the book. Rather, I suspect that what has happened here is that the authors simply took it as obvious that if you want to measure the components of happiness, you just have to measure satisfaction with such domains as work, marriage, leisure, health care, and so on. And if you want to measure happiness in general, you just have to measure satisfaction with life as a whole. I suspect that van Praag and Ferrer-i-Carbonell took these assumptions to be beyond question. They don't discuss them; they don't attempt to defend them. Perhaps they are unquestioned presuppositions of their research.

If van Praag and Ferrer-i-Carbonell did assume that happiness could be identified with satisfaction with life as a whole, then they shared a very popular assumption. Indeed, the most popular concepts of happiness among psychologists and philosophers nowadays are concepts of happiness according to which happiness is defined as 'satisfaction with life as a whole.' Such concepts are "Whole Life Satisfaction" (WLS) concepts of happiness.

In this chapter, I show that there are hundreds of non-equivalent ways in which a WLS conception of happiness can be developed. I go on to show that every precise conception either requires *actual* satisfaction with life as a whole or requires *hypothetical* satisfaction with life as a whole. I show that a person can be "happy" (in any familiar sense that might be relevant to eudaimonism) at a time even though he is not actually satisfied with his life as a whole at that time. I also show that a person can be "happy" at a time even though it is not correct to say that if he were to think about his life as a whole at that time, he would be satisfied with it as a whole. My thesis here is that if you think that happiness is The Good, you should avoid defining happiness as whole life satisfaction.

5.2 *Whole Life Satisfaction Theories of Happiness*

WLS concepts of happiness have been proposed by many philosophers, including Richard Brandt, John Kekes, Robert Nozick, Wayne Sumner, Wladyslaw Tatarkiewicz, Elizabeth Telfer, and G. H. von Wright. While every one of these concepts of happiness requires "whole life satisfaction" in some form or other, they are not equivalent.[1]

a. Tatarkiewicz says that happiness (in the most important sense of the term) is 'satisfaction with one's life as a whole.'[2] He apparently means to defend the view that if a person is happy then he must not only be fully satisfied with the current segment of his life, he must be satisfied with the past segment of his life and the segment of his life that is yet to come.[3] In his discussion of happiness and time he makes the point explicitly:

Satisfaction with life as a whole must be satisfaction not only with that which is, but also with that which was and that which will be, not only with the present, but also with the past and the future.[4]

b. Elizabeth Telfer formulates the theory in a different way.[5] She says:

My suggestion for a definition of happiness, then, is that it is a state of being pleased with one's life as a whole.[6]

---

[1] Each of these philosophers offers a WLS concept of happiness. In some cases, it is offered simply as an account of the nature of happiness. In other cases, it is offered as a stipulative definition as part of a larger project about welfare. In yet other cases, it is offered in other ways. I do not mean to suggest that all of these philosophers propose the *same* account of happiness, or that they use the account of happiness in the same way.   [2] Tatarkiewicz (1966: 1).

[3] In his (1976), Tatarkiewicz maintains that 'happy' is multiply ambiguous and vague in ordinary language. He claims, however, that in one of its two main ordinary senses, it means satisfaction with life as a whole. He claims that this is the crucial sense since happiness, thus understood, is 'one of the greatest goods accessible to man' (4). After further reflection, Tatarkiewicz revises this account, saying instead that ideal happiness is 'lasting, complete, and justified satisfaction with life' (16).   [4] Tatarkiewicz (1976: 140).

[5] Telfer also claims that 'happy' is ambiguous in ordinary language. Like Tatarkiewicz, she claims that in the most important sense, and the sense of greatest interest to moral philosophers, it expresses the concept of whole life satisfaction.   [6] Telfer (1980: 8–9).

Telfer expands upon this by saying that 'a happy man does not want anything major in his life to be otherwise; he is pleased with, that is wants (to keep), what he has got; there is nothing major which he has not got and which he wants (to get).'[7]

c. Richard Brandt states two conditions for happiness. Brandt says:

the following proposal for a definition of "happy" may be suggested . . . . in order to be happy it is necessary that one like . . . those parts of one's total life pattern and circumstances that one thinks are important. To say that one likes them is in part to say that one is "satisfied" with them—that one does not wish them to be substantially different, and that they measure up, at least roughly, to the life ideal one had hoped to attain; . . . [We] would not call a man happy if he did not frequently feel joy or enthusiasm or enjoy what he was doing or experiencing.[8]

Brandt apparently means to be proposing an account of what it means to say that a person had a happy life, or was a happy person. His idea seems to be that in order to be a happy person, one must meet two conditions. First, one must be satisfied with the life one in fact has lived—that life must measure up (or must be believed to measure up) sufficiently to the "life ideal" one had hoped to attain. Second, one must have felt joy or enthusiasm frequently during that life.

d. Like Brandt, Wayne Sumner claims that in order to have a happy life, a person must (a) be satisfied with his life as a whole, and (b) enjoy certain moods or emotions.[9] Sumner describes the first component in these words:

The cognitive aspect of happiness consists in a positive evaluation of the conditions of your life, a judgement that, at least on balance, it measures up favourably against your standards or expectations. This evaluation may be global, covering all of the important sectors of your life, or it may focus on one in particular (your work, say, or your family). In either case it represents an affirmation or endorsement of (some or all of) the conditions or circumstances of your life, a judgement that, on balance and taking everything into account, your life is going well for you.[10]

The second component of Sumner's analysis is the affective component. Sumner requires that a happy person experience "a sense of well-being" that is directed upon a specific object—his life as a whole.

---

[7] Ibid. 8.   [8] Brandt (1967: 413–14).
[9] Neither Sumner nor Brandt claims that a person's welfare level is directly determined by the amount of happiness he enjoys. Sumner, for example, claims that welfare 'consists in authentic happiness, the happiness of an informed and autonomous subject' (1996: 172).
[10] Ibid. 145.

The affective side of happiness consists in what we commonly call a sense of well-being: finding your life enriching or rewarding, or feeling satisfied or fulfilled by it.[11]

Views relevantly like these have been proposed by many other philosophers and psychologists. But for present purposes this brief catalogue should be sufficient. All these definitions—and others relevantly like them—introduce WLS concepts of happiness.

5.3 *Two Preliminary Problems*

WLS conceptions of happiness seem to confront two closely related problems right at the outset. For purposes of discussion, imagine a view (like Brandt's or Sumner's) according to which a person is happy if and only if he judges that important aspects of his life match up with his expectations. One problem arises because a person might judge at one time that important aspects of his whole life do match up with his expectations; but the same person might judge at another time that important aspects of his whole life do not match up with his expectations. This sort of change in judgment is unproblematic in itself. Just as your blood pressure may vary through time, so may the extent to which you judge that important aspects of your life as a whole match up with your expectations.[12] However, the advocate of the WLS concept of happiness surely does not want to say, in such a case, that the person both did have a happy life and also did not have a happy life. That would simply be a contradiction. This is the *instability problem*.

A second problem can be described as the *lability problem*. Empirical testing has demonstrated that an individual's judgment about whole life satisfaction can be affected by seemingly trivial features of the context in which he is making the judgment.[13] Thus, for example, if a subject is first allowed to discover a "lost" dime, and then is asked to make a judgment about whole life satisfaction, he is likely to indicate

---

[11] Sumner (1996: 146).

[12] In Diener et al. (1985), Ed Diener and his colleagues presented a little questionnaire designed to determine a person's satisfaction with life. They claim that their Satisfaction With Life Scale has "favorable psychometric properties." Among these properties is "high temporal reliability." People tend to get the same score on this scale when they retake the test two months later. I cannot imagine why Diener and his colleagues thought that this sort of reliability is a "favorable psychometric property." Surely the corresponding feature in a blood pressure test would be cause for concern about the test. Similarly, unless we have independent reason for thinking that happiness levels remain constant through life, temporal reliability is neither "favorable" nor unfavorable.

[13] For a popular sketch of some of the relevant research, see Nettle (2005: ch. 1).

greater satisfaction than he would if he had not found a dime. Many other contextual factors—the weather, the decor of the room in which the subject is questioned, the attractiveness of the questioner—have been shown to affect life satisfaction judgments. This seems to suggest that such judgments are somehow "wrong"—that they fail to track our actual levels of life satisfaction. Could a subject genuinely become more satisfied with his life as a whole simply because he recently came across a dime? That may seem incredible.

Some have suggested that these problems could be avoided if there were some ideal moment for measuring life satisfaction. For example, we might say that a person has a happy life if, at the moment of death, when he looks back and surveys his life as a whole, he judges that important aspects matched up with his expectations. The problems with this approach should be obvious: some people don't look back and survey their lives on their deathbeds. Surely we cannot just conclude that these people were not happy. Some who do thus survey their lives may make a favorable judgment even though they in fact led miserable lives. Maybe they have lapsed into delirium as they approach death. Others may not make favorable judgments even though their lives were very happy. And it's also possible that someone might find a lost dime shortly before he dies. Clearly, it is unreasonable to link a person's lifetime happiness level to the life assessment he makes *in extremis.*

I believe, however, that neither instability nor lability is a genuine problem. In each case, a problem seems to arise primarily because the theory has not been formulated clearly. In order to state it clearly, we must start by drawing a distinction between two WLS concepts. The fundamental concept is a concept of *whole life satisfaction at a moment.* This is just the amount of the relevant sort of whole life satisfaction that a subject has at a moment. The second concept would be a concept of whole life satisfaction *during an interval* based upon some sort of aggregation of information concerning whole life satisfaction levels at moments within the interval.[14]

Let me sketch one way of making use of this distinction. Suppose a subject, S, is satisfied with his life as a whole to different degrees at different moments. At t1, he is satisfied to degree 4 with his life as a whole. At t2, he is satisfied to degree 6, and so on. Suppose he is dissatisfied with his life as a whole at some other moments during the interval. At t16, for example, he is satisfied to degree −2 with his life

---

[14] For a discussion of this so-called "instability problem" and a different solution, see Valerie Tiberius (2003, unpublished). I discuss this approach later in section 5.5.

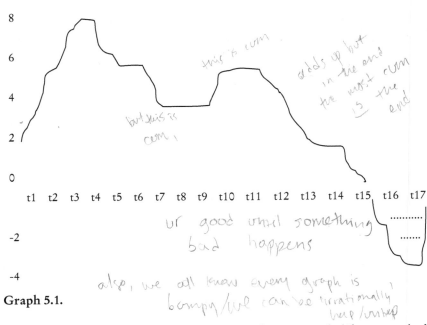

Graph 5.1.

as a whole. If all of these momentary satisfaction-with-life-as-a-whole levels are plotted on a graph, we get a line as shown in Graph 5.1.

We can define the subject's whole life satisfaction for the interval t1–t17 simply as the integral of his momentary life satisfactions for the moments during the interval. Thus, we recognize the fact that whole life satisfaction varies from time to time. We incorporate this fact into our calculations, letting life satisfaction during a stretch of time be determined (roughly) by the total amount of life satisfaction the person experiences during that time, minus the total amount of life dissatisfaction.[15]

Advocates of the WLS approach to happiness can then say that a person's happiness at a moment is equal to his level of whole life satisfaction at that moment; and happiness in life as a whole is equal to his whole life satisfaction for the interval that is his whole life. The fact that the subject had different levels of whole life satisfaction at different times does not give rise to a contradiction; we just take account of

[15] There are other ways of doing the aggregating. We might focus instead on *average* levels of momentary life satisfaction; we might focus on highs and lows; there are other options. I presuppose this method of aggregation primarily for simplicity in exposition.

all these different whole life satisfaction levels when calculating whole life satisfaction for the life as a whole. Thus the instability problem does not arise.

What of the lability problem? Suppose a subject finds a lost dime at a certain time. Suppose that a moment later he judges his life as a whole to be going very well. Suppose he would not have made such a favorable judgment about his life as a whole if he had not found the dime. Must we then worry that his judgment is somehow "wrong" and needs to be disregarded in our calculations? I think not. I think this lability is not a problem. Advocates of the WLS approach can simply claim that in fact subjects are temporarily made somewhat happier by seemingly trivial facts. Their outlook on life as a whole can be brightened even by finding a lost dime or sitting in an interview room with an attractive interviewer. Thus, there is nothing wrong with saying that they are somewhat happier (for a moment) even though the increase in happiness is based on quite a trivial factor.[16]

If we choose to formulate the theory in this way, these two problems are solved. But then the crucial question concerns whole life satisfaction at moments. Precisely how are the satisfaction-with-life-at-a-moment points determined?

5.4 *Some Distinctions and a Multitude of Concepts*

It should be obvious even from the smattering of quotations at the outset that it is not the case that advocates of the WLS approach have committed themselves to precisely the same view. Let us consider some of the respects in which these formulations differ.

a. Some of these formulations suggest that whole life satisfaction is something very "cognitive" and "judgmental." Others suggest that it is something much more emotional. According to a judgmental view, in order to be satisfied with his life a person must *make a judgment* about his life—perhaps (as Sumner says) the 'judgement that, on balance and taking everything into account, your life is going well for you.' According to a more emotional view, it would not be necessary to make any judgment. All that would be necessary is that the person should "feel good" about his life as a whole. Telfer seems to advocate

---

[16] In ch. 4 of his (2008b), Daniel Haybron discusses this problem. He points out that some researchers worry that this "fickleness" of life satisfaction reports indicates that such reports have 'little grounding in any important reality and are not to be taken seriously.'

this sort of approach. She says that what's necessary is that you be 'pleased with' your life as a whole. It should be obvious that a person could "feel good" about his life without making any judgment, and that a person could make a judgment without "feeling good" about anything. Brandt and Sumner apparently want to say that happiness involves both something judgmental and something emotional.[17]

b. Some of these formulations suggest that happiness essentially involves making a judgment about one's life *as a whole*. This provides the rationale for the name of the theory. Tatarkiewicz clearly opts for something like this. But other formulations weaken the requirement. They say that happiness essentially involves making a favorable judgment about *important aspects of the life*. Brandt, Sumner, and Telfer all say things like this. Sumner seems to commit himself to a still weaker view. In one parenthetical remark, he says that happiness requires merely that the subject make a favorable judgment about *some aspect of his life*.[18] Clearly, a person could judge that some aspect of his life is going well without judging that any *important* aspect of his life is going well; and he could judge that some important aspect is going well without judging that *all* the important aspects are going well; and a person could judge that all important aspects are going well without judging that the *life as a whole* is going well.

c. There is a striking difference between versions of the view according to which the happy person must *actually* make the judgment of life satisfaction, and versions according to which the happy person must merely be such that *he would have made such a judgment, if he had thought about the matter* (or if some other counterfactual condition had been satisfied). Tatarkiewicz clearly chooses the hypothetical version when he says, 'it is enough that he would be satisfied if he were to think of it.'[19] Again, the difference is obvious. Someone might never think about his life as a whole, and might never form any judgment about whether it was satisfactory, yet he might be the sort

---

[17] Tatarkiewicz seems also to opt for a conception of satisfaction that involves both an intellectual and an emotional element. See Tatarkiewicz (1976: 12).

[18] Sumner says that a person is happy if she is satisfied with 'some or all of the conditions or circumstances of her life' (1996: 156). I am puzzled by the suggestion that a person could be declared happy if she were satisfied with merely *some* of the conditions of her life. Surely that is far too weak. Suppose she is profoundly dissatisfied with most of the conditions of her life (including her health, her wealth, her level of freedom, her marriage, and her job), but satisfied with just two minor ones (her Internet access is fast; her TV reception is good). Perhaps (though he never says quite this) Sumner's idea is rather that a person is happy *in a certain area of life* if she is satisfied with the conditions of her life *in that area*.

[19] Tatarkiewicz (1976: 10).

of person who would have formed a favorable judgment about his life, if he had given it any thought. Let us introduce some terminology here to mark this difference. An *actualist* view would say that such a person is not happy because he did not actually form the judgment; a *hypotheticalist* view would say that he is happy because he would have formed the judgment if he had given it some thought.

d. Tatarkiewicz claims that to be happy one must be satisfied with one's *whole* life—past, present, and future. It appears that his idea was that the ideally happy person somehow conceives of everything that has happened to him, that is happening to him, and that ever will happen to him. He is fully satisfied with *all of it*, from beginning to end.[20] Tatarkiewicz recognizes that this is beyond the intellectual powers of any actual human being and accordingly concludes that no one is happy (in this robust "ideal" sense). A different view would maintain that to be happy at a time one must be satisfied with the temporal slice of one's life that is then current. Perhaps an advocate of this approach would say that to be happy in life as a whole is to be happy at enough of these moments. This could happen even if there was no moment at which the happy person were satisfied with anything in his past or future relative to that moment.[21] Yet another view would maintain that to be happy at a time requires that one be satisfied with everything that has happened to him up until that time.[22]

e. There are people who are confused about their lives. They think certain things have happened to them, but in fact those things have not happened. We might say that happiness requires being satisfied with the things that have *actually happened* in your life as a whole. Alternatively, we might say that happiness requires being satisfied with the things that *you think have happened* to you in your life as a whole. Depending upon the details of formulation, these views could yield different judgments concerning the case of a person who is mistaken about what has happened to him. I will characterize a view as a form of "objectivism" if it says that happiness requires satisfaction with the life you are actually living. I will characterize a view as a form

[20] This comes out especially clearly in one of the passages I cited earlier: 'Satisfaction with life as a whole must be satisfaction with that which is, but also with that which was, and that which will be, not only with the present, but also with the past and the future' (Tatarkiewicz 1976: 140).
[21] There might then be a question about the extent to which such a view still deserves to be classified as a form of "whole life satisfactionism." But if we aggregated information about momentary satisfaction levels so as to generate the subject's whole life satisfaction level, the resulting theory would be in important respects similar to the other theories under consideration here.   [22] I am not aware of anyone who actually defended this view.

of "subjectivism" if it says that happiness requires satisfaction with the life you think you are living.[23]

f. When we say that a person is satisfied with his life, we may have in mind (a) that he has a very detailed conception of what has happened in his life, and he is satisfied with that; or we may have in mind (b) that he has only a vague and superficial conception of what has happened in his life, but that (insofar as he is aware of it) he is satisfied with that. Thus, there is a further dimension on which WLS definitions of happiness can be located. This dimension involves the degree of detail and specificity of awareness that is required for happiness. Let us say that a definition is "maximally epistemically demanding" if it requires that the happy person have a complete and detailed conception of his own life; let us say that it is "epistemically lax" if it requires no such detail. Obviously, there are many intermediate degrees of demandingness between these extremes. For every such degree, there is a collection of distinct forms of WLS.

These are six independent distinctions. Judgmentalism can be combined either with actualism or with hypotheticalism; important aspectivalism can be combined with currentism or with up-to-nowism. The same is true for all the distinctions. The result is that we can formulate hundreds of different WLS definitions of happiness. Let's briefly consider some of the possibilities.

We can formulate a definition of happiness that is: (a) judgmental; (b) "important aspectival;" (c) actualist; (d) up-to-now-ist; (e) objective; and (f) moderately epistemically demanding. It looks like this:

WLS6: A person, S, is happy to degree n at a time, t, =df. there is a certain life that S has actually lived up to t, and at t S actually has a life ideal, and at t, S knows what his life ideal is and has a moderately detailed conception of what has transpired in important aspects of his life up to t, and at t, S judges with respect to the up-to-t segment of his life that important aspects of that life segment match up to degree n with the life ideal that he maintains at t.

A different definition would replace the (b) "important aspectivalism" of WLS6 with "universalism." It would also replace the (d) "up-to-now-ism" with "current slicism." The resulting definition is:

---

[23] In choosing this terminology to mark this distinction, I follow Tatarkiewicz (1976: 16).

WLS7: A person, S, is happy to degree n at a time, t, =df. there is a certain slice of life that S is actually living at t, and at t S actually has a life ideal, and at t S knows what his life ideal is and S has a moderately detailed conception of what is transpiring in the current slice of his life at t, and at t S judges with respect to *the current-at-t slice of his life* that it matches up *as a whole* to degree n[24] with the life ideal that he maintains at t.[25]

By making suitable substitutions, we can construct hundreds of other WLS concepts of happiness. No pair of these will be exactly equivalent. They give different accounts of happiness at a moment; accordingly, they yield different assessments of happiness in intervals and lives. My claim is that no matter which one we adopt, the version of eudaimonism based on it is seriously implausible.

5.5 *Actualism and Hypotheticalism*

Obviously, however, a detailed discussion of all these WLS concepts of happiness would be tedious. I will proceed in a different way. I will focus on the distinction between actualism and hypotheticalism. First, I will attempt to show that any actualist WLS definition of happiness generates an implausible form of eudaimonism. Then I will attempt to show that any hypotheticalist WLS definition of happiness generates an implausible form of eudaimonism. Since every WLS concept of happiness is either actualist or hypotheticalist, this should suffice to show that none of them figures in a plausible form of eudaimonism.

Let's consider a form of actualism that is judgmentalist, holistic, temporally universal, objective, and epistemically demanding:

WLS1: A person, S, is happy to degree n at a time, t, =df. there is a certain life that S actually will end up having lived, and at t S actually has a life ideal, and at t, S knows what his life ideal is and has a detailed conception of what will transpire in his life

---

[24] There is a question about what sense we can make of the notion that a momentary slice of life can "match up with" an ideal for life as a whole. I assume that the slice "matches up" if what goes on in that slice is consistent with the satisfaction of the ideal in the long term. Thanks to Brad Skow for pointing out that this needs explication.

[25] It may seem that WLS7 is not a genuine form of *whole life* satisfactionism, since the holistic elements of other versions seem to be missing. But it is important to keep in mind that WLS7 gives the criterion for happiness at a moment; to determine how happy a person is in life as a whole, we would have to determine the implications of WLS7 for every moment in the person's life and then aggregate the results. Thus, the holism would return when it comes time to do the aggregating.

as a whole, and at t, S actually judges with respect to his whole life (from beginning to end) that it matches up to degree n with the life ideal that S maintains at t.

In addition to being actualist, WLS1 is highly judgmental. It requires that the happy person actually constructs a suitable life ideal, and that he actually judges, with respect to the whole life that he actually will have lived, that it matches up to some specific degree to that ideal. In addition, WLS1 requires the happy person to have a comprehensive conception of the life about which he is making this judgment, and it requires him to make a favorable judgment with respect to that life. I believe that WLS1 is a fair interpretation of the concept of happiness that Tatarkiewicz had in mind in several passages, including one of the passages cited at the outset.[26] If we were to add a clause requiring some sort of favorable emotional attitude, the resulting definition would be similar to Brandt's.

WLS1 introduces a very strange concept of happiness. An incontrovertible empirical fact entails that no actual human being has ever been happy in the sense defined in WLS1. The relevant fact is that no actual human being has the mental capacity to have a sufficiently comprehensive awareness of his whole life from beginning to end. Even Tatarkiewicz—who endorses something like this concept—is well aware of this problem. He says, 'Happiness is to be satisfied with life as a whole; on the other hand, satisfaction of this kind is impossible. It is so because our minds are incapable of comprehending the whole of our life.'[27] As a result, if we define happiness in this way, and then say that a person's welfare level at a time is determined by his happiness level at that time, then we have to say that no actual human being has ever enjoyed positive welfare.

There are various ways in which the requirement for happiness could be weakened. For example, we might replace the universalism of WLS1 with important aspectivalism; we might replace the epistemic demandingness with laxness. The result is:

WLS2: A person, S, is happy to degree n at a time, t, =df. there is a certain life that S actually will end up having lived, and at t S actually has a life ideal, and at t, S knows what his life ideal is and has at least a vague conception of what will

---

[26] It seems also to be the central view he defends in Tatarkiewicz (1966).

[27] Tatarkiewicz (1976: 9). It's interesting to see that Tatarkiewicz himself is aware of the epistemic difficulty that arises if happiness is defined in something like WLS1. That independently confirms my claim that he must have been understanding ideal happiness in something like this form. Otherwise, why would he say that it has the unfortunate implications that he cites?

transpire in his life as a whole, and at t, S actually judges with respect to important aspects of his whole life (from beginning to end) that they match up to degree n with the life ideal that S maintains at t.

WLS2 is clearly different from WLS1 (and it is perhaps an improvement). But so long as the definition requires *actual judgments* about one's life, the central problem will remain. Things could be going well for a person at a time even though he is not making any judgment about his life at that time. Imagine that Timmy is a happy-go-lucky guy who has friends, and a job, and an apartment, and a car that he likes. He always has a smile on his face. Suppose we catch him at a time when he is singing and dancing at a party. He is apparently enjoying himself immensely. We may assume that appropriate "happy" neurotransmitters are flowing in abundance in Timmy's brain. Yet Timmy has not given any thought to the project of constructing a life ideal. He has no views about what is "important." If we were to ask him at this moment to reveal his judgment about the extent to which important aspects of his life measure up to his life ideal, he would say that he needs a few minutes to reflect. He never thought about such matters. He has never formulated any life ideal, and as a result he cannot make a judgment concerning the extent to which the most important aspects of his life measure up with his life ideal. So, if we accept WLS2 as our account of happiness, we will have to say that Timmy is not happy at this moment. If Timmy is always like this, we will have to say that he is never happy. If we use this concept of happiness in our formulation of eudaimonism, we will have to say that Timmy's life is not going well for him.[28]

It seems to me that those who are attracted by the fundamental eudaimonistic intuition would want to say that Timmy is (in the relevant but obscure sense) a very happy person. Accordingly, they would want to say that his life is going well for him. Thus, the concept of happiness defined in WLS2 generates a form of eudaimonism that does not adequately capture the idea that eudaimonists want to endorse.

It may appear that Timmy's happiness is shallow and undignified. It may seem that the WLS conception would be more appropriate for cases in which happiness arises from deeper engagement with more serious activities. Let us consider a case that shows that this appearance is misleading.

[28] Haybron discusses this problem in section 3 of ch. 5 of Haybron (2008b). He refers to it as 'the problem of attitude scarcity.'

Imagine some philosopher deeply engaged in serious philosophical contemplation. Suppose he is thinking about a problem in metaphysics, trying to untangle some profound conceptual knots. Suppose this philosopher is doing philosophy for its own sake—it's not "just a job" to him. Suppose that this philosopher is so engrossed in his metaphysical reflections that he is giving no thought to himself or his own life. He is focused entirely on the puzzle at hand and, let us imagine, he is beginning to think he sees a possible solution to the metaphysical puzzle that intrigues him. He is excited about the prospect of solving this puzzle.[29]

The crucial fact about this philosopher is that at the moment described he is not making any judgment about his life as a whole. He is not thinking about his life as a whole. He is not thinking about himself or his circumstances at all. Rather, he is thinking about the metaphysical puzzle. As a result, he is not happy in the sense defined by WLS2; and, as a result of that, he would be given a welfare rating of zero by the form of eudaimonism that employs the WLS2 concept of happiness. But surely the philosopher is in fact quite happy at the moment described—he is wholeheartedly engaged in an activity he loves. Those who think that happiness is The Good would want to say that the imaginary philosopher is enjoying very high—perhaps maximally high—welfare at this moment.

This problem would arise with respect to any definition of happiness that requires actual judgments either about whole lives, important aspects of lives, or even some aspects of lives. It would arise for any definition that required such judgments about life as a whole, the current slice of life, or life up till now. I think it would arise if it required a judgment about life as it actually is, or if it required a judgment about life as the happy person takes it to be.

The main critical point here is simple: *a person can be very happy at a time even though she is not making any judgment about her life as a whole at that time; she can have a happy life even though she never makes any judgment about her life as a whole.*[30]

Some actualist definitions do not require *judgment*. Such definitions require something more emotional. Consider a version of the view

---

[29] I am thinking here of the philosopher as described by Aristotle in bk. X, ch. 7 of the *Nicomachean Ethics*.

[30] The actual moral of this story is a bit more complex: you can be happy at a time even though you are not making any judgments about the extent to which you are satisfied with your life up to that time, or about the extent to which you are satisfied with the current slice of your life, or about the important aspects of your life up to that time, etc.

(similar perhaps to Telfer's) that requires nothing more than that the happy person be *pleased with* his life as a whole.

WLS3: A person, S, is happy to degree n at a time, t, =df. there is a certain life that S has lived up until t, and at t, S takes pleasure of degree n in the fact that she has lived that life so far.

The concept of happiness defined in WLS3 is more easily satisfied than the one defined in WLS1. It does not require the happy person to have any life ideal; it does not require that she make any judgment about her life as a whole; it does not require that she contemplate the way her life is going to progress in the future, or that she have any attitude toward her future prospects. It demands far less. It demands only that the person take pleasure in the life she has so far lived.

Even this modest requirement is still too stringent. To take pleasure in something at a time, one must at least consider that something. One must at least form some thought about that thing. But surely a person could be happy at a time even though he does not at that moment consider the life he has lived up until then. Suppose the metaphysician described earlier is too engrossed in metaphysical contemplation at a certain moment to give any thought to the life he has lived up until today. He may be taking pleasure in the fact that a solution seems to be at hand, but he is not thinking about his own life and is not taking pleasure in any autobiographical facts. If we employ the WLS3 definition of happiness, we will have to say that the metaphysician is not happy at that moment. But in spite of this even someone who endorses the underlying eudaimonistic intuition would want to say that things are going well for the metaphysician and that he is happy. After all, he is happy about[31] lots of things—primarily, in this example, he is happy to be on the verge of solving an interesting puzzle in metaphysics.[32] The main point here is also simple: *a person can be happy at a time even though he is not actually pleased about or feeling good about, or otherwise emotionally focused upon his life as a whole; a person can have a happy life even though he never is actually pleased about, or otherwise actually thinking about his life as a whole.*[33] I conclude, then, that every actualist WLS definition gives us a concept

---

[31] I here use 'happy' in some vague, pre-theoretical, but familiar sense.

[32] The case of Timmy seems to me to establish the same point. While singing and dancing, Timmy is not thinking about his life up until that point. Yet eudaimonists should want to say that his life is going very well for him. He seems to be precisely the sort of person they would describe as "happy."

[33] The further options mentioned in fn. 30 apply here as well, suitably revised so as to apply to the more purely emotional versions of WLS.

of happiness that does not serve well in a eudaimonistic theory of welfare.

Let us turn to hypotheticalism. Let us consider versions of the view that make use of the concept of a "would-be" judgment and a "would-be" life ideal. We can say that a person's happiness level at a time is determined not by the judgment he *actually* makes at that time about the life ideal he *actually* has at that time, but by the judgment he *would have made* at that time if he had made one. Consider this:

WLS4:   A person, S, is happy to degree n at a time, t, =df. at t, S is such that if he were to reflect on his life as a whole at t, and if he were to formulate a life ideal at t, he would judge that his life as a whole measures up to degree n to that ideal.

WLS4 is intended to define a momentary happiness level for every person, for every moment, whether the person makes a judgment at that moment or not. Information about these momentary happiness levels can then be aggregated so as to yield happiness levels for any interval, including a life as a whole. These happiness levels can then be employed in a eudaimonistic theory of welfare.

The case of the unreflective Timmy may now seem to be resolved. Although he did not think about his life, and did not formulate a life ideal, and did not form any judgments concerning the extent to which his life as a whole measured up to his ideal, it may appear reasonable to suppose that there is, for each moment in his life, a judgment that he would have made if he had thought about his life as a whole in the appropriate ways. These hypothetical judgments then yield happiness levels for all the moments in Timmy's life. These can then be aggregated so as to yield a lifetime happiness level for Timmy. Presumably, the lifetime happiness level would be positive.

It is not entirely clear that the proposed method does yield the requisite numbers. Perhaps there are several different numbers, each of which is such that Timmy *might have* given it if asked about satisfaction. Perhaps if the question were put to him in one way, he would come up with a certain response; but if the question were put to him in a different way, he would come up with a different response. Let us put this worry aside. Maybe there is an ideal way to frame the question. Let us assume that there are such numbers. Are the numbers of genuine theoretical interest? Is happiness so defined relevant to welfare?

Reflecting upon one's life and ideals and considering the extent to which the life measures up to the ideals very well may have some impact on a person's emotional state.[34] Just getting someone to think about the question might make him less glum. In a different sort of case it might make him less cheerful. Consider the case of Timmy again. He is a happy-go-lucky person who in fact never reflects on his life as a whole and hasn't formulated a life ideal. It is consistent with this to suppose that if he were to think about these things, he would become depressed. He might judge that his life as a whole has been a pointless waste. In such a case it would be cruel to force him to face reality; it would be better to leave him to his happy and unexamined life.

We can imagine that every waking moment of Timmy's adult life is like this: he is cheerful, active, smiling, and engaged in activities that he enjoys at that moment, but also such that if he were to reflect at that moment on his life as a whole, and if he were to formulate a life ideal, he would promptly become despondent and would judge his life as a whole to have been worthless. In this case, the judgments that Timmy would make would not reflect his actual happiness levels. For every moment in his adult life, Timmy's would-be judgment gives a number that is lower than the number that a perceptive observer would assign to him for that moment. The observer would focus on such things as his smile, his cheerful activity, his engagement in activities that he apparently likes, the fact that he keeps coming back eagerly to activities of the same sort. Thus, Timmy seems to be very happy. But his happiness is in part dependent upon the fact that he is doing things that he enjoys, rather than thinking about his life and his ideals.[35] If he were to turn his attention to questions about these things, he would cease being so happy. Thus, the concept defined by WLS4 does not correspond very well to anything we would normally call 'happiness' and is not suitable for use in a eudaimonist criterion of welfare.[36]

---

[34] This seems to be one of the guiding intuitions behind Cognitive Behavioral Therapy.

[35] My remarks are not intended to presuppose an undefended commitment to some specific analysis of the concept of happiness. I mention the smile, the cheerfulness, the enjoyment, etc., simply because I think these things would normally be taken to be indicators of happiness—even if we haven't got any precise account of the nature of happiness. *Whatever precisely happiness may be,* Timmy seems to have it.

[36] The opposite problem is also possible. Consider the case of an unhappy person—Tammy. Tammy in fact never formulates any life ideal and never makes judgments of satisfaction. She's just too glum to think about such things. It might be the case that, at every moment of her adult life, she is such that if she had been asked about her life and her ideals, she would have given these matters some thought; and if she had given them some thought, she would have formulated a life ideal, and she would have realized that her life has not been so bad; and, as a result of that, she would have been a lot happier than she in fact was. Tammy is thus an ideal candidate for CBT. The proposed theory yields in Tammy's case a number that is much higher than it should be. She is in fact not a happy person, but the theory says that she is.

The case of the contemplative philosopher highlights the problem for WLS4 from a different perspective. Suppose again that at a certain time he is deeply engrossed in philosophical contemplation. He might be like this: he would not think about his life as a whole unless someone were to interrupt him and ask the question; yet if someone were to ask him how he feels about his life as a whole, the interruption would annoy him. He was working on a problem in metaphysics, and now someone is breaking his train of thought and asking him to think about something else—his own life. Perhaps he finds this question trivial and narcissistic. He doesn't like to think about such things. Right at this moment he prefers to be thinking about metaphysics. The implication seems pretty clear: if at the selected moment he were to think about his life as a whole and his ideals, he would report that his life is not matching up very well to his ideals. He would have to say that the match would have been better if he had been permitted to continue thinking about metaphysics rather than his own personal affairs.

It seems to me that what I have said about WLS4 would hold equally for any hypotheticalist concept of WLS happiness. So long as we define a person's happiness level at a moment by appeal to some counterfactual judgment, there is always the chance that the numbers will be wrong.

Some philosophers have suggested that the best form of WLS would be one that defines happiness as the amount of life satisfaction that a subject would have if he were to contemplate his own life from an epistemically ideal perspective.[37] In one form, the idea is that a person's level of happiness is to be defined as the amount of whole life satisfaction he would have had if he had been fully informed, logically consistent, and not subject to emotional disturbances. The considerations I have raised here are directly relevant to any such hypothetical form of WLS. Consider a person who for all practical purposes seems to be very happy (again using the word 'happy' in some familiar, vague, ordinary sense), but who is also in an epistemically poor situation for life evaluation. Suppose he is confused about the actual circumstances of his life. We may imagine that if he were in an epistemically ideal situation for evaluating his life, he would know much more about his life and he would judge it to be much

---

[37] This seems to be at least part of what Valerie Tiberius claims in her 'How's It Going?' (2003, unpublished) when she speaks of the "reflective perspective," though it should be noted that she is proposing an account of happiness as an evaluative concept, not as an empirical concept.

less satisfactory. His is a case in which the old adage "ignorance is bliss" is apt. But note that the proposed definition would declare him to be *unhappy*. Obviously, any such conclusion would have no relevance to the question we mean to ask. He is blissful in fact. But his blissfulness is in part dependent upon the fact that he is misinformed about his own life. Thus, the happiness rankings generated by the imagined forms of WLS would be wide of the mark.

The opposite case is perhaps even more striking. Suppose Tammy is glum and miserable. She has a frown on her face all the time. Many of her desires are being frustrated. She thinks that her life is pathetic in all important respects. She is contemplating suicide. Her misery, let us suppose, is largely due to some faulty judgments. She thinks she is a worthless sinner; she thinks everyone hates her; she thinks her life has been a waste. Anyone with eudaimonistic leanings would want to say that Tammy is very unhappy and thus that her life is not going well for her. Yet it is consistent with all this to suppose that if Tammy were to view her life from an epistemically ideal perspective, she would find it far more satisfactory. If she knew that she was in fact not a sinner, and that she was in fact well liked by others, she might sincerely declare that her life had matched up in many important ways to her ideals. So an "ideal information" concept of WLS happiness would count Tammy as already happy. Thus, the proposed definition does not yield the theory of welfare that the eudaimonist finds attractive. The eudaimonist wants to say that Tammy would have been a lot happier and a lot better off if she had been better informed about her circumstances. If we define happiness by appeal to the level of satisfaction Tammy would have had if she had been well informed, we end up saying that she is already very happy and faring well.

5.6 *Conclusion*

The most popular concepts of happiness among psychologists and philosophers nowadays are WLS concepts of happiness. I have attempted to show that there are hundreds of logically distinct ways in which a WLS conception of happiness can be developed. However, every precise conception is either a version that requires *actual* satisfaction with life as a whole or a version that requires *hypothetical* satisfaction with life as a whole.[38] I have presented considerations designed to show that a person can be happy (in any familiar sense that might be relevant to eudaimonism) at a time even though he is not actually making any judgment about his life as a whole at that time. I have also presented considerations designed to show that a person can be happy (again in any relevant sense of term) even though it is not correct to say that if he were to form a judgment about his life as a whole at that time, it would be a favorable judgment. These considerations strongly suggest that those who are attracted by the eudaimonistic intuition ("happiness is The Good") should avoid defining happiness in terms of whole life satisfaction.

---

[38] To avoid needless repetition, I have not mentioned all the variants. I could have said, 'Or actual satisfaction with the current slice of life, or actual satisfaction with the important aspects, or actual . . . etc.'

Happiness and Time: More Nails in the Coffin of Whole Life Satisfactionism

I showed in Chapter 5 that Whole Life Satisfaction conceptions of happiness can be developed in a wide variety of different ways. In many of its popular forms, however, the theory implies that a person's level of happiness at a time depends upon the judgment he makes (or would make) at that time concerning his *whole life*. This appears most starkly in Tatarkiewicz. In a passage I quoted earlier, he says, 'Satisfaction with life as a whole must be satisfaction not only with that which is, but also with that which was and that which will be, not only with the present, but also with the past and the future.' Many other versions of whole life satisfactionism define happiness in such a way as to make these judgments concerning the past and future at least a necessary condition for happiness. But no matter how it is incorporated, this concern with other times generates a collection of messy problems.

I want to describe one of these problems by showing how it arises in the case of a simple version of whole life satisfactionism. The problem also arises in connection with other forms of WLS, but I leave it to the interested reader to work out the details. For present purposes, let us consider this conception of happiness at a moment:

WLSn: A person, S, is happy to degree n at a time, t, =df. there is a certain life that S has lived up to t, and at t S has a life ideal, and at t, S knows what his life ideal is and has a fairly accurate conception of the main things that have transpired in his life up to t, and at t, S judges with respect to his life up to t, that it matches up to degree n with the life ideal that S maintains at t.

WLSn makes satisfaction with the past of one's life a necessary condition for happiness in the present.

The crucial point of interest here concerns the fact that S's happiness level at a given moment depends upon the judgment S makes at that moment concerning the main things that have happened in his life up to that moment. Thus, the judgment concerns a portion of S's life that *includes the past*. Reflection on some examples will make it clear that this is a mistake; there is no conceptual connection between a person's happiness level at a time and the judgments he makes (or would make) at that time about the things that have happened to him in the past.

Suppose Tristan had a miserable childhood. Suppose he suffered from severe depression for many years. Suppose this depression infected all aspects of his life. He had no friends, he did poorly in school, he did not engage in any hobbies, and so on. His parents took him to a number of different psychiatrists, but the treatments they offered never worked. Tristan was by anyone's account an unhappy child.

Suppose that at age 24 Tristan was introduced to a new psychiatrist, Dr. Goldberg. After interviewing Tristan, Dr. Goldberg prescribed a drug. Tristan started taking the drug and was thrilled when he found that the drug was amazingly successful in his case. His mood lifted; his attitude changed; he started smiling and laughing (at appropriate times). Soon he got an interesting job and a charming girlfriend. After a few months, his emotional life was completely changed. Everyone said that Tristan had become a very happy person. At a follow-up visit, Tristan said to Dr. Goldberg, 'You are a miracle worker, and the drug you prescribed is a miracle drug. You have changed my life. I am now a happy person. I only wish we had met earlier.'

Suppose Tristan now volunteers for a psychological study. He is asked to make a judgment about his life. The question is clear and specific:

Q1: Thinking back on your life as a whole up until the present time, to what extent would you say the main things in your life have matched up with your ideals?

Obviously, if Tristan gives an honest answer to this question he will have to say that for 24 years the main things in his life did not match up at all well with his ideals. He took certain things to be essential to the good life (friends, hobbies, success in school, hope for the future, etc.) and he had none of them. Things changed dramatically in the most recent year. Reflecting on his life as a whole up to the present, he has to say that it consists of 24 completely unsatisfactory years and one satisfactory year. Thus, Tristan judges that he is overwhelmingly *not satisfied* with the important aspects of the life he has lived up to the present. For most of his life, those aspects of his life diverged dramatically from his life ideals. He is well aware of the fact that he had a long, miserable childhood.[1]

---

[1] Dan Doviak pointed out that there is some obscurity about these life ideals. Is the subject supposed to evaluate the match between his past experiences and his *current* ideals? Or is it rather the match between his past experiences and the ideals he *then* held? I finesse this question by assuming that Tristan has maintained the same ideals throughout his life.

WLSn then implies that Tristan is very unhappy *now*. That's because he *now* judges that his life up until now has not matched at all well with his ideals. But this assessment of Tristan's current level of happiness is clearly and dramatically wrong. Tristan joyfully claims that he is very happy now. His friends agree. Dr. Goldberg agrees. All the evidence agrees. The drug worked like a miracle. Tristan's emotional life has been transformed. The claim that he is unhappy today is just wrong.

Someone may object that Tristan's current emotional state would probably be adversely affected by his recollection of 24 years of depression. This seems plausible. Since Tristan recalls those 24 years of misery, it very well may be a source of regret for him. Maybe he is a bit less happy today when he thinks of those lost years. But, on the other hand, maybe he is a bit more happy today when he thinks about the emotional transformation he has enjoyed. Different people in this sort of situation might be affected differently.

We can clarify one thing that might be going on by introducing some numerical ratings. Let us suppose that when Tristan is asked to make a judgment about the quality of fit between the main aspects of his life and his ideals, he is given a numerical scale. Let us suppose that he is to give a number between −10 (utter, complete mismatch) and +10 (perfect fit). Tristan may reason as follows: 'For 24 years, there was a complete mismatch between my ideals and important aspects of my life. Thus, I give each of those years a score of −10. But in my 25th year, shortly after I met Dr. Goldberg, many aspects of my life began to match my ideals very well. I would give a score of +10 to the present year were it not for the fact that one of my ideals is to have had a good past, which of course I didn't have. So I give my 25th year a score of +9. Therefore, my life as a whole up until the present gets a score of −231. Up until the present it has been a very unsatisfactory life. I wish my parents had taken me to Dr. Goldberg when I was a baby.'

We can imagine that, instead of Q1, Tristan is asked a different question:

Q2: On a scale of −10 (extremely unhappy) to +10 (extremely happy), how happy would you say you are right now?

Tristan wants to say '+10.' He's happy for a lot of reasons: his new job; his new girlfriend; his optimistic hopes for the future. Perhaps most of all, he's happy because his emotional life has undergone a remarkable transformation.

Maybe '+10' is the wrong number. Maybe Tristan's actual happiness level is really only +9. It's hard to say. It would depend upon the extent to which he is bothered about the fact that he had an unhappy childhood. But it should be obvious that his current happiness level is not −231. It is not negative at all. He is now a happy person, though he is well aware of the fact that his life as a whole up until now has been far from satisfactory. This shows that WLSn defines a concept of happiness that does not coincide with any common-sense concept of happiness.

Furthermore, it should be clear that there is no connection between the WLSn concept of happiness and *welfare*. Any reasonable observer would say that Tristan is doing well today. His current welfare level is surely positive. Yet he judges (correctly) that there has been a dramatic mismatch between his ideals and things that were going on in the most important aspects of his life up until the present.

These considerations suggest a different way of thinking of Whole Life Satisfaction. Following Tatarkiewicz, I took the 'whole' in 'whole life' to mean *temporal completeness*. A person's whole life, on this conception, is that person's life *from beginning to end* (or from beginning *to the present moment*). On a different interpretation, we could take a person's "whole life" to encompass all the main aspects of his life *at the present moment*. So, for example, if Tristan currently has a job, a girlfriend, some hobbies, a health status, and so on, then we could ask him how he is doing *at the present moment* in each of these different domains; or we could ask him how he is doing in his life as a whole *at the present moment*. This question is designed to elicit a response that disregards past satisfaction or dissatisfaction. It is focused only on the present.

In fact, the questions employed by some psychologists reflect this focus on the present. Thus, for example, Schwarz and Strack mention these questions:

Q3: Taking all things together, how would you say things are *these days*...?

Q4: How satisfied are you with your life as a whole *these days*? Are you very satisfied, satisfied, not very satisfied, not at all satisfied?[2]

I believe that these questions are intended to encourage the subject to report on his level of satisfaction with his *current* situation either in life in general, or in several different domains of life. It should be obvious that a person like Tristan could be satisfied with his *current* situation in all domains while being seriously dissatisfied with his *former* situation in all of those domains. If we just ask about "whole life satisfaction" we blur this distinction. Hence it is important to note that there are different ways of understanding what is in question when we ask about "whole life satisfaction."

---

[2] Schwarz and Strack, in Kahneman, Diener, and Schwarz (1999: 61); emphasis added (FF).

Perhaps it will seem that this provides the basis for a solution to the problems I discussed in connection with Q1. Recall that Q1 is:

Q1: Thinking back on your life as a whole up until the present time, to what extent would you say the main things in your life have matched up with your ideals?

Perhaps a better question would be:

Q5: Thinking across all domains of your life *at the present time*, to what extent would you say that the main things in those domains of your life are *currently* matching up with your ideals?

Maybe it will seem that answers to this question give a better measure of a person's happiness at a time.

Consider Tristan's brother Trustam. Trustam never suffered from the depression that messed up Tristan's life. However, his observation of his brother's depression has given rise to a different problem: he is always worried about the future. No matter how well things may be going in the present, he is constantly convinced that it will all fall apart in the future. He thinks he might be headed for trouble. This makes him worried and anxious and unhappy.

Suppose that Trustam is a subject in some happiness research. Suppose he is required to answer Q5. Suppose he is trying his hardest to be accurate. He knows that his marriage is currently fine. He and his wife get along well in all respects. He certainly has nothing to complain about there. He is satisfied to degree +10 in that domain. He also knows that his work is going well. He likes his job, his boss, his coworkers, his pay, and so on. He is satisfied with that domain of life as well. He gives himself another +10. Same for his leisure activities, his health, and all other domains that he takes to be important. Thus, when he answers Q5, Trustam has to say that the main things in the various domains of his life match up very well with his ideals. Things are currently going just as he thinks they ought to be going. So far, it appears that his whole life satisfaction level is +100.

Of course, there is one domain in which Trustam knows that things are not going well. That is the domain of mental health. He knows that he is entirely too pessimistic. So his whole life satisfaction level must accordingly be reduced a few points to reflect this disappointment in one domain. Instead of getting a rating of +100, he gets a rating of only +90.

Yet, if we were to ask Trustam whether he is happy, we would get a different reaction. In virtue of his anxieties about the future, Trustam is unhappy. He might say that he knows that while everything is currently OK in his marriage, he nevertheless takes no joy in his marriage because he fears that it will soon fall apart. Similarly, though he knows that all is well at work, he takes no pleasure in his job because he is so worried that he will be fired. Even racquet ball is no longer a source of joy, since every time he plays he worries that he may break his ankle and thus be unable to play. All these fears have been nagging at him quite a long time. Though he recognizes that they are completely unfounded, and that everything is in fact currently going quite well, still these fears about the future conspire to make him unhappy. Sometimes he thinks he should schedule a meeting with Dr. Goldberg, who was so helpful with Tristan.

The example of Trustam demonstrates that a person can be unhappy at a time even though he judges that things are going reasonably well in all domains of his life at that time. Another example demonstrates the reverse: a person can be happy at a time even though he judges that things are going poorly in every domain of his life at that time. Imagine the case of Bruce, who is well aware of the fact that his current situation is rotten in all respects. He just sits at the bar and reminisces about his "glory days." After he has had a few beers, he is joyfully (and boringly) recounting his exploits as an athlete, a prankster, and a lover.[3]

If someone were to ask Bruce about his *present* standing in the important domains of his life, he would tell a different story. He now judges that his current situation in all domains diverges utterly from his ideals. He is divorced, unemployed, sickly, and so on. He knows full well that things are now going poorly. Yet he has a wonderful capacity to forget his troubles. As soon as he has had a few beers, and has started to regale the barflies with tales of days gone by, Bruce stops thinking about his current situation. So Bruce is happy, but he is aware of the fact that his current situation in the important domains of life does not match up with his ideals.

The example involving Bruce can be developed in different ways. In one form it refutes many forms of hypothetical whole life satisfactionism. In these forms, we stipulate that Bruce is currently happy but that if he were to form a judgment about the important domains of his life he would judge that his current situation in each domain falls short of his ideals. In another form, it refutes many forms of actual whole life satisfactionism. In these forms, we stipulate again that Bruce is currently happy, we in addition we imagine that something has caused Bruce to emerge for a moment from his bleary reminiscences and he has actually judged that his life is currently a wreck in all domains. (Fortunately for Bruce, he doesn't care much about the present. He "lives in the past.")

---

[3] The example of Bruce is derived from the song 'Glory Days' by Bruce Springsteen. The lyrics to this song can be found at the website: <http://www.brucespringsteen.net/songs/GloryDays.html>.

This shows another way in which judgments about whole life satisfaction may diverge from levels of happiness. Later, in Chapter 7, I will explain how my own theory of happiness—Attitudinal Hedonism about Happiness—evaluates Tristan, Trustam, and Bruce in way that coincides much more closely with our intuitions.

Appendix B

Happiness =df. Whatever the Happiness Test Measures

Years ago, in connection with the debate about IQ tests, questions were raised about the nature of the item that was being measured by such tests. Some critics claimed that they knew of children who were by any reasonable account "intelligent" but who nevertheless did not achieve high scores on the standardized IQ tests. Others pointed out that a student's score on a second IQ test might be much higher than his score on an earlier test, though there was no reason to suppose that his intelligence had changed. When groups of psychologists were invited to submit definitions of intelligence, it often turned out that the number of distinct definitions was equal to the number of psychologists submitting them. Thus, there was confusion and controversy about what was allegedly being measured by IQ tests.

In this context, some defenders of the tests adopted the approach of saying that there is no clear and unambiguous common-sense concept of intelligence. Thus, there is no point in trying to measure such a thing, since it does not exist. Rather, we should just focus on whatever is measured by the IQ tests. Since this factor is known to correlate with school performance, later job performance, and other observable outcomes, it might be best just to redefine intelligence as "whatever is measured by IQ tests." In the introductory essay in her 1976 book, *The Nature of Intelligence*, Lauren Resnick expresses this idea straightforwardly: 'For many years, the term intelligence has been used by psychologists in a particular and very pragmatic sense to refer to the level of performance on tests designated intelligence tests.'[1]

If we adopt this approach, we can simply stop worrying about whether the IQ tests are "accurate" measures of intelligence. That claim simply becomes tautological. This can be codified in a definition:

D1: x is intelligent to degree n =df. x achieved a score of n on the IQ test.[2]

---

[1] Lauren B. Resnick, ed., *The Nature of Intelligence* (1976: 1).

[2] Resnick goes on to discuss the problem induced by the fact that there are several different IQ tests, and an individual might get different scores when taking different tests.

If we adopt D1 as our definition of intelligence, we can simply bypass all the thorny puzzles about the nature of intelligence. We can move on immediately to the more interesting (but soluble) questions. To what extent is intelligence heritable? To what extent can intelligence be altered by training? What is the connection between intelligence and economic status? What is the connection between intelligence and gender? What is the connection between intelligence and race? All these questions then become amenable to relatively straightforward empirical investigation, since we now have a simple way to determine the intelligence of each person. (Of course, if we adopt this approach we should be sure to warn uninformed readers: what we mean by 'intelligence' is neither more nor less than what D1 says.)

I want to focus attention on a profoundly important question that (so far as I know) has been overlooked in the debate over the proposed definition. The question is this: *what shall we say about people who do not take the IQ test?* Shall we say that each of them has a level of intelligence of zero? That each of them has *no intelligence*? That seems preposterous. Surely there are plenty of smart people who by some accident never got around to taking the test. Surely there were intelligent people before the test was formulated.

Another proposal would be to say that in the case of any individual who has not taken the test, the level of intelligence is simply undefined. It's not that the individual has zero intelligence; rather, the claim might be that there is no number (not even zero), such that the individual's intelligence is equal to that number. But this proposal is problematic too. For we surely recognize that any common-sense notion of intelligence does not function in this way. We all think that it makes perfectly good sense to speak of the intelligence of an untested person. Even if we agree that the concept of intelligence is vague and possibly ambiguous, we assume that it makes sense to speak of the intelligence (or intelligences) of individuals who have not yet taken any IQ tests. Thus, the concept defined in D1 is surprisingly different from any common-sense concept of intelligence.

For those who are drawn to the pragmatic outlook mentioned by Resnick, the natural response is to say that, in the case of an individual who has not taken an IQ test, his IQ is equal to the score he would have gotten if he had taken the test. This can be understood as acceptance of a revised definition:

D2: x is intelligent to degree n =df. if x were to take the IQ test, then x would achieve a score of n on the IQ test.

The subjunctive conditional in D2 is to be understood in the obvious way: to find the level of intelligence of a person, go to the nearest possible world where the person takes the IQ test. The person's intelligence is equal to his score on that test. (If a person in fact has taken an IQ test, then the nearest world in which he takes the test is the actual world. His intelligence is equal to the score he actually achieved.) If a person has not taken the test, then imagine a situation in which he has taken the test, but which situation is otherwise as similar to the actual situation as possible consistent with his taking the test. The score he achieves in that situation is his intelligence in the actual world.

Suppose Myron has not taken an IQ test. Then we must determine his score on the test in the nearest possible world where he takes it. That world cannot be *exactly* like the actual world in all respects except that Myron takes the test. There would have to be some further differences so as to make that world internally consistent. Thus, for example, if in fact Myron has never talked face to face with a psychologist, we would have to locate a world that differs in that respect so as to accommodate his taking of an IQ test. But there seems to be no reason to suppose that he would have different parents in that world, or that he would have enjoyed several years of intensive IQ test preparation, or that he would have a much more active brain. There is no need to imagine such changes to accommodate the taking of an IQ test. So the idea is this: to find out how intelligent Myron is, imagine the possible world most similar to the actual world, except that Myron takes an IQ test (and whatever else is changed so as to accommodate the fact that he takes the test). Consider the score he gets on the test there. That is Myron's level of intelligence here in the actual world (where he never takes the test).

The patient reader may be wondering what all this has to do with happiness. I will explain.

Some of the most popular psychological tests for happiness are tests that ask respondents a bunch of questions about "whole life satisfaction" (or "WLS"). The tests ask respondents to contemplate their lives as wholes, as well as various domains of their lives (work, income, housing, health, marriage, social life, leisure). They ask respondents to think about their hopes and dreams for their lives and for their experiences within these domains. They then ask respondents to judge the extent to which their lives match up with their ideals. A typical question on such a test might ask:

Q1: Reflecting on your life as a whole and your ideals, would you say that your life as a whole (a) matches up very well with your ideals; (b) matches up fairly well with your ideals; (c) matches up fairly poorly with your ideals; or (d) matches up very poorly with your ideals?

A domain-specific question might be:

Q2: Reflecting on your work (job location, co-workers, type of work done, chances for advancement, etc.) would you say that what goes on in your work (a) matches up very well with your ideals; (b) matches up fairly well with your ideals; (c) matches up fairly poorly with your ideals; or (d) matches up very poorly with your ideals?

Some formula may then be used to generate an overall "whole life satisfaction rating" for the subject. This would then be said to indicate how happy the subject is.

As in the case of intelligence tests, there very well could be complaints about the use of the test in an effort to quantify happiness. 'How can we be sure that people who are in fact happier will get higher scores on the test?' 'What justifies the assumption that happiness varies so closely with scores on the test?' 'Isn't it possible that someone might in fact not be very happy, yet might say that his life matches up fairly well with his life ideal?' These are all legitimate complaints. They are indeed reasons to worry that the test is not measuring happiness.

One common response to these complaints goes like this: the word 'happy' in ordinary English is vague and possibly ambiguous. Different people may mean different things when they use the word. Selecting any one such possible meaning would at best be arbitrary. So, following the lead of the intelligence testers, perhaps we should just say that a person's level of happiness is defined as his score on the happiness test. Then we can get on with the exciting business of doing empirical research on the connections (if any) between happiness and age, or happiness and gender, or happiness and income level.

This, in effect, amounts to the acceptance of a definition:

D3: x is happy to degree n =df. x got a score of n on the life satisfaction test.

But again this leaves us with a puzzle: what shall we say about the people who have not taken the life satisfaction test? We could just say that they are all happy to degree zero—but this seems preposterous in light of the fact that some of them seem very happy, and others seem very unhappy, and they certainly do not appear to be equally happy. Zero seems the wrong number in just about every case. A slightly better option would be to say that every such person has an undefined happiness level. In other words, to accept this option is to say that there is no number (not even zero) that measures the amount of happiness that a person has if he has not taken the test.

This "undefined" option seems unacceptable as well. For it reveals a striking divergence between anything we might pre-analytically mean by 'happy' and the thing defined by D3. Even if our pre-analytic concept of happiness is obscure or vague or ambiguous, one datum is that a person can be happy to some non-zero degree whether he has taken the life satisfaction test or not. That's not true of the concept defined in D3. If we define happiness with D3, we are committed to the claim that no one can be happy to any degree unless he has taken the life satisfaction test.

As in the case of intelligence, the natural solution is to go hypothetical:

D4: x is happy to degree n =df. if x were to take it, x would get a score of n on the life satisfaction test.

The corresponding move solved the problem in the IQ case, and so this may seem to solve the trivial problem of finding a suitable number for those who have not taken the life satisfaction test.

It seems to me that the concept defined in D4 is defective in a way that the concept defined in D2 is not. The defect is this: there are many cases in which the taking of a life satisfaction test would affect the happiness level of the person taking it. Some simple examples should clarify the point.

Example 1. Suppose Tammy (discussed above in Chapter 5) is glum and suicidal. She has never thought much about her life; she has never formulated any life ideals. She has been leading a miserable and unexamined life. However, she is a good candidate for Cognitive Behavioral Therapy. If she were to think about her life, and if she were to formulate some life ideals, she would pretty quickly see that there has been no reason for her to have been so miserable. She would cheer up. She would become a happier person.

In this case, things that Tammy would have to do if she were to take the life satisfaction test would inevitably have psychological consequences. If she were to take the test, she would think about various domains of her life; she would construct some life ideals; she would then see that in fact her life does match up fairly well with her (newly formulated) ideals. The results on the test would indicate that she is quite a bit happier than she in fact is.

I am not suggesting that taking the test would make Tammy instantly become blissful. I am just saying that if she were to take the life satisfaction test, she would be somewhat less miserable than she in fact is. But this is enough to show that D4 is wrong. For the level of life satisfaction that Tammy has in the nearest world where she takes the life satisfaction test is not coordinated with the level of happiness that she in fact has here in the actual world.

The example involving Timmy (also discussed in Chapter 5) illustrates a similar point but in the opposite direction. Suppose Timmy is a cheerful, unreflective, party-loving playboy. Suppose he has never taken a life satisfaction test. Nor has he taken a philosophy class in which he was introduced to the Socratic maxim about the unexamined life. His own life is unexamined and apparently quite cheerful. Everyone thinks that Timmy is a very happy guy.

Let us assume that Timmy's emotional state would be adversely affected if he were to contemplate his life. If he were to think about such things as his marital status (he's still a bachelor, even at age 38), his employment status (still no job; living off the dwindling inheritance); his health (OK for now, but beginning to have some problems with the old ticker), he would become worried. And if he were asked about his life ideals, he would at first have to admit that he has no such ideals. But if he were to construct such ideals, he would come to the conclusion that he admires solid family life, steady work, and vigorous exercise. As a result of all this, when we go to the nearest world where Timmy takes the life satisfaction test, we find that in that world he first constructs his life ideals, and then (for the first time in his life) contemplates the extent to which his actual life matches up. He finds that the quality of fit is *terrible*. He there judges that his life matches up very poorly with his ideals.

The implication then should be clear. If we define happiness hypothetically as we do in D4, we have to say that Timmy is already very unhappy. But this is clearly wrong. He is in fact happy. The thought experiment merely shows that *if he were to take the life satisfaction test, he would become much less happy*. This has no implications for his actual level of happiness.

A defender of the WLS approach to happiness might insist that I have applied the test incorrectly in the cases I have discussed. They might claim that it is unfair to imagine cases in which the taking of the test would affect the subject's level of happiness. In order to make clear that this is not the sort of hypothetical test-taking they have in mind, they might propose:

D5: x is happy to degree n =df. If x were to take the life satisfaction test *while remaining just as happy as x in fact is*, x would get a score of n on that test.

With D5 in hand, the proposal is this: to see how happy Tammy is, go to the nearest world where she takes the life satisfaction test *but remains just as miserable as she is in the actual world*. Surely there is such a possible world. Her score there indicates her happiness level at the actual world. Similarly for Timmy. His actual happiness level is determined by the score he gets on the life satisfaction test *at the nearest possible world where he takes the test while remaining just as happy as he is here in the actual world.*

The obvious circularity of this proposal makes it a non-starter. Precisely what is meant by 'happy' on the right-hand side of D5?

PART II

WHAT HAPPINESS IS

CHAPTER 6

What is This Thing Called Happiness?

6.1 *Where We Stand*

In Part I of this book, I discussed some of the most interesting and popular theories about the nature of happiness. Among these are sensory hedonism (Chapter 2), Kahneman's theory of "objective happiness" (Chapter 3), a form of subjective desire satisfactionism defended by Wayne Davis (Chapter 4), and whole life satisfactionism of many varieties (Chapter 5). In each case, I pointed out features of the proposed analysis that seem to me to make it unsuitable as an explication of the relevant concept of happiness. Thus, in opposition to Kahneman, I pointed out that a person could be very happy even though he does not want his present experiences to continue. In opposition to Davis's form of subjective desire satisfactionism, I described several ways in which the satisfaction of our desires can fail to have any impact on happiness. In opposition to whole life satisfactionism, I pointed out that it's possible for a person to be very happy even though he never makes any judgment about the extent to which his life measures up to his ideals. I also argued that among people who do not make any such life assessment, there very well might be some who are in fact happy, but who would make negative judgments about their lives if they were called upon to make such judgments. Thus, these popular theories about the nature of happiness confront difficulties. None of them seems to give a completely plausible account of what happiness is.

In Chapter 2, I discussed a form of hedonism that has been associated with Bentham, Mill, and Sidgwick. I cited a passage from Mill in which he seems to be giving an account of happiness:

The creed which accepts as the foundation of morals, Utility, or the Greatest Happiness Principle, holds that actions are right in proportion as they tend to promote happiness, wrong as they tend to produce the reverse of happiness. *By happiness is intended pleasure, and the absence of pain*; by unhappiness, pain, and the privation of pleasure.[1]

I pointed out a problem with the wording of Mill's statement and then went on to give a clearer statement of Sensory Hedonism about Happiness. This account made use of the concept of "hedono-doloric balance." I said that a person's hedono-doloric balance at a time is equal to the number of hedons of sensory pleasure he is then experiencing, minus the number of dolors of sensory pain he is then experiencing. I then defined a person's momentary happiness level in this way:

D1: x is happy to degree n at t =df. x's hedono-doloric balance at t = n.

I said that the defender of Sensory Hedonism about Happiness can also say that a person is happy at a time if and only if he is happy to some positive degree; and unhappy if and only if happy to a negative degree. I mentioned a slightly more plausible form of sensory hedonism according to which there is a certain lowest positive threshold, H, such that a person should not be called happy at a time unless his hedono-doloric balance is greater than H. Other components of the theory involve happiness during intervals, in domains of life, and in life as a whole. On Sensory Hedonism, all of these concepts are defined by appeal to net amounts of sensory pleasure.

I claimed that Sensory Hedonism about Happiness is false. A person could be unhappy at a time even though he is feeling more sensory hedons than dolors at that time. I cited the example of Wendell who, after being bombarded by email advertisements, has purchased an orgasm enhancer. He has paid for, and is expecting a 400 hedon orgasm. I asked the reader to suppose when the orgasm comes, it is a mere 12 hedon orgasm. Wendell is disappointed. He thinks he has wasted his money. He is also somewhat embarrassed, since he had been warned that the email advertisements were just scams. However, at the moment of orgasm, his hedono-doloric balance is definitely positive. He feels 12 hedons of sensory pleasure, and no dolors of sensory pain. Yet he is not happy. This refutes the form of Sensory Hedonism about Happiness that I formulated.

I claimed that H2 goes wrong in the opposite direction too. I described the case of Dolores who has been suffering from serious chronic pain for a long time. I asked the reader to imagine that

---

[1] Mill (1957: 10); emphasis added (FF).

Dolores's doctor informs her of a new pain management drug, which Dolores then takes. Suppose it works. The pain is dramatically reduced. Instead of suffering with constant 400 dolor pain, Dolores is now suffering with pain somewhere in the 12 dolor range. She might be very happy about this reduction in pain. If asked, she might say that she is surprised, delighted, and in general fairly happy since taking the drug. Yet she still has a negative hedono-doloric balance. She still feels more dolors of sensory pain than hedons of sensory pleasure.[2]

One of the most striking examples that I discussed in Chapter 2 was the example involving the new mother. In the example, the new mother was giving birth to her first child. She was experiencing a wild collection of intense sensations and emotions. On the purely sensory side, she was suffering the intense pains associated with childbirth. She was not feeling any sensory pleasure. Thus, Sensory Hedonism about Happiness implies that she was unhappy at that moment. But I claimed that the new mother might describe the moment of childbirth as the happiest moment of her life. Though she was in serious pain, she was joyous about the end of her uncomfortable pregnancy, the successful birth of the baby, and the beginning of her career as a mother.

These examples remind us that a person can be unhappy at a time even though he is feeling more sensory pleasure than pain at that time; and that a person can be happy at a time even though she is feeling more sensory pain than pleasure at that time. Thus, hedonism of the Bentham-Mill-Sidgwick variety is false.

6.2 *A Crucial Distinction*

Nevertheless, I want to defend a form of hedonism about happiness. How can this be done?

There is a crucial distinction between two different sorts of pleasure. One is the familiar sort of *sensory pleasure*, where pleasure is taken to be a feeling, or sensation, perhaps relevantly like the feeling of warmth, or the feeling of pressure, or a tickle or an itch. But there is in addition a different sort of pleasure—*attitudinal pleasure*. This sort of pleasure is a propositional attitude rather than a feeling, or sensation. We attribute this sort of pleasure to a person when we say that he is pleased about something, or when we say that he "takes pleasure in" some state of affairs. Consider, for example, the statement that Tom

---

[2] For an extended attack on hedonism about happiness, see Haybron (2001).

is pleased *to be living in Massachusetts*. In this case, there is explicit mention of the *object* of Tom's pleasure. It is the state of affairs of Tom's living in Massachusetts. The pleasure attributed to Tom in this case in attitudinal pleasure, not sensory.[3]

In some cases we attribute attitudinal pleasure to a person but we don't explicitly identify the propositional object of his pleasure. Thus, consider the statement that *Tom is pleased about the weather*. Presumably, this just means that there is some fact about the weather that is the object of Tom's pleasure. Perhaps we can put it like this: there is some way that the weather is, such that Tom is pleased that the weather is that way. We are saying that Tom is taking attitudinal pleasure in some state of affairs, and we are saying that this state of affairs involves some fact about the weather, though we don't know precisely what state of affairs it is.

I am going to try to explain happiness by appeal to attitudinal pleasure.[4] Roughly, I am going to offer a reductive account of happiness according to which a person's momentary happiness level at a time is the amount of this attitudinal pleasure he takes in things at that time, minus the amount of attitudinal displeasure he takes in things at that time. On my account, to be happy is to be on balance attitudinally pleased about things. I am doubtful about the prospects for defining attitudinal pleasure, and so I propose to take it as my starting point. I will not offer an analysis of attitudinal pleasure, but will try to explain it in other ways.

On the view I want to defend, the amount of happiness that a person enjoys at a time depends upon the occurrence at that time of certain "atoms" of happiness. The atoms of happiness are states of affairs in which a person is attitudinally pleased to some determinate degree about some specified propositional object at some specified moment. So, for example, if at a certain moment Tom is very pleased to be living in Massachusetts, then this might be an atom of his happiness:

1. Tom is pleased at 9:00 p.m. on July 5, 2006, to degree 9 that he is living in Massachusetts.

---

[3] I discussed the distinction between attitudinal pleasure and sensory pleasure first in 'Two Questions about Pleasure' (1988), which was reprinted in Feldman (1997). I returned to that theme in Feldman (2004b).

[4] Wayne Sumner says 'there is no algorithm for computing your level of happiness from the intensity or duration of your particular enjoyments or sufferings.' See Sumner (1996: 148). One of my main aims in this chapter is to formulate an algorithm of precisely the sort that Sumner seems to be saying does not exist. Of course, when I say this, I assume that Sumner meant to be talking about *particular attitudinal enjoyments and sufferings*, not merely sensory ones.

Of course, in ordinary English we don't often talk in quite that way. Tom might say that he is glad that he is living in Massachusetts; he might say that he is delighted to be living in Massachusetts; he might even say that he is enjoying living in Massachusetts.[5]

In an effort to clarify the nature of the undefined concept of attitudinal pleasure that figures in these atoms, I want to state a series of theses about attitudinal pleasure.

i. Attitudinal pleasure is a "pro attitude." If Tom is pleased in this way about living in Massachusetts, then he is in some sense "in favor of it" or "for it" rather than "against it." Of course, there are a lot of different pro attitudes (liking, wanting, preferring, being amused by, hoping for, etc.) and so merely saying that it is a pro attitude does not serve to identify the relevant positive propositional attitude. We need to say more.

ii. Sometimes when we say, using the term in the relevant way, that a person is pleased about some state of affairs at some time, we mean to indicate that *at that very time* he is thinking about, and taking pleasure in, that state of affairs. His attitudinal pleasure is then consciously focused on the state of affairs. So, for example, suppose an old friend comes to visit Tom. Suppose they are sitting on Tom's deck, overlooking his wife's flower garden. Suppose the friend asks Tom how he feels about living in Massachusetts. Tom might stop to think for a second about the fact that he lives in Massachusetts. Maybe this has not been on his mind lately. Then he might say that he is very pleased to be living here. He might then express *occurrent* attitudinal pleasure; he might mean to say that *right now* he is actively pleased about this state of affairs. Perhaps his heart beats a bit more quickly. Perhaps he gets some sort of "cheery feeling."[6] He thinks about living here in Massachusetts; he is occurrently pleased about it. This could not happen at a time when he is asleep; or at a time when he is totally engrossed in some other activity.

On another occasion, someone might say that throughout the time Tom lived in Massachusetts he was always pleased to live here. He

---

[5] A somewhat misleading and possibly confusing expression employs 'because.' He might say that he is pleased because he is living in Massachusetts. This could express the relevant thought, but very well might not. It might express a causal claim not about the object of Tom's attitudinal pleasure, but about the cause of his sensory pleasure, which would be a completely different topic.

[6] I do not mean to suggest that Tom's attitudinal pleasure is to be identified with any of the feelings that I mention. I think it's obvious that Tom could be pleased even if he didn't feel any of those cheery feelings.

might intend to express the idea that Tom never had any complaints about living in Massachusetts and that, whenever he thought about it, he was occurrently pleased about it. When these things are true, Tom may be said to be *dispositionally pleased* about living in Massachusetts. If we are talking about dispositional pleasure, it would be acceptable to say that Tom is pleased to be living in Massachusetts throughout a certain interval of time even if Tom happens to be asleep at many moments during that time, or if he is not thinking about the fact that he lives in Massachusetts during some of those moments. Perhaps he just got another speeding ticket and is not pleased at all. Still, he is dispositionally pleased about living in Massachusetts. If he were able to calm down; if he could direct his attention to his living arrangements, he would be occurrently pleased about them.[7]

Every atom of happiness attributes occurrent attitudinal pleasure to a person (or other suitable creature). It says that he or she (or it) is occurrently pleased about some state of affairs. It also indicates the specific time at which the person is occurrently pleased about the state of affairs. If S is occurrently pleased about p throughout a stretch of time, then S is occurrently pleased about p at every instant within that stretch. From the fact that a person is dispositionally pleased about something during a stretch of time, it does not follow that that person is occurrently pleased about that thing at any moments during that time.

iii. One important fact about occurrent attitudinal pleasure is that it comes in degrees. Surely it makes sense to say that a person is pleased about p, and pleased about q, but more pleased about p than he is about q. Thus, for example, Tom might be pleased about the fact that he is the world champion (in his age group) in indoor rowing, and also pleased about the fact that he lives in Massachusetts, but he might be far more pleased about the former fact than he is about the latter.

iv. Although I would not want to take the numbers very seriously, I want to say that these different amounts of attitudinal pleasure can be represented numerically. So I will say that whenever a person, S, is attitudinally pleased about a state of affairs, p, there is a number, n, such that S is pleased to degree n about p. When a person is pleased

---

[7] I am grateful to Brad Skow for impressing upon me the fact that we cannot *define* dispositional pleasure by the unexplained use of the subjunctive conditional 'if he were to think about it, he would be occurrently pleased.' The conditional is not sufficiently sensitive to unusual circumstances. So it's better just to leave the concept of disposition unanalyzed, hoping that the idea will be sufficiently familiar.

about something, the relevant number is positive. Higher numbers represent greater degrees of attitudinal pleasure. I see no reason to suppose that there is any upper limit to possible degrees of attitudinal pleasure. No matter how pleased you are about something, you (or someone else) might be more pleased about something else. I assume that the numbers can be assigned in such a way that if S is twice as pleased about p as he is about q, then the number representing his degree of pleasure concerning p will be twice the number representing his degree of pleasure concerning q.[8]

v. Attitudinal pleasure has an opposite—attitudinal displeasure. While Tom may be pleased to be living in Massachusetts, he may be displeased about his receipt of another speeding ticket. We can understand displeasure to be "negative pleasure;" in other words, to be displeased about a thing is to be pleased about it to some negative degree. Let us assume that one unit of displeasure is equal in absolute magnitude but opposite in "sign" to one unit of pleasure. Whereas attitudinal pleasure is a "pro" attitude, attitudinal displeasure is the corresponding "con" attitude.

vi. There is also the case in which a person contemplates a proposition and is neither pleased nor displeased about it. It just leaves him cold. This gives us a non-arbitrary zero point in our scale of measurement for occurrent attitudinal pleasure—the point that represents the case in which a person is neither pleased nor displeased about some state of affairs. I have assumed that each unit increment is equal in absolute size to each other unit increment. As a result of these assumptions, we may now say that there is a ratio scale on which we can locate every atom of happiness. In each instance in which a person is attitudinally pleased or displeased about a proposition at a time, there is some number on this scale that indicates precisely how pleased he is then about that proposition.

vii. What things are possible objects of attitudinal pleasure? About what can a person be pleased? As I see it, there is no conceptual limit to the things about which a person might be pleased. Any state of affairs is something about which someone might be pleased. I grant, of course, that there might be some contingent barriers to attitudinal pleasure. Perhaps there are some things about which no

---

[8] I certainly do not mean to suggest that there is any easy way for observers to determine the amount of pleasure that a person experiences at a time. Indeed, as I will say in my comments in item xiv below, even the person experiencing the pleasure may be unable to specify its magnitude correctly.

one could (psychologically) be pleased. Still, such barriers would not be conceptual, or "logical." My point here is that there are no such logical barriers to pleasure.

viii. One implication of this is that, on my view, a person might be pleased about things that are in the past or future, as well as about things that are in the present.[9] Tom might be pleased about temporally present things (as in example (1)) or about past things. Thus, he might now be pleased *that he spent his childhood—many years ago—in Massachusetts.* He might now be pleased about future things; for example, *that he will some day enjoy his Golden Years in Massachusetts.* He might even be pleased about things whose temporal location is somewhat obscure—such as the fact *that 1937 ends long before 2037 begins.* It is not clear that we can assign any particular date to such a fact as that.[10]

ix. A person might be pleased about huge "global" facts about his life, and he might be pleased about minor, trivial, and "local" facts about the immediate present.[11]

Earlier, in Chapter 5, I mentioned Elizabeth Telfer's form of Whole Life Satisfactionism about happiness. Telfer offered a definition of happiness according to which a person is happy at a time if and only if she is pleased about her life as a whole at that time.[12] Perhaps Telfer would agree that a person could be pleased about all sorts of facts, but she would say that one's level of happiness is affected only when the object of one's pleasure is a certain global fact: the fact that one's life as a whole has gone in the way it has gone. I am going to present a view according to which a person's level of happiness is affected by such global pleasures, but also by non-global pleasures.

x. A person might be pleased about things that are happening, or did happen, or will happen, to others; Tom might be pleased *that*

---

[9] In saying this, I believe I am denying Wayne Sumner's claim in Sumner (2000: 13) that pleasure must always be directed toward temporally present states of affairs.

[10] This marks an interesting difference between attitudinal pleasure and enjoyment. I think enjoyment is also a propositional attitude, but its objects are restricted to the present. If Tom is now enjoying living in Massachusetts, then he must think he is living in Massachusetts *now.* We don't say that he now enjoys the fact that he lived here in his childhood, or that he now enjoys the fact that he will live here in the future. Of course, we can say that he now enjoys *thinking about the fact that he lived here in his childhood,* but that object is in the present.

[11] Although many philosophers appeal to the alleged distinction between local and global facts, I am not entirely clear on it. I cannot recall ever having seen it drawn precisely.

[12] Telfer (1980: 8–9).

his daughter will be coming home again to live in Massachusetts. He might be pleased about things that don't happen to anyone, such as the fact about 1937 mentioned above.

xi. In my view, if a person is occurrently pleased about some state of affairs at some time, then he is thinking about it at that time.[13] I do not mean to suggest that every such state of affairs must be at the very forefront of consciousness. But if it is correct to say that right now Tom is occurrently pleased to be living in Massachusetts, then he must, at least to some extent, be aware of the fact that he is living in Massachusetts. If right now he's giving no thought at all to the idea that he lives in Massachusetts, then at best he could now be dispositionally pleased about it.

This indicates at least one class of objects about which no one could be pleased. Consider the class of things that no one can grasp. If you can't grasp, or entertain, a certain proposition, you can't believe it or be pleased about it. So there is this limitation on your attitudinal pleasure: if you can't think of something, you can't be pleased about it.[14]

xii. In my view, occurrent attitudinal pleasure entails belief.[15] If Tom is pleased to be living in Massachusetts, then he must think that he is living in Massachusetts. If he thinks he does not live in Massachusetts, or if he has no opinion about where he lives, then he cannot be pleased about living here. At best he might be pleased about some related thought—perhaps he is pleased about the fact that he *might* be living in Massachusetts. But in that case he must believe that he might be living in Massachusetts.

xiii. I doubt that attitudinal pleasure entails knowledge. I think the phenomenon of "false pleasure" is possible. A person can be pleased about something that turns out to have been false. 'Whoopee!' says Tom, 'We are moving to Massachusetts!' He's pleased that he is going to live in Massachusetts. Later it turns out to be a mistake. Tom misunderstood what Alice said. She said that they are moving to

---

[13] Davis seems to maintain a very similar view about happiness. See Davis (1981b: 113).

[14] Of course, there is an indirect way in which a person can be pleased about a proposition he cannot grasp. Suppose there is some mathematical proposition that is too complicated for Tom to grasp. He knows it only by the description 'the theorem that Wile has recently proven.' Tom cannot be pleased about the theorem itself, but he can be pleased *that the theorem that Wile has recently proven is true.*

[15] Davis accepts something relevantly like this too. See Davis (1981b: 113). Davis goes further and says that happiness about p entails *absolute certainty* about p. This seems to me to go a bit too far.

Mississippi. But Tom was pleased for a while; and he was pleased about something. I think he was pleased about moving to Massachusetts even though it was not true that he was moving to Massachusetts. He had a false belief. It was not knowledge but he was pleased about it anyway. This example also shows that occurrent attitudinal pleasure does not entail truth.

xiv. There is another way in which attitudinal pleasure might be thought to be connected to knowledge. Someone might think that if you are pleased about something, then you must know that you are pleased about it. This seems not true. At least, it is not true as a matter of conceptual necessity. I think it is possible for there to be a person who is confused or self-deceived about his own mental states. Consider the case of Stan, the overly competitive indoor rower. He finds that one of his rivals has just been diagnosed with a serious illness. Perhaps Stan is pleased about this, but is too ashamed of himself to acknowledge that he is pleased about it; perhaps he finds it difficult to admit to himself that he is the kind of person who could be pleased about a rival's illness. In such a case, Stan is pleased about something but seems not to know that he is pleased about it.

xv. Although occurrent attitudinal pleasure and desire are both "pro" attitudes, no one supposes that they are the same attitude, or even equivalent. Suppose Tom knows he's in Vermont, but wishes he were in Massachusetts. In this case, he wants to be in Massachusetts, but it would be wrong to say that he's pleased to be in Massachusetts. The main problem, obviously, is that he does not believe that he is in Massachusetts.

xvi. A more plausible view is that attitudinal pleasure can be identified with the combination of belief and desire. Assuming that belief and desire are propositional attitudes that come in suitable amounts, we might say that a person, S, is pleased about a state of affairs, p, if and only if S desires p and S believes that p is true.[16] Loosely, to be pleased about something is to want it and to believe that it is happening.

It seems to me that the combination of belief and desire is not sufficient for attitudinal pleasure. It is possible to want a thing and to think that you're getting it without having a favorable emotional outlook on that thing. To see this in a clear example, consider a case in which a person has a desire that he thinks is shameful and hurtful. He wishes he

---

[16] Compare Davis (1981b: 113).

did not have that desire. Suppose, for example, that Nicko is addicted to cigarettes but has been trying to quit. He knows that if he succumbs to his desire to light up on some occasion, his eventual quitting will be delayed even longer. He now wants to light up, and thinks he is lighting up; but he takes no pleasure in the fact that he is lighting up.

In many cases, of course, we want certain things because we think we will enjoy them. But there are other reasons to want things. Our sense of moral obligation provides another reason to want something. Suppose, for example, that a rigid Kantian moralist, Otto, believes that he has a duty of perfect obligation to visit an elderly neighbor who is recuperating in the hospital. Since he thinks it is his moral duty to do this, Otto wants to do it. He desires to visit his neighbor. But at the same time Otto does not enjoy visiting this neighbor. In fact, he finds visits to the neighbor somewhat unpleasant because the neighbor is boring and unfriendly and ungrateful. Suppose Otto goes to the hospital and grimly fulfils his obligation.

In this case (a) Otto wants to visit his neighbor and (b) believes that he is visiting his neighbor, but (c) does not take pleasure in visiting his neighbor. He does not enjoy the visit. It's "no fun." The examples could be multiplied. The point is clear: getting what you want is one thing; being pleased about it is another. Though they often come together, they can come apart.

xvii. Surely it is possible for a person to be pleased about several things at once. Tom might be pleased to be living in Massachusetts, pleased to be sitting on his deck, and pleased to be smelling the roses, all at one time. And, equally surely, a person can be pleased about several things at a time, and simultaneously displeased about several other things. Tom is still displeased about his latest speeding ticket.

xvii. It seems to me that there is an important distinction between *intrinsic attitudinal pleasure* and *extrinsic attitudinal pleasure*. In some cases a person is pleased about a certain fact, but only because he takes this fact to be a sign of another fact that he is pleased about. For example, Tom might be pleased to see the beads of sweat breaking out on his rival's forehead. Tom might be pleased about this, but only because it suggests that his rival is tiring fast, and he's pleased about that. And he's pleased that his rival is tiring fast only because it suggests that Tom is going to be able to defeat him.

I will say that a person is *intrinsically attitudinally pleased* to some degree about some state of affairs, p, if and only if he is pleased about p to that degree for its own sake, and not because there is some other state of affairs, q, such that he is pleased about p only because he takes p to be suitably related to q, and he is pleased about q. I will say that a person is merely *extrinsically attitudinally pleased* about some state of affairs if and only if he is pleased about it, but not intrinsically.[17] Every atom of happiness is an attribution of occurrent *intrinsic* attitudinal pleasure or displeasure to a person, at a time, to a degree, in a specific propositional object.

This concludes my discussion of attitudinal pleasure and the atoms of happiness. I now turn to questions about aggregation.

6.3 *Happiness at a Time, During an Interval, in a Domain, and in a Life*

Suppose Tom and Alice are having a romantic dinner. Suppose that as they sip their champagne, Alice asks Tom if he is happy: 'Are you happy right now, dear?' she asks. 'And furthermore, if you are happy, precisely *how happy* are you?' Tom may be nonplussed. This is not the sort of question he expects from Alice. He may not know the answer. But, in my view, there is an answer.

The answer is this: consider all the states of affairs that Tom is occurrently intrinsically attitudinally pleased (or displeased) about, at the moment. For each, consider the extent to which he is intrinsically pleased (or displeased) about it. Add up these numbers, making sure to make use of *negative* numbers for all the things Tom is intrinsically displeased about at the time. This sum represents how happy Tom is at the moment.

Kahneman uses the term 'instant utility' to refer to something like this number.[18] Davis uses the expression 'degree of occurrent happiness.'[19] I will instead speak of a person's *momentary happiness*. It is defined in this way:

D1:   S's momentary happiness at t = the sum, for all propositions, p, such that S is occurrently intrinsically (dis)pleased about p at t,

---

[17] There are further complexities here. A person might be *partially* intrinsically pleased about some state of affairs. Suppose, for example, that Tom is pleased to degree 10 to be living in Massachusetts. Suppose that he is, in part, pleased about this because it enables him to live near his children, who also live in Massachusetts. Suppose that he would still be pleased, though only to degree 5, to live in Massachusetts even if his children didn't live there. Suppose that this other component of his pleasure is not dependent upon anything else that he is pleased about. Then half of his pleasure is intrinsic, and half is not. In such a case, we can say that Tom gets 5 units of intrinsic attitudinal pleasure out of living in Massachusetts.

[18] Kahneman (1999: 4).   [19] Davis (1981b: 113).

of the degree to which S is occurrently intrinsically (dis)pleased about p at t.[20]

I have introduced and described the items that I take to be the atoms of happiness. These involve *attitudinal pleasure and displeasure.* They are states of affairs in which a person is intrinsically (dis)pleased to some determinate degree at some moment about some specified object. D1 purports to define a person's momentary happiness level as a function of the set of all the atoms of happiness that the person is experiencing at that moment. But this is hardly a complete account of the nature of happiness. I have not said anything about a person's happiness during an interval, or in a life, or in a domain of life. I now turn to these questions.

Suppose Tom drives down the Mass Pike during a period of time starting at t1 and ending at t15. Suppose that, for each of 15 instants during this period, Tom's momentary happiness level has been calculated. At t1, Tom's happiness level is +4; at t2 it is +6; etc. These 15 momentary happiness levels could easily be plotted on a simple graph. It would look like Graph 6.1.

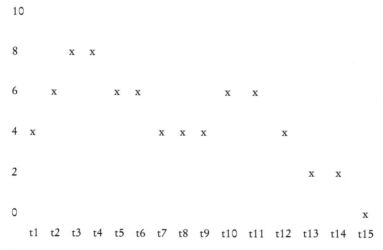

Graph 6.1.

---

[20] The reader may wonder whether there might be a problem in cases in which a person is pleased about infinitely many things at the same time. The sum will not be properly defined in such cases. I think this problem will not arise, since attitudinal pleasure entails "thinking about" and belief. Since human beings cannot think of infinitely many things at one time, they cannot be occurrently pleased about infinitely many things at one time. The sum, then, will always be the sum of finitely many addends.

On the graph, numbers on the up-and-down axis indicate momentary happiness levels; numbers across represent times; each 'x' represents Tom's momentary happiness at the indicated moment.

But, of course, the interval contains more moments—presumably infinitely many. If we plot the position of Tom's happiness level for *all* of these moments during the interval t1–t15, we will get a line instead of a disconnected collection of x's. Perhaps it will look like Graph 6.2.

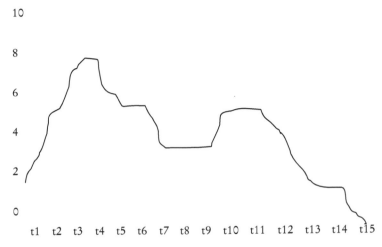

Graph 6.2.

We can call this line "Tom's happiness curve for t1–t15." It shows, for every instant in the specified interval, Tom's momentary happiness level for that instant.

The area under the happiness curve (down to the zero line) represents the total amount of happiness that Tom experiences during the whole period of time.

Suppose that during the period t15–t17, Tom is engaged in some discussion with a Massachusetts State Trooper. Perhaps the conversation includes such remarks as 'May I see your license and registration, please?' and 'Do you have any idea how fast you were going?' Suppose Tom was intrinsically displeased about a number of things during this period of time. In that case, his happiness curve would go below the zero line. Then the graph as a whole might look more like Graph 6.3.

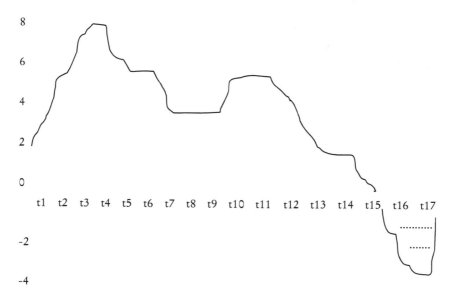

Graph 6.3.

Tom's total unhappiness during t15–t17 is represented by the dotted area between the "unhappiness curve" and the zero line above it. To find Tom's total net happiness during the period t1–t17, subtract the unhappiness area from the happiness area.

The principles illustrated in this example can be applied to any person, and any period of time. It will give answers to such questions as the following: 'How happy were you in your childhood?' 'Were you happy during your years in Providence?' 'How happy was Helen during March?' It also provides a clear sense for such familiar remarks as 'have a happy birthday,' 'have a happy new year,' and 'happy days are here again.'

Sometimes, when we talk about happiness during an interval, we do not mean to be discussing the total amount of happiness experienced during that interval. For example, consider the case of a person who was in elementary school for six years and in middle school for only three. Suppose his average happiness level remained fixed throughout this time. The principle I have so far mentioned would entail that he was half as happy in middle school as he was in elementary school—simply because there were half as many minutes of middle school in which he was happy. But the more natural way to view the situation would be to say that he was just as happy in middle school as he was in elementary school, since his average momentary happiness level for the moments of middle school were the same as his average momentary happiness level for the moments of elementary school. So this gives us a second way of understanding talk about happiness during intervals.

We need next to say a few words about happiness in various domains of life. What might be meant by saying that a person is happy in his marriage, but not happy in his work? Surely this is not to be explained by appeal to happiness during different intervals of time—it's not as if certain periods of time are "work intervals" and others are "marriage intervals." A married person is still married when he goes to work.

Suppose Tom tells us that he enjoys his work. If we are nosy, we may ask him to expand upon his comment. We may ask him to be more specific: 'precisely what about your work do you enjoy, or take pleasure in?' Suppose Tom says that in particular he is pleased about the fact that has friendly colleagues, and the fact that he gets to think about Leibniz all the time, and the fact that he can take time off to go rowing any time he feels like doing so. That's what he enjoys about his work. Let us say that these are the happifying features of his work. I assume that there are some unhappifying features of his work too.

Now we need only to do a tiny bit of simple arithmetic to find out how happy Tom is in his work during a period of time. Select a time, t, during the period. Take the sum, for all the happifying and unhappifying features, p, of his work, of the degree to which Tom is occurrently intrinsically (dis)pleased about p at t. That sum represents the extent of Tom's (un)happiness with his work at t. Do the same for all other times in the period. Plot the points representing Tom's happiness with respect to his work at all those times. Draw the curves as before. Do the subtraction if necessary. The result is Tom's happiness with his work during the period of time you have selected. The same could be done for any domain of life and any period of time.

Now let us turn to the question about the happy life. Aristotle seems to endorse the maxim attributed to Solon: 'Count no man happy till he's dead.'[21] The present approach provides a convenient way to make sense of Solon's maxim. When we say that someone is a happy person, we may mean that he has led a happy life; in other words, we may

---

[21] Aristotle, *Nicomachean Ethics*, bk. 1, ch. 10.

mean that his net happiness for the whole interval during which he lives is positive. According to the view presented here, a person's net lifetime happiness is determined by the magnitudes of two areas—the area below his lifetime happiness curve and the area above his lifetime unhappiness curve. The person is said to have had a happy life if the difference between these areas is positive. The person's net lifetime happiness is the magnitude of the difference.

A pessimist will be sure to point out that even if a person has been pretty happy throughout his life so far, and even if he is very happy right now, if he's still alive, there is still time for him to experience enormous unhappiness, and in this way ruin what otherwise might have been a happy life. As the pessimist sees it, there is always time for things to go bad. But, on the other hand, an optimist will be sure to point out that, even if a person has been pretty unhappy, there is always the chance that his final hours will bring such great happiness that, in the end, his life will turn out to have been a happy one. There is always time for things to improve. 'Count no man *unhappy* till he's dead' will be the optimist's motto. So we take a certain risk if we say, while a person is still alive, either that his is a happy life or that his is an unhappy life.

This reveals an ambiguity in the statement that a certain person "is a happy person." For the statement might mean (a) that the person is happy *at the moment of utterance*. In that case the statement would be true if the person has a positive momentary happiness level at the moment of utterance. Since (under this interpretation) the statement has no implications about future happiness levels, impending good or bad fortune could not affect such a claim. It's merely a statement about the person's present happiness level. We don't need to wait for the person to die to determine that the statement is true. The statement that a certain person is happy might mean (b) that the person is generally, or typically, happy. In that case the statement would be true if the person generally, or typically, has a positive momentary happiness level. We don't need to wait for the person to die to say this, either. But, finally, the statement that a certain person is a happy person might mean (c) that the person has (or *will end up having had*) a "happy life." In that case, the statement is true only if the person's net lifetime happiness is positive. If the person is still alive, this statement is much riskier. Its truth depends on things that have happened in the past and other things that will happen in the future. Since things can always take a turn for the worse, perhaps it's best to wait until the person is dead before making such a bold claim. If this is what Solon meant, his motto is a judicious piece of ancient philosophical wisdom.

6.4 *Wendell, Dolores, and the New Mother*

In Part I of this book I formulated several competing theories about the nature of happiness. Among these was a form of sensory hedonism that I attributed (somewhat hesitantly) to Bentham, Mill, and Sidgwick. I then presented the cases of Wendell, Dolores, and the new mother in an attempt to show that our common-sense concept of happiness diverges from the concept defined in the sensory hedonistic theory. I now want to reconsider those cases to see what attitudinal hedonism says about them.

Since the cases involving Wendell and Dolores are structurally similar, we can focus on just one of them. Let's look at the case of Dolores.

Dolores's situation was described as follows: she had been suffering with unrelenting pain in the 400 dolor range for some time. She was feeling somewhat hopeless. But then her doctor prescribed a new drug that promptly reduced her level of pain to something like 12 dolors. Since she was feeling no other sensory pleasures or pains at the moment in question, her hedono-doloric balance was −12. Sensory hedonism implies that she was unhappy; but I said that she was thrilled and delighted and filled with new hope. She was very happy, though still in pain. This case refutes sensory hedonism about happiness. What does my attitudinal hedonism about happiness imply about this case?

Attitudinal hedonism says that Dolores's momentary happiness level is the sum of the attitudinal pleasure or displeasure levels of all the atoms of happiness that Dolores is experiencing at the moment. (Let's call the moment when she realizes that the drug is really working '*tn*.') What are Dolores's atoms of pleasure and displeasure at *tn*? Earlier, I specified that Dolores was thrilled about the dramatic reduction in pain, and that she was hopeful about the future. Consider these possible atoms of happiness:

2. Dolores is attitudinally pleased at *tn* to degree 10 about the fact that Dolores is feeling 388 fewer dolors than she had been feeling recently.
3. Dolores is attitudinally pleased at *tn* to degree 10 about the fact that there is reason to hope that her pain will soon be removed entirely.

4. Dolores is attitudinally pleased at *tn* to degree 10 about the fact that she likely will not have to suffer any pangs of 400 dolor pain anytime in the near future.

Of course, it's not all good news for Dolores. She is still feeling 12 dolors of sensory pain. Let us grant that she takes attitudinal displeasure in various sensations that she is having. I will indicate the relevant sensations merely by saying that Dolores feels "like *this*," where '*this*' is a demonstrative term that Dolores uses to indicate her painful sensation. Since presumably Dolores does not like feeling like *this*, the following atom of happiness must be taken into account:

5. Dolores is attitudinally displeased at *tn* to degree 12 about the fact that she feels like *this* at *tn*.

For ease of calculation, let us assume that these are the only atoms of happiness and unhappiness involving Dolores at *tn*. In that case, her momentary happiness level is +18. The moment counts according to attitudinal hedonism—correctly, as I see it—as a happy time for Dolores. Thus, whereas sensory hedonism yields the wrong result in the case of Dolores, my theory yields the right result. She's happy, though in pain.

Since the example involving Wendell is structurally identical to the case involving Dolores, there is no need to discuss it in detail. Attitudinal hedonism declares that Wendell is unhappy, even though his hedono-doloric balance is positive. His unhappiness results from the fact that he takes attitudinal displeasure in several facts, including the fact that he has permitted himself to be duped.

I also pointed out that Sensory Hedonism about Happiness implies that the new mother was unhappy at that moment when she gave birth to her baby. This is clearly an incorrect assessment of the situation; though she was in pain, the new mother describes it as the happiest moment of her life. Attitudinal hedonism yields a more attractive result. Note that the new mother was taking great attitudinal pleasure in several facts. For one thing, she was delighted that her long and uncomfortable pregnancy was coming to its end. For another, she was very pleased that the new baby was being born and that it was healthy. And, third, she was thrilled that she would soon begin the exciting process of raising the child. Suppose we say that she took 15 units of intrinsic occurrent attitudinal pleasure in each of these facts; suppose we say that she took 20 units of intrinsic occurrent attitudinal displeasure in the fact that she felt like *this* (where '*this*' is intended to refer directly to the intense painful sensations that the new mother was feeling). Then we can say that the new mother was enjoying a net balance of +25 units of attitudinal pleasure. In this case, Attitudinal Hedonism about Happiness implies that the new mother was very happy in spite of the intense pain. This assessment corresponds to her (imagined) statements as well as to my intuitions about the case.

I discussed the case of the new mother in connection with Kahneman's theory as well. According to that theory, a person's momentary happiness level is equal to the strength of the person's desire for her present experiences to continue. It is reasonable to suppose that, at the moment when she is giving birth, the new mother would not want her present experiences to continue. I think it's more likely that the thought of prolongation of those labor pains would seem just about unbearable. One of the features that make her current situation so thrilling for her is the fact that it marks a major transition. Pregnancy is ending; new motherhood is beginning. Surely she does not want to linger at the point of transition; she wants to get into the next stage. So Kahneman's theory implies that the new mother is unhappy. Again, this seems wrong. Though there are tears in her eyes, she is very happy. Attitudinal Hedonism about Happiness again evaluates the case correctly. The new mother is happy because she is taking great pleasure in several important facts at the moment when the baby is being born.

I claim, then, that even though it is a form of hedonism, Attitudinal Hedonism about Happiness generates acceptable evaluations of the three cases that I mentioned in connection with Sensory Hedonism about Happiness. Of course, before we can reach any conclusion about the overall merits of Attitudinal Hedonism about Happiness, we need to see whether it can deal adequately with various objections, and we need to evaluate its implications for other hard cases. I turn to these topics in the next chapter.

Appendix C
The Meaning(s) of 'Happy'

C.1 Some Claims of Ambiguity

A number of philosophers and others have claimed that 'happy,' as a term of ordinary English, is ambiguous.[1] Tatarkiewicz is perhaps the prime example. At the beginning of *Analysis of Happiness* he claims that the term has four distinct senses. In one sense, 'happy' signifies 'a state of intense joy, bliss and rapture.'[2] In a second sense, it does not mean bliss or rapture, but instead it means 'lasting satisfaction with life.'[3] In its third sense, 'happy' is synonymous with 'successful.'[4] And in its fourth sense, 'happy' is alleged to mean the same as 'possesses the highest good.'[5] Tatarkiewicz goes on to say:

These four meanings are a copious source of confusion in our ideas about happiness; four concepts each designated by the same word are apt to fuse in our minds into a single nebulous notion hovering between the four. Even though most philosophers who have written about happiness have accepted only one of them and eliminated the rest, the average man is still inclined to lump these four different things under a single label.[6]

Nettle seems to endorse the ambiguity thesis. He talks of 'three different senses of the term "happiness"'[7] and even provides a chart to make the alleged senses clear. In the first sense, 'happiness' means 'joy, pleasure.' In the second sense, to say that a person is happy seems to mean that '. . . upon reflection on the balance sheet of pleasures and pains, they feel the balance to be reasonably positive over the long term.'[8] In the third sense, 'happy' applies to a person if he has 'a life in which the person flourishes, or fulfils their true potential.'[9] Happiness (if we use the term in this third sense) does not have any distinctive phenomenology; it is a term of evaluation.[10]

---

[1] Obviously, if philosophers or psychologists introduce multiple novel stipulative definitions of 'happy,' the word will have as many such senses as they stipulate. The claim about ambiguity does not concern introduced technical senses; it involves the meaning of the word as it appears in natural languages.   [2] Tatarkiewicz (1976: 1).

[3] Ibid. 2.   [4] Ibid. 6.   [5] Ibid.   [6] Ibid.

[7] Nettle (2005: 18).   [8] Ibid. 17.   [9] Ibid. 19–20.

[10] I think it's interesting to note that while Tatarkiewicz and Nettle agree that 'happy' is ambiguous, and they agree that it sometimes means 'feels joy or pleasure,' they are in serious disagreement about all the other senses.

Telfer claims that 'happy' "refers to" several different concepts. She says:

A happy *temperament*, often attributed to young children, is a disposition to be cheerful, to find things agreeable. One can speak of someone as a *'naturally* happy person' in this sense, meaning among other things that he is likely to manage to be happy in life even in very difficult circumstances. A happy *mood* is a (temporary) inclination to look on the bright side or find things agreeable, sometimes coupled with a recognition that in fact things are in a bad way; like other moods, its existence can often be explained by causes rather than reasons, in this case such things as a good dinner. 'Happy' meaning 'enjoyable' or 'pleasant' occurs in sentences like 'I spend a happy evening looking through old photographs', and a similar use is exhibited when we say of a child paddling in the mud 'He's very happy,' meaning 'He's enjoying himself.' Happiness *in life* is the kind which is in question when someone says, 'At last he has found happiness', or 'I'm a very happy man.'[11]

A few pages later, Telfer gives her "definition" (her term) of this final sense of 'happy' when she says that happiness is 'a state of being pleased with one's life as a whole.'[12]

Merely by focusing on these three writers, we seem to have about eleven alleged senses of 'happy.' They are as follows:

WT1: x is happy =df. x experiences intense bliss, joy or rapture.
WT2: x is happy =df. x has lasting satisfaction with life.
WT3: x is happy =df. x is successful.
WT4: x is happy =df. x possesses the highest good.

N1: x is happy =df. x experiences joy or pleasure.
N2: x is happy =df. upon reflection on the balance sheet of x's own pleasures and pains, x believes that the balance of pleasure over pain is reasonably positive.
N3: x is happy =df. x flourishes, x fulfills x's true potential.

ET1: x has a happy temperament =df. x is disposed to be cheerful.
ET2: x is in a happy mood =df. x is temporarily disposed to look on the bright side.
ET3: x is happy =df. x is enjoying himself.
ET4: x is happy =df. x is pleased with x's life as a whole.

I take these to be claims about the meaning of the word 'happy' in ordinary English. By 'meaning' here I mean *intension*, or sense, where the sense of a word is the concept that the word expresses. If one of these definitions were correct, the term to the right of the '=df.' sign

---

[11] Telfer (1980: 1–2). [12] Ibid. 8.

in that definition would be a synonym of 'happy.' If several of these definitions are correct, then 'happy' is ambiguous.

Of course, sometimes we use the word 'happy' to refer to someone who is experiencing intense joy or rapture. Suppose a person behaving in such a way as to make it obvious that he is experiencing intense joy or rapture. We don't recognize the person. We ask, 'who is that happy guy over there?' On another occasion we might use the word 'happy' to refer to someone who is successful. Imagine that we see Donald Trump smiling broadly but we don't recognize him. We ask, 'who is that happy guy over there?' It does not follow that the word 'happy' *means* 'intense joy or rapture,' or that it means 'successful.' (Sometimes we use the word 'happy' to refer to someone who is left-handed or who has his hair combed over in an odd way; the word is not a synonym of 'left-handed' or 'has a comb-over.' From the fact that a word correctly applies to a person who has a certain feature, it does not follow that that feature is the meaning of the word.)

The question here is not whether the word 'happy' correctly applies to people of several different sorts—obviously it does. The question is whether the word has multiple meanings.

C.2 Quine on Ambiguity

In his characteristically amusing and insightful discussion of ambiguity in *Word and Object*, Quine draws an important distinction between two different ways in which a general term may have "multiple applicability."[13] On the one hand, there are cases in which a term has a single meaning, but the meaning is sufficiently broad so that the word applies to a wide variety of items. Quine characterizes these as cases of mere generality. On the other hand, there are cases in which a term has a couple of different meanings. In these cases, the term is actually ambiguous. It has a plurality of senses.

Sometimes it is hard to tell whether we are dealing with mere generality or genuine ambiguity. Quine cites the case of 'hard.' We speak of hard chairs and of hard questions. It's not clear whether 'hard' has a single meaning that is sufficiently broad so that it correctly applies both to chairs and to questions, or whether 'hard' has one sense ('resists deformation when pressure is applied') in which it applies to certain chairs and another sense ('not easily answered') in which it applies to certain questions. In the former case 'hard' would be a

[13] Willard Van Orman Quine, *Word and Object* (1960: 129–34), section 27, 'Ambiguity of Terms.'

univocal term with a single broad meaning; in the latter case it would be an ambiguous (or perhaps innocently polysemous) term with two meanings. Quine wonders whether we are ' . . . in effect calling "hard" ambiguous, if at all, just because it is true of some very unlike things?'[14]

There is no surefire test for ambiguity. There are some suggestive hints. One of these involves counting and jokes. Consider this statement:

1. I have three planes: two Stanleys and a Cessna.

(The Stanleys are woodworking planes; the Cessna is a small airplane.) If you think the word 'plane' is ambiguous as between one sense in which it means 'woodworking tool used to smooth and flatten surfaces' and another sense in which it means 'heavier-than-air flying machine,' then you will find statement (1) amusing. It's a joke because it runs together these two senses in a surprising way. It involves counting up "planes" and "planes" as if they were things of the same countable kind.

But the joke test is inconclusive. Consider Quine's example 'hard.' Suppose I say this:

2. I confronted three hard things in the examination room: a chair and two questions.

If you find (2) amusing, perhaps that is because 'hard' is ambiguous in your idiolect. On the other hand, you may just find it a bit surprising because it points up a similarity between items normally thought to be very unlike: chairs and questions. Quine leaves the matter unresolved.

Another test for ambiguity involves sentences that would be self-contradictory on the assumption of a single sense. Here is an example:

3. I have a plane—but I don't have a plane.

Imagine that as the first 'plane' is uttered, the speaker first makes motions as if operating a woodworking plane, but when the second 'plane' is uttered, he makes motions as if flying through the air. In this case, the hearer would probably understand (3) to mean the same as:

3a. I have a *woodworking* plane—but I don't have an *airplane*.

In this case, the term 'plane' would seem to be ambiguous.

But again, the test is inconclusive. Consider this sentence:

4. I confronted something hard this morning—but it was not hard.

---

[14] Quine, *Word and Object*, 130.

If 'hard' is ambiguous, it should be possible to understand (4) to mean the same as:

4a. I confronted something hard *in the "resists deformation" sense* this morning—but it was not hard *in the "difficult to answer" sense.*

I am not sure what the test reveals in this case.

Quine makes some amusing remarks about 'true.' He says that he is baffled by philosophers who "stoutly maintain" that 'true' means one thing when applied to necessary propositions and another thing when applied to contingent propositions. He says, 'What mainly baffles me is the stoutness of their maintenance. What can they possibly count as evidence?'[15,16]

C.3 Is 'Happy' Ambiguous?

Let us apply our admittedly inconclusive tests to see if 'happy' is ambiguous in any of the suggested ways. To do this, let us imagine a case involving three people. Let one of them be Timmy, a happy-go-lucky party-goer who was discussed earlier in Chapter Five. Timmy enjoys spicy food and sparkling beverages; he likes loud music and fun-loving companions at parties. He never thinks "deep thoughts" about his life as a whole. Let the second of them be Woody, who is a mild-mannered fellow who does not enjoy any sensory pleasures, but who has reflected deeply on his life as a whole and who has found it satisfactory. Let the last of them be the philosopher, who enjoys very few sensory pleasures and who doesn't think about his own life. He is deeply engrossed in philosophical contemplation, just as he prefers. Suppose that while I have this trio in mind, I say:

5. I know three happy people: Timmy, Woody, and the philosopher.

The joke test suggests that if 'happy' were ambiguous in the way claimed by Tatarkiewicz, there would be something amusing about sentence (5). It would be a play on words, or a joke. For if Tatarkiewicz is right, when I say that Timmy is happy all I can mean is that he is happy in the "joy, bliss, rapture" sense—but neither of the others

---

[15] Ibid. 131.

[16] The suggestive tests seem to imply that 'true' is not ambiguous. There is nothing funny about the claim that many propositions are true—some of them necessarily and some contingently. Nor can I find a suitable reading for 'this proposition is true; but it is not true.'

is happy in this sense. When I say that Woody is happy, all I can mean is that he is happy in the "satisfied with life" sense—but neither of the others is happy in this sense. And when I say that the philosopher is happy, perhaps what I mean is that he is happy in the "has the highest good" sense—but neither of the others is happy in this sense. Perhaps my sense of humor has atrophied. In any case, (5) does not seem at all funny to me. Though the three characters are happy for three different reasons, and may perhaps be said to be happy in three different ways, each of them seems "happy." What I say about Timmy seems to mean the same as what I say about Woody and the philosopher. I see no evidence of ambiguity here.

Now let's consider the second test. Consider this sentence:

6. Timmy is happy all right; but he is not *happy*.

The self-contradiction test suggests that if 'happy' were ambiguous, we could read the first 'happy' in one way and the second 'happy' in another. Just as in the case of the two 'plane's, we could find a way to make sense of the sentence.

However, when I reflect on (6) I cannot find any way to make it seem plausible. Even when I give myself some hints, it still seems wrong:

6a. Timmy is happy all right (in the sense that he has plenty of sensory pleasure), but he is not happy (in the sense that he has not judged his life as a whole to be satisfactory).

(6a) seems to me to be a lexical disaster. When I see a sentence like (6a), my first inclination is to think that the author doesn't know what 'sense' means. I assume that when he speaks of "senses of 'happy' " what he really means is "ways of being happy." Thus, if I am in a charitable mood, I assume that the author meant to say:

6b. Timmy is happy; but only because he has plenty of sensory pleasure. His happiness does not depend upon his having judged his life as a whole to be satisfactory, since he hasn't done that.

But of course (6b) provides no evidence in favor of the ambiguity thesis. It just suggests that 'happy' is sufficiently broad in meaning so that it can correctly apply to people whose happiness has a variety of different sources.

In the end, I am like Quine. I know that some philosophers and psychologists stoutly maintain that 'happy' is ambiguous in ordinary English. What baffles me is the stoutness of their maintenance. I cannot see any reason to think that the word is ambiguous in the ways indicated.

C.4 Does 'Happy' Have Any of the Suggested Senses?

Subject to certain obvious restrictions, if WT1 were true, then there would be a certain class of sentences of ordinary English that contain the word 'happy' and such that it would be possible to substitute 'experiences intense bliss, joy, or rapture' for 'happy' without changing the meaning of the sentence—the sentence as a whole would still express the same proposition. Consider these two sentences:

7a. When Tom took third place in the rowing contest, he was only moderately happy.
7b. When Tom took third place in the rowing contest, he was only moderately experiencing intense bliss, joy, or rapture.

When I look at those sentences, it seems obvious to me that they don't express the same proposition. I cannot contort my mind in such a way as to get (7a) just to mean the same as (7b). (7b) seems to me simply to be a mess. No competent speaker of English would utter such a monstrosity. (7a), on the other hand, seems perfectly in order. So my linguistic intuition tells me that (7a) does not mean the same as (7b); I conclude that 'happy' in (7a) does not mean the same as 'experiences intense bliss, joy, or rapture.'[17]

I should admit at the outset that I don't take this to be a *proof* that WT1 is false. After all, I have claimed only that the words are not synonymous in one pair of sentences. They might be synonyms in some other pair of sentences. I don't know how to demonstrate that a certain word does not have a certain alleged sense in ordinary English. I can point out that I have been speaking English for more than sixty years; I am familiar with the word; I think I understand others when they use it. It simply does not seem to me that the word has the alleged sense. People just don't mean that when they say it. That's what I am saying about WT1. It seems to me that the word 'happy' in ordinary English simply is not synonymous with the phrase 'experiences intense bliss, joy, or rapture.'

WT3 seems to me to be equally erroneous. Of course, many successful people are happy; many happy people are successful. But

---

[17] When I speak here of 'linguistic intuition' I do not mean to suggest any special sort of epistemic faculty. Linguistic intuition is just a person's sense of the syntactical or semantic appropriateness of expressions. It is the product of observational experience with the language, plus memory, plus (perhaps) some inductive or analogical reasoning. Linguistic intuition yields knowledge of contingent facts about the language, and its operation can be explained by appeal to familiar epistemic capacities. It should not be confused with the far more controversial sort of conceptual intuition that is sometimes alleged to give us insight into a priori necessities.

the non-synonymy of 'happy' and 'successful' should be pretty clear when we reflect on such pairs as these:

8a. Marilyn Monroe was a successful actress.
8b. Marilyn Monroe was a happy actress.

(8a) tells us something about the rate at which Marilyn managed to achieve her theatrical goals. The sentence seems to be saying that it was pretty great. (8b) says nothing about her achievement of goals. It says (as I see it) that she took on balance a positive amount of attitudinal pleasure in things relating to her career as an actress.

I think it is very likely that if a person possessed the highest good, then he would be happy. But it does not follow from this that definition WT4 is correct. If WT4 were correct, then the word 'happy' (when used in a certain sense) would mean the same as 'possesses the highest good.' If the word were used in that sense, then this sentence would be analytic:

9. Every happy person is a person who possesses the highest good.

When I reflect on (9), it strikes me that there is no such sense. No matter how I squint and stare at (9), it does not look analytic. In fact, it just goes on looking false. The word 'happy' simply does not mean what WT4 says it means.

Two definitions call for special attention. These are WT2 and ET4. According to these definitions, 'happy' means the same as 'has lasting satisfaction with life' or 'is pleased with life as a whole.' In Chapter Five and Appendix A, I tried to show that a person can be happy at a time without thinking about or passing any judgment on his life as a whole at that time. If successful, my arguments would establish that there is some sense of 'happy' in which it does not mean what WT2 and ET4 say it means. But my arguments would not establish that there is no such sense. Again, it seems to me that while the word surely could apply to some people who are satisfied with or pleased about their lives as wholes, the word does not have either of these meanings. There is no sense of the word 'happy' that would make this analytic:

10. Every happy person is a person who has lasting satisfaction with his life as a whole.

I do not know how to show that (10) is not analytic. (Of course, I do not know how an advocate of WT2 or ET4 could show that it is analytic.)

I will leave it to the interested reader to contemplate the plausibility of the other definitions.

C.5 The Meaning of 'Happy'

So if there is no proof that 'happy' has multiple senses, and none of the definitions offered by Tatarkiewicz, Nettle, and Telfer is correct as an account of the meaning of the term in ordinary English, the question remains: what does 'happy' mean?

My view is that 'happy' is used loosely and vaguely in ordinary English. In some cases, as when it appears in ritual phrases such as 'happy birthday,' it has very little determinate meaning. But when it is used seriously as part of a description of someone's mental state, it seems to me that it is generally used in such a way that its meaning would be made somewhat more precise and articulate but not seriously distorted if it were replaced by 'takes more attitudinal pleasure than displeasure in things.' As I see it, when we say that someone is happy, we are saying (in a vague way) that he takes more pleasure than displeasure in things; when we say that someone is in a "happy mood" we are saying (again, in a vague way) that he is in a mood wherein he is likely to be taking more pleasure than displeasure in things; when we say that someone has a "happy temperament," we mean to indicate that he is by nature a person who tends to take more pleasure than displeasure in things. Most importantly, in my view, when we say that someone had a happy life, our statement means (roughly) that the person took more pleasure than displeasure in things during his life.

I am not suggesting that every speaker of ordinary English will instantly recognize that 'happy' and 'takes more attitudinal pleasure than displeasure in things' are synonyms. My suggestion is more modest. I think that 'happy' is (like so many familiar words) often used without any clear sense. Speakers need not have anything very precise in mind when they describe someone as being "happy." No harm is done; their remarks succeed in getting across some vague notion; a rough but helpful idea is communicated. However, it also seems to me that fairminded and thoughtful speakers would agree, if they gave it proper thought, that a more precise and articulated version of what they intended to say when they described someone as "happy" is that the person in question takes more attitudinal pleasure than displeasure in things.

I think that when we speak of a 'happy temperament' we are using 'happy' in the same sense. We just mean to indicate the sort of temperament that would make a person tend to take more attitudinal pleasure than displeasure in things. Similarly for a 'happy mood.' This is just a mood in which a person is moved to take more pleasure than displeasure in things. A happy life is one in which the person takes more pleasure than displeasure in things. Thus, as I see it, Telfer's four senses of 'happy' are not needed. All the uses she cites can be accommodated on the assumption that there is really only one central sense of 'happy' in ordinary English. The differences in meaning for the phrases are not due to differences in the meaning of 'happy.' They are the result of differences in the meaning of 'mood,' 'temperament,' and 'life.'

A question remains concerning my claim (Chapter One) that 'happy' has a descriptive sense and an evaluative sense. I seem to have committed myself to the claim that 'happy' is ambiguous in at least that way.

In fact I do think that 'happy' is ambiguous in the cited way. However, in saying this I have not taken sides in the ambiguity debate. That's because the ambiguity debate concerns the meaning of 'happy' *as a term of ordinary English.* I think 'happy' is used in the evaluative sense only by philosophers and others whose good linguistic instincts have been perverted by them. Perhaps this usage harks back to a fumbled attempt to find a good English word to translate 'eudaimonia.' As a result of this, I am inclined to treat such uses of 'happy' as semi-stipulative, semi-technical uses. It is not clear to me that ordinary speakers of English, completely innocent of philosophy, ever use 'happy' to mean the same as 'having sufficiently high welfare.' In my view, the claim that welfare tracks happiness is not analytic. It is a substantive claim in axiology.

A final comment: the OED reminds us that we sometimes speak of "happy coincidences," where a happy coincidence is just a lucky, or fortunate coincidence. The OED also says that 'happy' can be used to mean 'drunk.' I am inclined to think that these claims may be right. Perhaps the word does have these two additional senses when used in ordinary English. But again, I am not aware of any decisive test that would put either of these claims beyond question.

CHAPTER 7

Attitudinal Hedonism about Happiness

Attitudinal Hedonism about Happiness (AHH) has now been presented. According to this theory, to be happy at a time is to have a positive net balance of intrinsic occurrent attitudinal pleasure over intrinsic occurrent attitudinal displeasure at that time. More simply, to be happy at a moment is to be taking more pleasure than displeasure in things at that moment. Happiness in an interval is the integral of happiness at moments within the interval. Happiness in a domain is happiness taken in objects suitably associated with the domain. Happiness in life as a whole is happiness in the interval that is your whole life.

In this chapter, I want to clarify the conception of happiness I have now introduced. I will do this first by discussing some objections. Then later I will discuss a series of hard cases. These are cases that were introduced earlier in connection with competing theories of happiness. I claimed that those other theories of happiness are not able to deal with these cases adequately. In this chapter, I try to show that the hard cases pose no problem for AHH.

But, first, some objections to AHH.

7.1 The Problem of Objectless Moods

Critics of AHH sometimes raise a question about "objectless mood states." As examples of such states, they may mention such things as anxiety, depression, and irritability. It is reasonable to suppose that if a person is to some extent anxious, depressed, or irritable during a period of time, he is to that extent less happy during that time. This would be true even if the person were suffering from anxiety, depression, or irritability that was diffuse and generalized—even if the anxiety, depression, or irritability were a more or less "free-floating" mood.

It is here that the difficulty may seem to arise: according to AHH, a person's happiness or unhappiness depends essentially upon the extent to which he takes attitudinal pleasure or displeasure *in things*. All attitudinal displeasure must ultimately be displeasure *about some propositional object*. Yet the unpleasant mood states under scrutiny here are distinctive in part because it is not clear that they have any objects. It may seem that a person can be anxious or irritable during a stretch of time without being anxious or irritable about anything in particular.

Although he apparently is not prepared to pursue this objection,[1] Dan Haybron mentions the relevant features of objectless moods in this passage:

> if you are feeling uneasy *in general*, about nothing in particular, to what do you attend? This feeling attaches to nothing in particular; it just forms a part of the background of your experience of everything. . ,. The same seems true of moods in general . . . Unlike emotions and sensory affects . . . moods have no particular location or object. . . . Yet moods are quite central to the experienced quality of our lives.[2]

In this context, Haybron goes on to mention some other relevant moods:

> A vague sense of malaise . . . Likewise for depression, anxiety, and related mood states, at least in their milder forms. . . . Presumably being tense, anxious, or stressed detracts substantially from the quality of one's experience, even when one is unaware of these states.[3]

It might be easier to understand and evaluate the objection if we have an example to work with. Let us assume that Ira is anxious, depressed, and irritable. Let us assume that his bad mood has really gotten to him. There is nothing else going on that counterbalances these bad moods. Ira and all his friends agree: Ira is unhappy. Let us furthermore assume that when his friends ask Ira to specify the states of affairs in which he is taking intrinsic attitudinal displeasure, he is not able to give a satisfactory response. He just claims to be feeling anxious, depressed, and irritable in general. If his moods are not directed on any states of affairs, then AHH will be at a loss to explain Ira's unhappiness. The theory implies that he cannot be unhappy unless he is unhappy *about something*.

I think it may be helpful, in this context, to reflect more carefully on anxiety, depression, irritability, and similar mood states. Let's consider anxiety first. As I understand it, anxiety typically involves excessive or

---

[1] In earlier unpublished work, Haybron did present the objection.
[2] Haybron (2008b: 202–3).   [3] Ibid. 203.

irrational worry.[4] An anxious person is one who is troubled by a lot of such worries. Some sorts of anxiety are conceptually linked to certain objects. Thus, social anxiety involves excessive worry about meeting people or embarrassing oneself when giving a public performance. The critic cannot be thinking of this sort of anxiety, since it clearly does have an object. The objection concerns "objectless mood states." I checked the discussion of anxiety disorders in DSM-IV and found that of all the options listed there, the most likely is "Generalized Anxiety Disorder." After mentioning that those suffering from Generalized Anxiety Disorder have worries that are 'far out of proportion to the actual likelihood or impact of the feared event,' the description goes on to say:

Adults with Generalized Anxiety Disorder often worry about everyday, routine life circumstances such as possible job responsibilities, finances, the health of family members, misfortunes of their children, or minor matters (such as household chores, car repairs, or being late for appointments).[5]

Suppose that Ira's problem is Generalized Anxiety Disorder. Then, over a period of time, he might first be excessively worried about his finances, and then about the health of his children, and then about something else. He might realize that his level of apprehension about these things is excessive. He might also realize that his constant worrying is interfering with his work or with his enjoyment of his leisure activities. Thus, his happiness is adversely affected.

If this description of Ira is correct, then it appears that there are plenty of states of affairs in which he is taking attitudinal displeasure. He is displeased about the fact that he might lose his job, or that the chances of his losing his job are too great. He is displeased about the fact that his children might get sick. He is displeased about the fact that he is wasting a lot of time and energy worrying about things that are probably not going to happen. Most importantly, perhaps, he is displeased about the fact that his constant worrying is interfering with his enjoyment. If this is what is going on with Ira, then his case seems not to be a problem for AHH. Ira is unhappy, but there are plenty of things that he seems to be unhappy about.

Irritability is another component of generalized depression. According to DSM-IV, people who are suffering from increased irritability have 'a tendency to respond to events with angry outbursts or blaming

---

[4] Thanks to Noah Lemos for reminding me that sometimes anxiety involves *rational* worry—worry about things that deserve to be worried about.
[5] American Psychiatric Association Task Force on DSM-IV (1994: 433).

others, or an exaggerated sense of frustration over minor matters.'[6] A typical example of this sort of irritability is a proclivity to road rage. Let's suppose that Ira has this symptom too. Suppose that Ira flies off the handle when he gets stuck in traffic or when someone passes him on the wrong side. Then there are other states of affairs in which he takes displeasure—he is displeased about the fact that he is stuck in traffic, or that he will be late for work, or that some knucklehead is passing on the wrong side. If he is irritable in this way for an extended period of time, then he will be angry about a lot of things; we may assume that he takes an inordinate amount of displeasure in each of them. It is, in addition, reasonable to assume that Ira will take further displeasure in the fact that so many things seem to be bothering him so much. He may take displeasure in the fact that he is going to get very angry about trivial things (such as traffic) that do not merit such a strong emotional response. So there are "higher-order" displeasures present in this case as well. Again, if this is Ira's problem, then his case does not constitute a difficulty for AHH. His irritation has plenty of propositional objects.

According to DSM-IV, when a person is suffering from depression, 'loss of interest or pleasure is nearly always present, at least to some degree.' Individuals who have depression report 'not feeling any enjoyment in activities that were previously considered pleasurable.'[7] So here are some more burdens for Ira to bear: whereas he formerly did take pleasure in many activities, he no longer does so while in the grip of depression. AHH then implies that his level of happiness is lower than it formerly was. If he notices his lack of pleasure, he may take displeasure in the fact that he no longer takes pleasure in things that he formerly enjoyed. He may be sad about the fact that he is not happy, or the fact that he very well may never be happy again. In such cases, his level of happiness is declared to be even lower by AHH.

The upshot is that AHH seems to be able to explain what has gone wrong with Ira. He has a kind of generalized depression, anxiety, and irritability. But each of these states (depression, anxiety, irritability) manifests itself in episodes in which Ira takes displeasure (or decreased pleasure) in specific propositional objects. In some cases, he takes displeasure in "first-order" objects such as the fact that he is stuck in traffic. In other cases, he takes displeasure in "higher-order" objects such as the fact that he is taking an inordinate amount of displeasure in things.

---

[6] American Psychiatric Association Task Force on DSM-IV (1994: 321).   [7] Ibid.

If developed in the way I have imagined, the example involving Ira is apparently not relevant to the objection that critics have had in mind. For, as I have imagined it, Ira's bad mood involves displeasure in a constantly changing array of objects. The objection would arise in a case in which there are no such propositional objects. Let us try to imagine what it would be like for Ira to have genuinely "objectless" anxiety and depression. Let us imagine that during a certain day he is anxious, but there is nothing that he is worried about; he is irritable, but there is nothing that he gets angry about; he is depressed, but there is nothing that he is sad about. In order to make the case relevant to AHH, we must also assume that during this period of time Ira does not take displeasure in the fact that he is objectlessly anxious, irritable, and depressed. So we must imagine that, during this period of time, none of these objectless states becomes itself an object of displeasure. Thus, we must also imagine that Ira does not take displeasure in the fact that he is then anxious, irritable, or depressed. I am prepared to agree that someone could be in such a condition.

If Ira does not take pleasure or displeasure in anything during the day, then AHH implies that his happiness level for the day is zero—he is neither happy nor unhappy. I see no reason to suppose that this implication is problematic. I grant that Ira is steadily on the verge of becoming unhappy; but if he never actually gets angry or sad or worried about anything, it appears to me that he never becomes actually unhappy. So this case seems to me to be no threat to AHH.

In a different context in his book, Haybron calls attention to a further feature of moods such as "objectless irritability." Some of these remarks suggest a slightly different difficulty for Attitudinal Hedonism about Happiness (though it is not clear that Haybron himself would want to raise this difficulty). Haybron says that irritability 'is presumably (un)happiness constitutive.'[8] As I understand this, the idea is that merely being in an irritable mood constitutes being at least to some extent unhappy. Haybron goes on:

The problem is that my irritability need not at every moment impinge on my experience. Sometimes we only discover our disagreeable moods when we find ourselves inexplicably lashing out over some trivial offense. . . . at times one experiences nothing untoward until some provocation comes along and generates a disproportionate reaction. . . . It is *logically* possible for a bad mood to recede completely from consciousness.[9]

If untriggered irritability is "unhappiness constitutive," and if it is so even when the subject "experiences nothing untoward," then we have

[8] Haybron (2008b: 70–1).   [9] Ibid. 71.

a problem for AHH. For AHH is based on the idea that unhappiness arises only when the subject takes displeasure in something. We need to look into this possibility. To do this, we need to make some further assumptions about Ira's psychological condition.

Let's suppose that throughout a certain day Ira is in an irritable mood. Let's also suppose that his irritability is never triggered. He never actually lashes out at anyone or anything in particular. So his mood is "objectless"—at least during the day in question. In addition, let us suppose that Ira's mood is not a mere disposition, or propensity. Let us suppose that Ira's irritability has a certain phenomenology. This amounts to the claim that there is something that it feels like to be in this way objectlessly irritable. So let us suppose that during the day Ira has feelings of objectless irritability. Let us refer to these as "moody feelings."

Perhaps Haybron's point is this: merely having these moody feelings constitutes being to some extent unhappy. This, it might be claimed, illustrates a way in which AHH goes wrong. For the mere having of these moody feelings is not a matter of any propositional attitude. It has been stipulated that Ira does not "lash out," or become angry about anything during the day. Merely being in the mood is sufficient to make him count as unhappy.

It is not clear to me that merely being irritable in fact does have any "feel." I am inclined to think that irritability itself is really just a disposition, and that the relevant phenomenology arises only when these dispositions are triggered. But my intuitions on this are unsettled. Let us suppose that the latest description of Ira is right. He is objectlessly irritable and this mood has its own distinctive phenomenology.

Now it seems to me that there are two main cases to consider. On the one hand, it may be unpleasant to experience this mood. That is, Ira might take displeasure in the fact that he is feeling moody in the specified way. In that case, the example poses no threat to AHH. Ira is unhappy and his unhappiness can be explained by appeal to the fact that he is displeased to be experiencing certain moody feelings.

On the other hand—and this is more in keeping with Haybron's claim that irritability might 'recede completely from consciousness'—Ira might never notice or care about the fact that he is in this irritable mood. He may be unaware of and untroubled by the fact that he is objectlessly irritable. In this case, assuming that nothing else is making trouble for Ira, AHH implies that Ira is not unhappy. Perhaps Haybron would insist that if Ira is in these moods, he is unhappy whether he cares about being in the moods or not. But my sense of the situation leads me to the opposite conclusion. If there are such unexperienced moody states, and if a person can be in them without being displeased about being in them, it is hard for me to see why anyone would want to say that the person is thereby made unhappy. He seems to be indifferent to these moods. He seems to be "unbothered" by them. Thus, while of course they don't make him any happier, I cannot see why we should think that they make him less happy. So, in this case, AHH generates the correct result: Ira is not unhappy.

7.2 *"The Missing Element"*

Attitudinal Hedonism about Happiness (AHH) is the view that a person's level of happiness is ultimately determined by the amounts of intrinsic attitudinal pleasure and displeasure she takes in things. Attitudinal pleasure and displeasure are propositional attitudes, in this respect like belief or fear. They are not "feelings;" a person can take pleasure in things without feeling any pleasurable sensations. One of the most frequent objections this conception of happiness is based on the claim that happiness so construed is 'desiccated' or 'thin' or 'overly intellectualized.'[10] Some have suggested that if we think of happiness in the way I have proposed, we will 'take all the fun out of it.'[11] The objection arises from the fact that, according to this view, all happiness is ultimately founded upon and defined in terms of a "cognitive" propositional attitude, whereas it may seem that happiness essentially involves something more emotional—something sometimes characterized as "cheery feelings" or "smiley-face feelings."

Part of the trouble here concerns "feelings." Sometimes we use the word 'feeling' in such a way that mere propositional attitudes count as feelings. For example, someone might say that he "feels confident" that the weather will clear. This seems to mean just that he *is confident* that the weather will clear; and if this is what the statement means, then it seems to be nothing more than a report of a propositional attitude—relatively firm, relatively unwavering belief that the weather will clear. Sometimes a person says that he "feels proud" of his achievement. This seems to mean just that he *is proud* of

---

[10] Roger Crisp, Elinor Mason, Michael Zimmerman, and Alastair Norcross have raised objections along these lines, though not in connection specifically with attitudinal hedonism about happiness. See Crisp (2006a: 154); Mason (2007: 382); Zimmerman (2007: 426–7); and Norcross (2007: 390).

[11] Haybron expresses the objection in this way. See Haybron (2008b: 64).

that achievement. If so, it is nothing more than another propositional attitude report. Let's distinguish this sort of feeling by use of the term "attitudinal feeling," since these so-called feelings are really just propositional attitudes.

If we use the word 'feeling' in this way to refer to attitudinal feelings, then it will be correct to say that intrinsic attitudinal pleasure is itself a feeling. It is impossible to be happy without taking up this attitude toward something. Thus, happiness certainly cannot lack feelings—if we think of feelings as attitudinal feelings.

But there is a different way of understanding feelings. Here the paradigm cases are such things as feelings of warmth or cold; feelings of pressure; itches; tickles; burning sensations; "pins and needles;" and so on. Many feelings (of this category) are typically identified by mentioning the circumstances in which people normally feel them. Thus, for example, there is a certain feeling that I get when I am in an elevator and it begins to rise. I feel this throughout my body, but perhaps mostly in my stomach. There is another feeling I get when a mosquito lands on the back of my neck. Let's call these "sensory feelings."

I think all these sensory feelings are alike in certain respects. They all occur, or phenomenologically present themselves as occurring, in some part of the body. In some cases, the relevant part of the body is a narrowly localized part of the skin, as in the case of an itchy feeling caused by a mosquito. In other cases, the relevant part seems to be pretty much the whole body, as in the case of the feeling caused by the rising elevator. I believe that in fact these feelings arise in us as a result of stimulation of some nerves. Perhaps the nerves whose stimulation is involved in feelings of this sort are distinctive in some way. I leave it to the experts to determine whether this is true. My point is merely that this indicates a respect in which sensory feelings differ from attitudinal feelings. Sensory feelings are associated with locations in the body and typically involve the stimulation of sensory nerves; attitudinal feelings are different in both respects.

Another crucial difference between sensory feelings and attitudinal feelings is that attitudinal feelings always have propositional objects, whereas sensory feelings do not. The mosquito case illustrates this nicely. It's one thing to have the sensory feeling that you get when a mosquito has landed on the back of your neck. It's another thing to "feel" that a mosquito has landed on the back of your neck. You could do the latter even if your neck were numb—maybe someone tells you that there is a mosquito there; maybe you see it in the mirror. But you don't really *feel* anything (in the sensory way). In the typical case what happens is this: you have the sensory feeling of some mosquito-y sensations on your neck; you then "attitudinally feel" (= believe) that there is a mosquito on your neck.

Another interesting thing about sensory feelings is that they often can be suppressed by anesthesia. This is obvious in the case of itches, tickles, feelings of warmth and coldness. If you have an itch, and your doctor gives you a shot of the correct anesthesia, you will stop feeling the itch. Ordinary sensation-stopping anesthesia does not work in this direct way to remove attitudinal feelings, though of course it may work in a more roundabout way: if the doctor gives you a shot of anesthesia, you may stop feeling the itchy feeling of the mosquito on your neck. In consequence of this, you may stop having the attitudinal feeling that there is a mosquito on your neck.

I have claimed that happiness can be explained by appeal to a certain propositional attitude: intrinsic, occurrent, attitudinal (dis)pleasure. When I say that this attitude does not essentially involve any feelings, I am thinking of sensory feelings like itches, pressure, warmth, coldness, "pins and needles," and so on. I mean to say that a person can be pleased about something even though he does not feel any special sort of "cheery feelings." Of course, I am not denying that there are such feelings; nor am I denying that happy people often feel them. I am just saying that they are not essential constitutive elements of happiness.

Suppose a researcher is trying to understand the neurological mechanism underlying the cheery sensory feelings that normally occur along with happiness. Suppose this researcher has located an area of the brain that seems to be activated when and only when these cheery sensory feelings are being felt. He thinks that activation of this brain region is responsible for the feelings. To test his hypothesis, he needs a human subject. He plans to disable the brain region, do something that would normally give rise to cheery feelings, and then ask the subject if he can feel any cheery feelings. Of course, he cannot get permission from the Human Subjects Review Board. He decides to perform the experiment on himself.

Let us imagine that this researcher finds a way to disable the relevant area of his own brain. Imagine that he then spends some quality time with his children. He has a lot of fun with them, but feels decidedly strange: though he is enjoying the time spent with his children, something is missing. He cannot feel any cheery feelings. The sensory background normally associated with happy times is simply gone. The researcher is delighted. This is good news. His hypothesis is confirmed. He will now be able to publish a paper in which he announces the discovery of the neural basis of cheery feelings.

It seems to me that this researcher could be happy during the stretch of time he spends playing with his kids. His happiness would be based in part on the fact that he takes pleasure in various activities with the children. Another component of his happiness would be the pleasure he takes in the fact that his neurological hypothesis has been confirmed. All of this could happen, it seems to me, even though the researcher was not feeling any cheery sensory feelings during this stretch of time. Indeed, as the example has been developed, he is happy in part precisely because he does not feel those feelings.

I grant of course that this example is a mere thought experiment. The case is imaginary. But it seems to me that there are real-life cases that illustrate the same point, though perhaps without the same sharp focus. One type of example has already been suggested. Recall the case of Dolores (discussed above in section 2.3). Dolores was suffering from a lot of sensory pain. Her doctor prescribed a drug that reduced the pain. Dolores was thrilled, delighted, and happy, though still in some pain. I originally mentioned the example in order to point out a problem for sensory hedonism about happiness. In fact, the example was based on a somewhat more complex actual case. We can make use of the actual case here.

An old friend of mine was plagued by a number of painful ailments. Among other things, he had psoriatic arthritis. His joints—especially his knuckles—were swollen and achy; his skin was covered with patches of scaly, painful lesions. His doctors seemed to be at a loss. Even powerful pain-relieving medications seemed to do very little to relieve my friend's pain. Then one of his doctors prescribed a new medication. For a while my friend thought it was going to work. For a while the intensity of the pain was reduced.

My friend told me that he was very happy about this development. His happiness, as he explained it, was founded in the fact that he had new hope for the future. He was beginning to think that his doctor had finally found a medication that would relieve his pain; he was hoping that he would soon be pain-free. He declared that he would be happy even if the pain could not be entirely eradicated. Just to have the intensity reduced to a manageable degree, so that he could think about philosophy again, would be wonderful. Throughout this period, he continued to be in pain, though the intensity was reduced. I had no reason to suppose that he felt any cheery sensory feelings during the whole episode. Of course, a die-hard defender of the theory of cheery feelings could simply insist that if my friend was happy, he *must have felt such feelings*. But my own view, based on conversations with my friend at the time, was that the only relevant sensory feelings he felt at the time were mild joint pain and moderately itchy skin. (Unfortunately, the symptoms soon returned in full force and my friend again fell into an unhappy mood. His condition worsened and after a period of time he became incapacitated and eventually died. I never had an opportunity to question him closely about the details of his experience.)

I think that cases such as this serve to remind us that a person can be happy at a time even though he is not feeling any "smiley-face sensory feelings" at the time. Thus, while it is true that AHH implies that we can be happy without such feelings, this is no defect in AHH. It is a feature of the theory that makes it more plausible than some of its competitors.

7.3   *In Praise of Shallow Happiness*

There seems to be a tradition according to which we are permitted—even encouraged—to make overblown and hyperbolic claims about happiness. Outrageous exaggerations are the norm. As examples I can cite frequent assertions to the effect that happiness is essentially "deep," "pervasive," or "life changing." Some have said that the more attractive forms of happiness give structure and meaning to our lives. These remarks often seem to claim that there are essential conceptual connections between happiness and such other good things as rationality, meaningfulness (of life), wisdom, humanity, and virtue.

While thus gushing with hyperbolic praise for happiness, some have suggested that these linkages show that hedonism about happiness must be wrong. For it is pretty obvious that a person could enjoy shallow and non-pervasive pleasures; the suggestion is that if hedonism about happiness were true, it would be correct to describe a person who enjoys shallow pleasures as "happy." Yet, according to the objection, if his pleasures are so shallow, his cheerfulness does not make him worthy of that august description.

It may appear that Philippa Foot was making this sort of remark when she said:

It seems that great happiness, unlike euphoria or even great pleasure, must come from something related to what is deep in human nature, and fundamental in human life, such as affection for children and friends, the desire to work, and love of freedom and truth.[12]

John Rawls seems to indulge in the same sort of overstatement in his discussion of happiness in *A Theory of Justice*. He explicitly claims to be defining happiness when he says:

> we can think of a person as being happy when he is in the way of a successful execution (more or less) of a rational plan of life drawn up under (more or less) favorable conditions, and he is reasonably confident that his plan can be carried through.[13]

Thus, Rawls suggests that happiness somehow involves *rationality* and carefully thought out plans of life.

Although his remarks are specifically about "authentic happiness," Haybron also suggests some important connections between happiness and deeper things. In this case, the nature of the self:

> The central contention of this chapter is that happiness—or rather, "authentic happiness"—has intrinsic prudential value as an aspect of self-fulfillment. This is because happiness bears a special relation to the self: the facts about what makes us (authentically) happy partially define who we are, our selves.[14]

I think none of these claims is true if taken as a claim about happiness. I think a person can be outstandingly happy even though his happiness is not founded upon anything "deep in human nature." I think a person can find happiness in trivial things. I think a person can be "authentically happy" without having a rational plan of life, and definitely without being confident that such a plan is on the way to execution.

It's not clear to me that it will be possible to present an explicit argument to support my view. At best I can say a few things that may cast some doubt on the opposing position.

Recall the case involving Timmy, the happy-go-lucky fellow discussed above in Chapter 5. In order to make the case relevant to the present context, let me say a few more things about Timmy. I stipulate that Timmy's pleasures do not come from things that are "deep and fundamental in human nature." He has lots of fun, but none of it arises in connection with "affection for children and friends, the desire to work, and love of freedom and truth." In fact, Timmy has no desire

---

[12] Foot (1979); reprinted in Foot (2002: 35–6). I say it "may appear" that she is making a hyperbolic remark about happiness in this passage. I note that her remark is confined to cases of "great happiness." Furthermore, I note that in later writings she seems to disavow the position. See, for example, Foot (2002: 97).   [13] Rawls (1971: 409).
[14] Haybron (2008b: 178).

to work and certainly doesn't want to have any children. He is not much interested in "truth" and while he may take pleasure in being able to attend the party of his choice, he has never reflected much on the value of freedom. I furthermore stipulate that Timmy has never taken the time to think about a rational plan of life. He simply lives in the moment, generally choosing to attend whatever party promises to be most enjoyable.

But I also stipulate that Timmy enjoys these parties. He likes the loud music, spicy food, and cold drinks. He enjoys dancing and flirting with the girls. Suppose that there is often a broad smile on his face and that close inspection of his brain would reveal that it is often flooded with "happy" neurotransmitters. Suppose Timmy continues for a long time in this way, and that he never suffers from a dark night of the soul; he never even considers the possibility that his life has been wasted. He sleeps soundly, and dreams of noisy parties.

Compare Timmy to his cousin Tommy. Assume that Tommy has been seeing a psychiatrist for many years. He has dissected his life with the sharpest psychoanalytic scalpel. He has reflected on his childhood, his relations with his parents, his work, his plans for the future, and even his dreams. He thinks long and deeply about his plan of life, and he grimly goes about trying to achieve the various well-integrated goals that he has established for himself. Yet the depression does not lift. Tommy remains glum.

Perhaps there is something valuable, important, and admirable about Tommy's introspective efforts. But, in spite of all this, I would still pity Tommy and view him as a deeply unhappy person. I would agree that Timmy is shallow and in some ways not an admirable person. I might prefer to have the despondent Tommy for a friend (since I don't like noisy parties). But when I focus on the question specifically about *happiness*, it seems to me that there cannot be any reasonable debate. Timmy is by far the happier fellow, in spite of the shallowness of his happiness.

If we find ourselves thinking that Timmy's happiness is not "real" or "authentic" or "great," then I think we may be falling for a persuasive high redefinition of 'happy.' We are allowing ourselves to be lulled into accepting a new definition of 'happy'—one that retains the generally favorable connotations of the term, but one that attributes to it a new and controversial "cognitive meaning." I see no good reason for doing that. Happiness, as ordinarily understood, does not need to be replaced with something grander.

This completes my discussion of these two familiar objections to AHH. I now turn to a review of some of the examples that were discussed earlier in connection with competing theories of happiness.

7.4   *Brett the Drag Racer*

In Chapter 3, I presented a theory of happiness that Daniel Kahneman defended in his essay 'Objective Happiness.' According to Kahneman's theory, a person's momentary happiness level is proportional to the strength of his desire for his present experience to continue. These momentary happiness levels are taken to be the atoms of happiness. Happiness in intervals and lives is calculated by aggregating information about the atoms. In an attempt to illustrate what I take to be a fundamental difficulty for Kahneman's theory, I described a case involving Brett the Drag Racer. The example of Brett was intended to draw attention to the fact that a person can be very happy during a stretch of time even though he does not want the experiences he has during that time to continue.

As Brett was speeding down the drag strip, he was having a series of intense and fleeting experiences. These were the sights and sounds and feelings that were produced by the rapid acceleration of his racing car as he gained speed, shifted gears, and observed the track from a succession of perspectives from the starting line to the finish. I made two main claims about Brett: (a) He did not want any of those experiences to continue, since they would continue only if he had come to some sort of weird halt in the middle of the dragstrip. But at the same time, since his car was performing flawlessly and he was winning the race, (b) Brett was very happy as he sped down the track. This shows that there is something awry in Kahneman's theory.

What does my theory of Attitudinal Hedonism about Happiness say about this case?

Let us select a suitable moment in the middle of Brett's run. Let us suppose that at this moment he hears the sound of his engine, sees the tachometer on his dashboard, feels the vibration and pressure of acceleration, and sees the drag strip from a certain perspective in the middle of the course. He does not want any of these experiences to continue. However, assuming that the race is going very well, we may naturally imagine that he is very pleased about these things. He is glad that the tachometer indicates (let us imagine) 7,500 rpm. He is glad that the engine is pulling so hard. He is pleased that he is now in second gear and that the tires seem to be gripping the pavement properly. He is very pleased that he is slightly ahead of the car in the adjacent lane. In general, then, he is taking pleasure in several facts as he speeds down the track. If, at the same time, Brett is not displeased about anything, then AHH declares that this is a happy moment for him.[15] If other moments during the race are similar to this one (aside from such details as that the tachometer is showing different rpms, Brett is viewing the track from different locations and hearing different sounds from the engine) AHH declares that Brett is happy at those moments, too. Finally, if all this is true and if at the end of the race Brett is very pleased to have won, then AHH declares that the whole interval was a happy time for Brett.

My intuitions about the case coincide with the implications of the theory. I think that a typical drag racer, speeding down the track to a victory in a tough drag race, would probably be quite happy—unless, obviously, there were other unrelated factors about which he was displeased. I think such a racer would be happy even though he did not want his experiences to continue. Thus, I think that while Kahneman's theory gets this case wrong, AHH evaluates it correctly.

7.5 *Susan the Pessimistic Student*

In Chapter 4, I described a case involving a philosophy graduate student. I called her Susan. I stipulated that Susan started off convinced that some of her most important desires would be frustrated. She wanted to write a good dissertation, get a good job, and have her papers published. She believed that none of these things would happen. She was unhappy. I then imagined that Susan sought help from Dr. Goldberg, who prescribed a psychoactive drug. Susan took the drug and her mood lifted. Susan continued to have the same set of desires. Since she was no fool, she continued to think they would be frustrated. So, while her desires and her beliefs about her desires remained fixed, she became happier.

I presented this case in an attempt to point out a difficulty for Wayne Davis's theory of happiness. According Davis's view, a person's momentary happiness level is defined as (roughly) the extent to which the person thinks her desires are being satisfied. Consider all the

---

[15] In a real-life case like this, Brett probably would not be taking *intrinsic* pleasure in the items I have mentioned. His pleasure in these items would be *extrinsic*. But it is reasonable to assume that for each of the mentioned items, there is some other item further along the line, and that Brett takes intrinsic pleasure in that other item. For example, he might take intrinsic pleasure in the fact that he is winning the race, or that the engine in his race car is running smoothly.

propositions that the person is thinking at a time; for each, consider the extent to which the person wants it to be true. Multiply by +1 if the person is certain it is true; multiply by −1 if the person is certain it is false. Sum the products. That is the person's momentary happiness level according to Davis's theory. So the theory seems to imply in this case that Susan's level of happiness after taking the medication should be about the same as her level of happiness before taking it. After all, it is stipulated that she has approximately the same desires and continues to think that they will not be satisfied.

However, if the medication worked as advertised, and Susan's depression lifted after taking it, it seems that her level of happiness did not remain constant. I would say, and I think that in real-life cases like this the subjects would say, that they are much happier after taking the drug, regardless of their level of subjective desire satisfaction.

Attitudinal Hedonism about Happiness can offer a plausible account of the change in Susan's level of happiness. It is reasonable to imagine that prior to taking the medication Susan was pretty seriously displeased about several things. We may assume that she was very displeased about the facts (as she saw them) that she would never finish her dissertation, or get her papers published in good journals, or have a successful career as a philosopher. These things really bothered her. AHH implies (together with further plausible assumptions about the case) that Susan was very unhappy before she took the medication. After taking the medication, Susan still believed that she would not finish her dissertation, and so forth, but she was no longer quite so displeased about these things. They didn't bother her as much as they did previously. As a result, AHH implies that she was somewhat less unhappy after taking the medication.

A further point may be relevant. I have imagined that at the earlier time, before she took the medication, Susan was suffering from depression. She felt glum about her career prospects. We may assume that Susan found her feelings of glumness unpleasant—she didn't enjoy being so glum. AHH then implies that Susan was experiencing further atoms of unhappiness. These were episodes in which she took intrinsic attitudinal displeasure in the fact that she was feeling glum. After she took the medication, she did not feel quite so glum. Her mood was brighter. We may assume that Susan found her feelings of brightened mood to be pleasant. AHH then implies that there are even more atoms of happiness present. These are the episodes in which Susan takes pleasure in the fact that she feels a brighter mood. As a result, on balance and depending upon the details of the case, AHH yields the result that Susan was less unhappy after taking the medication.

It's possible that this improvement in her mood could be sufficient to convert Susan from an unhappy person to a happy one—though of course the case is not described in enough detail to allow us to reach such a firm conclusion.

My intuitions about the case coincide with the implications of AHH. If there were a person like Susan, and if she had the experiences described in the scenario, and if there were no other important features to her story, then I would be inclined to say that the drugs worked. Susan went from being a pretty unhappy person to being a less unhappy person. This happened, in my view, because she went from being a person who took quite a lot of displeasure in things to being a person who took less displeasure in things and at the same time who also took some pleasure in some other things. Thus, I think the example indicates a way in which AHH yields plausible results.

7.6 *Lois and the Dinosaurs*

One of the more striking cases that I mentioned in connection with Davis's theory involved Lois and the dinosaurs. Lois was escorting some children through the museum of natural history. She had been to the museum many times before, and was finding the current trip pretty boring. As she stood before an exhibit displaying a ferocious-looking dinosaur, someone mentioned how horrible it would be to be eaten by such a thing. Lois believed that she would not be eaten by a dinosaur; Lois preferred that she not be eaten by a dinosaur; yet these thoughts did not make Lois any happier. Perhaps, as she contemplated the sharp teeth of the dinosaur in the exhibit, Lois was in an emotionally neutral state, neither happy nor unhappy. If such a case is possible, Davis's theory is false. For Davis's theory implies that a person must be happier if she believes that her desires are being satisfied.

Again, it seems to me that AHH handles this case more successfully. AHH declares that Lois's level of happiness depends not on her beliefs and desires, but on the extent to which she is taking pleasure in things. While she believes that she will not be eaten by dinosaurs, Lois apparently takes very little pleasure in this fact. Since she never thought she was running a serious risk of being eaten by a dinosaur, she is not relieved to learn that it is not going to happen. She is not cheered by this thought. It does not strike her as "good news." It just seems *obvious*. Nothing to get excited about.

Of course, there could be a person who does take pleasure in the fact that he will not be eaten by a dinosaur. Perhaps some of the children in Lois's group would be examples of this. Imagine that one of the children at first fears that he might be eaten by a dinosaur. Imagine that Lois explains that dinosaurs are long extinct—there is no chance that one will attack him. The child might then be relieved. He will be glad to learn that he will not be eaten by a dinosaur. In such a case, the child's level of happiness would rise when he stops taking displeasure in the notion that he is at risk of dinosaur attack and starts taking pleasure in the fact that there is no such risk. AHH handles the case in a smooth and intuitively appealing way.

7.7 *Tammy*

In Chapter 5, I presented a series of cases that (I claimed) show that various forms of Whole Life Satisfactionism are wrong. Among these was the case of Tammy. I presented this case in order to point out a defect in some "full information" forms of Whole Life Satisfactionism. According to these theories, a person's level of happiness is not determined by the judgments of whole life satisfaction that she actually makes. It is determined by the judgments that she would make, if she were fully informed about her own life.

As I described the case involving Tammy, she was confused and misinformed about her whole life. She had many false beliefs about herself. She thought she was a worthless sinner. As a result, Tammy was deeply unhappy—even suicidal. I went on to say that Tammy was an ideal candidate for Cognitive Behavioral Therapy. If a skillful therapist could get Tammy to have more accurate beliefs about her life, she would be a lot happier.

I pointed out that the full information form of Whole Life Satisfactionism then generates dramatically incorrect results concerning Tammy's happiness. Since she would have made a favorable judgment about her life if she had evaluated it from an epistemically ideal perspective, the theory implies that she is happy. But she is suicidally unhappy.

Attitudinal Hedonism yields correct results in Tammy's case. As I see it, Tammy is unhappy because she is taking attitudinal displeasure in several things. Here are some plausible examples:

1. Tammy is attitudinally pleased at *tn* to degree −10 about the "fact" that she is a sinner.

2. Tammy is attitudinally pleased at *tn* to degree −10 about the "fact" that everyone hates her.
3. Tammy is attitudinally pleased at *tn* to degree −10 about the "fact" that she has never accomplished anything worthwhile.

If we assume that Tammy has thoughts like these frequently, and that she rarely takes pleasure in anything, then Attitudinal Hedonism implies that she is an unhappy person. This seems to me to be precisely right. I recognize, of course, that Tammy would be a lot happier if she were better informed about her life. But, as the example has been described, she is not well informed about her life; and that in large measure explains why she is in fact unhappy.

7.8   *Tristan and Bruce*

In Appendix A, after Chapter 5, I discussed some examples that were intended to highlight some interesting facts about happiness and time. One case involved Tristan, who was seriously dissatisfied with most of his life. He had suffered from a bad case of depression for 24 years. Fortunately, in his 25th year, he was given some new medication that worked like a miracle. He became happy. The example was intended to show that certain forms of Whole Life Satisfactionism are wrong. Specifically, I was thinking of forms of Whole Life Satisfactionism (like one defended by Tatarkiewicz) according to which a person is happy at a time only if he is then satisfied not only with "that which is, but also with that which has been, and that which will be." I focused on a time in his 25th year when Tristan was very happy even though he was not satisfied with his life as a whole. In particular, he was not satisfied with "that which has been." He recognized that the first 24 of his 25 years were an emotional disaster.

This case presents a serious difficulty for any theory that implies that, in order to be happy at a time, a person must be satisfied with the way his life was going at earlier times. But the case does not present any difficulty for Attitudinal Hedonism about Happiness. According to AHH, in order for Tristan to be happy at the selected moment in his 25th year, all that is required is that he have a sufficiently favorable balance of attitudinal pleasure over attitudinal displeasure at that time. And it is reasonable to suppose that the condition would be satisfied in a case like Tristan's. We may assume that at the selected moment in his 25th year, there are many things in which he can take attitudinal pleasure. He may be pleased that he has a blossoming relationship with his new girlfriend; he may be pleased that his new job is off to a good start; he may be pleased that he has found a medication that seems to have cured the depression that marred his first 24 years. Most of all, he surely must be very pleased to be in such a bright, cheerful mood.

I recognize that if Tristan were to think about his first 24 years, he probably would take displeasure in the fact that he suffered from depression during that time. Indeed, he might take displeasure in lots of things about his past. Whenever he takes displeasure in some fact about his past, his displeasure diminishes his current happiness. However, there is no need to assume that he will spend a lot of time thinking about these things. Perhaps he will be able to repress his bad memories; perhaps he will learn to let bygones be bygones. If he can focus on the present and the future, he will find lots of things to be pleased about. It is possible that Tristan will just be a very happy person. So AHH seems to generate a correct assessment of Tristan's level of happiness.

The second case that I discussed in Appendix A involved Bruce. Bruce was described as a burnt-out drunk who spent his days perched on a barstool happily reminiscing about his "glory days" as an athlete, lover, and prankster. When we observe him, Bruce knows quite well that his current situation is pretty rotten in virtually all domains: he is unemployed, divorced, in poor health, and an alcoholic. Yet, because Bruce has a wonderful capacity to focus his attention on days gone by, he manages to be pretty happy in spite of all his current problems.

I stipulated that in fact Bruce does not think very much about the present. He does not contemplate his current standing in various domains of life. As a result, any form of Whole Life Satisfactionism that requires *actual* judgments about one's current standing in the various domains of life as a whole will imply that Bruce is not happy. He makes no such judgments. But Bruce seems to be very happy, especially after he has had a couple of drinks.

Hypothetical forms of Whole Life Satisfactionism also seem to yield an incorrect assessment in this case. If an investigator from Eurobarometer were to arrive at the bar, and were to ask Bruce to give his assessment of his current standing with respect to job, marriage, health, housing, income, etc., Bruce would smile broadly and declare that he has no job, he is divorced, his health is rotten, he lives in a shabby little apartment, and his pension is so small that he is barely able to afford his cigarettes and booze. 'No,' he would say with a sheepish grin, 'my life as a whole is currently a wreck.' Thus, these hypothetical forms of Whole Life Satisfactionism imply that Bruce is unhappy. It should be clear that the implications of these theories would be wide of the mark. Bruce is happy in large measure because he in fact does *not* think about these domains of his life. His happiness is based on the fact that he spends his time wallowing in reminiscences about his glory days.

Attitudinal Hedonism about Happiness yields a far more plausible evaluation of Bruce's status. When he focuses his attention on his youthful achievements, he takes pleasure in things he did years earlier. He takes pleasure in the fact that he was so successful in sports, and in romance, and elsewhere. Perhaps his recollections are not accurate. Maybe he was not really quite so successful as an athlete. No matter; if he now takes pleasure in the "fact" that he hit 60 home runs, then this pleasure serves to enhance his current level of happiness. Thus, we have a satisfactory explanation for the smile on his grizzled face, and the twinkle in his watery eyes. Bruce is happy to be living in the past.

7.9 *The Philosopher*

In Book X of the *Nicomachean Ethics*, Aristotle presents a series of surprising arguments apparently in support of the view that the happiest life is the life of the philosopher. He seems to argue that philosophers are outstandingly happy because (a) philosophizing makes use of the understanding, which is "the supreme element in us" (1177a20); (b) philosophizing is the virtuous activity that we can engage in most continuously (1177a23); (c) philosophizing is the most pleasant of activities in accord with virtue (1177a25); (d) other sorts of virtuous activity require the cooperation of colleagues, but the philosopher can go about his business by himself (1177b1); (e) philosophers engage in philosophy for its own sake—they are not using philosophy as a means to any further end (1177b4); (f) philosophizing is the most leisurely of virtuous activities (1177b6); and (g) philosophizing makes use of the divine element in us. Insofar as we philosophize, we are godlike (1177b30).

I suppose there have been some philosophers who found philosophizing to be leisurely and pleasant. Perhaps Aristotle himself found that he could go on philosophizing for many hours at a stretch without getting tired or bored. But if we take his remarks to apply to a typical twenty-first-century assistant professor of philosophy, they will seem oddly implausible. Surely many modern-day philosophers engage in the activity at least in part in order to make a living. For most of us, the idea that we do it for no further end seems hard to swallow. Similarly, the reader is bound to be perplexed at the assertion that philosophizing is the most "continuous" of virtuous activities. Couldn't someone engage in philanthropic activities just as steadily as the steadiest philosopher engages in philosophizing? And many of us find that after a short time we are burnt out and unable to continue doing philosophy. To say that it is the most leisurely of virtuous activities seems puzzling. One wonders if Aristotle meant to be making a remark that would apply to philosophers like us; and if he really meant to say that what we do is *leisurely*. Maybe there is something wrong with the translation. Maybe the passage is corrupt. Maybe it was not written by Aristotle.

In spite of all this, it does seem to me that there is a certain modest truth hidden among the remarks about philosophy in Book X. That truth is just this: it is possible for a person to be happy while engrossed in philosophical reflection. I tried to describe one such person earlier in Chapter 5, as part of my discussion of certain kinds of Whole Life Satisfactionism about happiness. I imagined a philosopher who was thinking about a puzzle in metaphysics. I stipulated that he was excited about the prospect of finding a solution to the puzzle. I also stipulated that he was not thinking about his own life and that he would have been annoyed if someone had interrupted him with questions about his personal affairs. I used the example to cast doubt on the idea that a person's momentary happiness level is equal to the degree to which he judges that his life as a whole matches up with his life ideals. The philosopher I imagined was happy; he was not making any judgments about his life as a whole.

It is interesting to note that the example of the happy philosopher might also refute some forms of sensory hedonism about happiness. It's possible that the philosopher is not feeling any pleasurable sensations while he philosophizes. It's also possible that he does not feel any "cheery feelings." So a bunch of popular claims about happiness are refuted by this example.

It seems to me, however, that Attitudinal Hedonism about Happiness is not refuted by the example of the happy philosopher. Suppose the philosopher thinks he may have discovered the solution to the metaphysical puzzle on which he is working. He may take pleasure in the fact that he has solved the puzzle. He may take pleasure in the fact that he will be able to publish his results, and that this may help him to gain the respect of his colleagues and to get tenure. He may take pleasure in the fact that he will continue to have the opportunity to think about metaphysical puzzles. If he takes pleasure in such things as these, or in further things that he thinks may result from these things, then AHH can easily explain his happiness. He is happy because he is taking pleasure in things—not because he is feeling pleasurable sensations or because he is making a favorable judgment about his life as a whole. Thus, it appears that AHH gives a satisfactory analysis of the happiness of the philosopher.

7.10 *Summary*

This completes the presentation, clarification, and illustration of my view about happiness. It is a form of hedonism about happiness, but it is not a form of sensory hedonism. It is instead a form of attitudinal hedonism. I am claiming, roughly, that to be happy is to take pleasure in things; the greater the extent to which you take occurrent intrinsic attitudinal pleasure in things, the happier you are (minus, of course, the extent to which you take a corresponding sort of displeasure in things). This seems to me to be an interesting and plausible account of the nature of happiness.

CHAPTER 8

Eudaimonism

8.1 *"Happiness is The Good"*

In Chapter 6, I explained Attitudinal Hedonism about Happiness (AHH). In Chapter 7, I discussed some objections and I reviewed a series of puzzle cases. Each of these cases had been presented earlier in an attempt to point out some shortcoming of some competing theory of happiness. In each instance, I tried to show that AHH handles the case correctly. If our best settled intuition about the case is that the character described therein is happy, then AHH implies that the character is happy. In addition, I also discussed the claim that AHH fails to account for the "joy" or "bliss" of happiness. My conclusion was that the conception of happiness provided by AHH is adequate; it is reasonable to say that a person is happy when, and to the extent that, AHH says that he is happy.

I have thus completed my discussion of the *nature* of happiness. Now I am ready to turn to a fundamentally different topic. The next topic concerns the *value* of happiness. More specifically, I turn to the thesis that "happiness is The Good." I take this to be the thesis that the good life is the life of happiness, or that what ultimately makes for welfare, or well-being, is happiness.

8.2 *Welfare, Well-Being, Quality of Life*

In accord with what has come to be standard usage, I have used the term 'eudaimonism' for the view that happiness determines welfare. So, in effect, I now turn to the defense of eudaimonism.

In order properly to understand this doctrine, we must understand not only what is meant by 'happiness,' but also what is meant by 'welfare.' What does the word 'welfare' mean when embedded in the maxim 'happiness determines *welfare*'?

It would not be sufficient just to say that 'welfare' indicates the *value* of someone's life, for each person's life can be evaluated in several different ways. For example, when speaking of a "good life" we might intend to be discussing a *morally good* life. A person might lead a morally good life while not enjoying high welfare. This could happen most obviously when the person's moral obligations required great personal sacrifices. Another kind of life evaluation is fundamentally *aesthetic*. If a person had a beautiful life—one that would make a good subject for drama, for example—we might describe it as a good life. But of course a life could be aesthetically excellent while being not very good for the one who lives it. It might have high aesthetic value but low welfare value.

So we can see that the *welfare value* of a person's life is distinct from these other sorts of value. Eudaimonism is a thesis about welfare value, not any of these other sorts of value. How can we be sure that we are thinking of the right sort of value when we debate the question whether happiness determines the *value* for that person of his or her life?

We might try to isolate the concept of welfare by mentioning some other terms that can be used to indicate the same sort of value. For example, instead of speaking of the welfare value of a person's life, we might speak of the amount of *intrinsic value that the life has for the person*, or *how good in itself it is for him*. We might use the term 'well-being,' or 'prudential value,' or 'self-regarding value,' or 'quality of life' to indicate the same thing. We might say that a life that has a substantial positive amount of this value is "well worth living." Each of these expressions can be used to express the concept of *goodness of life for the one who lives it*. But even if each of these expresses the same concept as 'welfare,' it's still not clear that we know precisely what concept that is.

The concept of welfare has some formal features. First, of course, welfare is value *for a certain person*. A certain state of affairs could have welfare value *for me* while having no such value *for you*. While this indicates that welfare value involves a relativization to a person, the relativity has nothing to do with what the person believes. The statement that a certain state of affairs has value *for Mary* does not mean just that Mary believes that it has value. Something can be good for Mary even though Mary takes it to be worthless; or even if Mary has no view about its value. Something can have no value for Mary even though she firmly believes that it is precisely what she most needs.

A person's welfare can vary through time. It makes sense to ask (as Ronald Reagan did in 1980) whether you are better off today than you were four years ago. As I understand it, this is a question about welfare. Reagan was asking voters to consider whether they then had an amount of welfare that is greater than the amount they had four years earlier. Welfare should be understood to be a relation between a person and a time. In some cases, the time is just a moment—Reagan could have asked 'how are you doing *now*?' In other cases, the time is an interval—Reagan could have asked 'how have things been going for you *recently*?' And in many cases, the time is a person's whole life—'how did things go for your grandmother *in her life as a whole*?'

Interpersonal comparisons are also possible. Reagan could have asked whether you are better off now than your parents were 30 years ago.

I think welfare levels can be represented by numbers, though of course there is no universally recognized scale on which to plot these numbers. Making use of this convention, we can agree to use positive numbers to indicate positive welfare. If a person's life is going well for him then we can use a positive number to indicate his level of welfare. If one person's life is going better for him than another person's life is going for her, we can use a higher number to represent the first person's welfare. If a person's life is going badly for him, we can use a negative number, with lower numbers representing lower levels of welfare. Zero, of course, will represent the welfare value of a life that is neither good nor bad for the one who lives it, but neutral.

I see no reason to suppose that there is any upper or lower bound to these numbers. No matter how well things are going for you at a certain time, they might be going better for you (or for someone else) at some other time. Furthermore, it seems to me that between any two levels of welfare, there is another. We can also be sure to select numbers in such a way that when one person's welfare is twice as great as another's, the number used to represent the first person's welfare will be just twice the number used to represent the other's. Thus, welfare levels fall onto a standard number line.

Of course, there are lots of different systems of evaluation that appear to have these same formal features. A person's level of moral virtue at a time, for example, might also be plotted on a number line. So might his net worth or his beauty or his athletic fitness; so might his value for others. Each of these can be conceived of as a function from an ordered pair of a person and time to a number. We need to make sure that, when we speak of a person's welfare, we are thinking of the right sort of value. Several philosophers have proposed informal tests that are intended to help us be sure that we have the right sort of evaluation in mind.

Brad Hooker has suggested that we might use "the Sympathy Test" to distinguish welfare from other sorts of value.[1] He pointed out that 'how sorry we feel for someone is influenced by how badly from the point of view of his own good we think that person's life has gone.'[2] Hooker's point—which he presents only tentatively—seems to be that there is a connection between the concept of welfare and the concept of sympathy, or "feeling sorry for someone." Suppose two people are alike in many respects except that one has a certain feature, X, that the other one lacks. Suppose that when we notice this, we feel sorry for the one who lacks X. Then this sorrow on our part indicates that we take the lack of X to indicate a diminution of welfare. The fact that we feel sorry for the one who lacks X shows that we take X to be associated with welfare.

Hooker's idea is suggestive, but I think it needs to be used with caution. It can yield misleading results. Suppose I am very keen on the Aristotelian moral virtues. I think that a truly upstanding person must be courageous, just, generous, great-spirited, friendly, witty, and so on. I don't think that having these virtues will necessarily enhance a person's welfare; but I do think having them will just make him a morally better person. I think it's important to be morally better. Now I meet a person who is cowardly. I pity him. I feel sorry for him. But I don't pity him because I think his welfare is low. I pity him because I think he lacks something that I take to be an important moral virtue; and I think this lack makes him a morally worse person. A careless application of the Sympathy Test might lead us to believe that I am worrying about this fellow's welfare (after all, I am feeling sorry for him because he lacks something); but in the present example, I am not worrying about the subject's welfare. I am worrying about his moral excellence.

In order to avoid this problem, an advocate of this approach would have to distinguish between two different ways of feeling sorry for someone. In some cases, we feel sorry for a person because we feel that he is missing out on something that diminishes welfare. We could call this "lost welfare sympathy." In other cases, we feel sorry for a person because we feel that he is missing out on some other sort of value. We could call this "lost non-welfare sympathy." Then we

okay but still wtf is welfare.

[1] Brad Hooker, 'Does Moral Virtue Constitute a Benefit to the Agent?,' in Roger Crisp, ed., *How Should One Live? Essays on the Virtues* (1996: 141–56).   [2] Ibid. 149.

could say that welfare is the sort of personal value such that we feel lost welfare sympathy when we think a person is missing out on it.

The proposal is plausible. It might even be true. But its obvious circularity makes it pointless as a test for welfare. We would be unable to make use of the test unless we already had a clear grasp on the concept of welfare.

Another approach involves a different emotional reaction. Instead of focusing on sympathy, we might focus on love. We might say that welfare is the type of value that a loving parent has in mind when she looks into the crib at her newborn innocent child and hopes that he will have a "good life." The idea here is that when the loving parent thinks of a "good life" for her child, she is thinking of a life high in welfare. This plausible idea has come to be known as the "Crib Test" and it has been discussed and defended by a number of philosophers.[3]

Again, however, the test is suggestive but inconclusive. Imagine a sternly moralistic parent gazing lovingly at her baby and praying that he gets to live a good life; imagine that as this parent utters her prayer, she is picturing her child growing up to be a moral saint. Surely it is possible that when this parent thinks of a "good life" for her child, she is not worrying about the child's future welfare. She is thinking about the child's future level of virtue. So the Crib Test would backfire in this case.

We can make the point a bit more dramatically. Suppose the loving parent utters a prayer: 'Please, God, allow my beloved child to have a *good life*.' Suppose that an emissary from God then appears to the mother and says that he can arrange to have the prayer answered, but first he needs some clarification. 'Your prayer is somewhat ambiguous. Are you just praying that the child has a life high in welfare?—that things go well for him in terms of prudential value? Or are you praying that the child has a life high in moral value?—that he leads a thoroughly virtuous life? The problem is that we can arrange for either one of these prayers to be answered, but we cannot arrange for both. If we give him a life of high welfare, he will have to be somewhat immoral. If he is perfectly virtuous, his welfare will suffer. Which were you praying for?' Surely the loving mother might say that she had been praying for the morally good life. Thus, appeal to the cribside prayers of a loving parent may not succeed in isolating the concept of welfare.

---

[3] Most notably, Stephen Darwall in *Welfare and Rational Care* (2002).

Other tests for welfare have been proposed. I will discuss these a bit later in a context in which the need for such a test becomes more apparent.

I am inclined to think that the best way to distinguish the concept of welfare from closely related but distinct value concepts is by "triangulation." By this, I mean the process of locating the concept by describing some of its important linkages to other related concepts. This may not yield a definition, but it may help to locate the concept we have in mind. The concept of welfare is located within a web of interesting and important concepts. Some of these are virtue concepts, such as *prudence, self-sacrifice,* and *benevolence.* Some are concepts indicating emotional states, or patterns of motivation, such as *love, selfishness,* and *altruism.* Others are associated with prima facie duties, such as *benevolence, maleficence,* and *gratitude.* Perhaps the most tightly connected concepts are the concepts of *harm* and *benefit.* Let us start with *harm.*

If we had a solid grasp of the concept of harm, we could explain the concept of welfare. We might think that I harm you if I injure you or damage something that you own. But this is inadequate. Suppose I ruin your lawn by driving my car across it. In such a case, it's not clear that I have harmed you. If driving my car across your lawn doesn't make you sad, or angry; if it doesn't force you to waste a lot of time planting new grass; if it doesn't force you to divert funds from things you enjoy, then it's not clear that I have harmed you even though I have damaged something you own. Maybe you don't care about tire marks on your lawn. To harm you, I must make you worse off. If ruining your lawn makes you unhappy, then it begins to look like I have harmed you. In order to harm you, I must decrease your level of welfare. So we can say that a person's level of welfare is the thing that is adversely affected when the person is harmed.

We might think that this provides the basis for a definition:

DWH: x's welfare =df. the type of value that x has such that, if x were to be harmed, it would be adversely affected.

One big problem here is that someone might sense a kind of circularity. This would emerge if he were to fuss about the concept of harm.[4]

---

[4] This would happen most obviously if the person suspected that there is such a thing as "moral harm"—this being the sort of harm that a person suffers when he is made morally worse.

Suppose he insisted on a definition. Surely there would be circularity if we offered this:

DHW: x harms y =df. x does something that adversely affects y's welfare.

So I should emphasize this: I am not proposing to define welfare by appeal to the concept of harm. Rather, I am just pointing out that the concepts are linked. If, by some good fortune, you have a satisfactory understanding of the appropriate concept of harm, you can make use of it to gain some footing with respect to the concept of welfare.

If we had a solid grasp of the concept of benefit, we could explain the concept of welfare. Suppose you don't care about money or anything you can purchase with money. Suppose I give you a gift of $100. In this case it is not clear that I have benefited you. If you don't care about having the money, and if giving it to you does not favorably affect you in any further way (e.g., it doesn't make you more popular, or more secure, or more relaxed), then it is hard to see how the gift makes you any better off. To benefit you, I would have to do something that would make you better off. In other words, I must increase your level of welfare. So we have another way of identifying the concept of welfare. We can say that a person's level of welfare is the thing that is favorably affected when the person is *benefited*.

These remarks about harm and benefit suggest another family of concepts that is connected to the concept of welfare. Ross says that we have prima facie obligations of beneficence and non-maleficence. Clearly, these are obligations that involve the welfare levels of others.[5] The former obligation is an obligation to enhance the welfare of others; the latter is an obligation to avoid decreasing their welfare. So, if we had firm and independent grasp of these kinds of prima facie obligation, we could then appeal to those concepts in order to explain welfare. We could say that welfare is the value in others that we have a prima facie obligation of beneficence to increase, and a prima facie obligation of non-maleficence to avoid decreasing.

If we had a solid grasp of the concept of *self-interest*, we would be able to explain the concept of welfare. Anything that is ultimately in your self-interest must be something that enhances your welfare. If you were completely selfish, and cared only about your self-interest,

---

[5] The situation is slightly more complicated. Ross suggests that you have a prima facie obligation of beneficence to help others by enhancing their level of virtue. If he's right about this, then while the prima facie duty of beneficence *sometimes* involves enhancements of welfare, it also *sometimes* involves enhancements of things other than welfare.

the thing you would be caring about is your own level of welfare. We can thus identify welfare in this way: a person's level of welfare is the thing he would be ultimately interested in if he were completely dominated by *self-interest*.

In one standard sense of the term, 'prudential rationality' refers to the virtue that a person has when he wisely seeks to maximize his own welfare. This may help to explain why some philosophers like to use the term 'prudential value' to refer to welfare. This gives us another point that may help us to locate welfare. Welfare: what the prudent person ultimately seeks to maximize in himself.

Correspondingly, we may be able to locate welfare by thinking about *altruism*. A genuinely altruistic person cares so much about others that he is motivated to do things that will benefit them—even at cost to his own welfare. If you could imagine a person who is completely altruistic, and cares only about others, this would give us another way of fixing the concept of welfare. We could say that welfare is the value such that the altruistic person is motivated to enhance the standing of others with respect to that value even when it means decreasing his own standing with respect to it. It's the thing that the altruistic person is willing to sacrifice in his own case in order to enhance in the case of others. Sometimes a person is described as "selfless." Surely this does not mean that he doesn't have a self. Rather, what it means is that he doesn't pay much attention to his own welfare. Again, we see how the concept of welfare pops up in the account of another concept.

Suppose a woman has become pregnant. At an appointment with her doctor, she learns that there are some anomalies in her pregnancy. If the baby comes to term, it will have some disabilities. The doctor begins to talk about "options," one of which is abortion. The woman is at first shocked and dismayed. She realizes that she has a hard decision to make. So she asks for more information. She wants to know as much as she can about the quality of life that the child would have, if it were to be born. Of course, she has other questions as well, but her primary focus at this point is on the baby. She might make it clear that her concern at the moment is entirely on the baby. 'I realize that raising this child may be hard on me and my husband; I realize that it might have consequences for the other children in the family; I realize that it might affect the school system in our town. But I want to put all of that aside. I want to know how things will go for this baby. If we all do our best, and luck is on our side, is it possible that this baby will have *a life worth living?*'

It's dangerous making this decision for someone else, granted fetus + baby.
But in general

I think that when this woman asks about "a life worth living," she very well may be asking about the level of welfare that the baby will experience. She may be asking whether the baby will get a life that has positive welfare. If this is her question, then she is asking for a prediction about the baby's standing with respect to the sort of value that is of interest here: welfare, or well-being.

In general, it seems to me that when questions about quality of life are raised in connection with medical decisions, those questions should (ultimately) be understood to be questions about the welfare of the affected patient. This can be seen if we consider a case in which there are two different procedures that can be used to deal with a certain condition. Suppose the procedures are fairly well matched in cost, painfulness, likelihood of success, and other features. But suppose they have different side effects. A patient might want to know about quality of life: 'What will be my quality of life if I opt for Procedure A rather than Procedure B?' If this is right, we have yet another way to locate the concept of welfare: we can say that a person's welfare is the sort of value that a caring parent or provider of medical assistance would be considering when thinking solely about the loved one's "quality of life."

I do not claim that these reflections yield a definition of welfare. My claim is more modest. I am assuming that most of us already have the concept of welfare. My remarks are intended to locate the concept of welfare by indicating how it fits into a larger conceptual scheme. The general point can be made by saying:

Welfare: the sort of value that is decreased when a person is harmed; the sort of value that we increase in a person when we benefit him. Additionally, when a person is selfishly trying to enhance his own self-interest, the sort of value that he is seeking to enhance is his own welfare. Contrariwise, it is the sort of value an altruistic or benevolent person tries to enhance in others. Welfare is the value that we have in mind when we worry about someone's quality of life, or when we consider whether he has a life worth living. Welfare is the kind of value in another that we are concerned to enhance when we love, or care for, that person. Welfare is the value about which we may be concerned when, at graveside, we reflect on the question whether the deceased "had a good life."

I should emphasize that this account of welfare is not entirely conclusive. Everything I have said here to locate welfare by triangulation could still misfire. Someone could follow all these remarks about the relations between welfare and other sorts of value and still end up confusing welfare with moral excellence. But I think this may be about the best we can do. In any case, it will have to suffice here.[6]

Eudaimonism is the view that it is ultimately only happiness that determines welfare. On this view, the welfare value that a person enjoys or suffers at a time is directly proportional to her level of happiness at that time; the amount of welfare that a person enjoys or suffers during an interval is proportional to the amount of happiness that she has during that interval; the welfare value of a person's life as a whole is proportional to the amount of happiness in her life as a whole. More succinctly: *welfare tracks happiness*.

However, since there are many different views about the nature of happiness, there are many different forms of eudaimonism. According to the form of eudaimonism that I mean to defend, welfare tracks happiness *as explicated by my theory of happiness*. I would not endorse the claim that welfare tracks happiness as explicated by competing theories of happiness, such as sensory hedonism, or local preferentism, or any form of whole life satisfactionism. Thus, in order to make this point clear, it may be helpful to make use of a suggestive bit of terminology. I call my theory "Attitudinal Hedonistic Eudaimonism," or AHE. My claim here is that AHE gives a plausible account of individual welfare.

It's not clear to me that it is possible to present arguments in favor of a view as fundamental as AHE. A better approach, as I see it, is just (a) to note how plausible and attractive it is on its face; (b) to appreciate its capacity to deal with objections that have been raised; and (c) to reflect on the implications of the theory for some hard cases. So that is what I propose to do here.

As I see it, eudaimonism is initially attractive. Some, following Aristotle, take eudaimonism to be obvious—hardly more than a platitude. When we care about a person, and hope that things will go well for her, and it is her birthday, we wish her a happy birthday. When we care in this way about our friends, and it is New Year's Eve, we wish them a happy new year. When a period of gloom is ending, and better days seem to be arriving, we declare that happy days are here again. Suppose your daughter informs you that she has decided to drop out of college. She is thinking of embarking on a career as a juggler. If you love her, and want things to go well for her, and don't want to interfere too much in her decisions, you may

---

[6] Thanks to Alex Sarch for many helpful discussions of this topic.

be uneasy about telling her that she has made the wrong decision. Perhaps you will express your concern by saying 'I just want you to be happy. Are you sure you will be happy with a career in juggling?' All of these familiar remarks suggest that we associate happiness with welfare.   *when we do this its problematic.*

I am inclined to think, however, that the most fruitful way to come to understand and appreciate my proposed form of eudaimonism is to think about some reasons that can be given for rejecting it. When we see that none of these objections is conclusive, we may both understand eudaimonism better and also come to have a better grasp of its plausibility.

8.3   *Eudaimonism and Survival Strategies*

According to the theory of happiness that was presented in Chapter 6, if a person takes pleasure in lots of things, and takes displeasure in few, then the person is happy. Such takings of pleasure and displeasure are, clearly, facts about the psychology of the subject. Happiness, on this view, is a mental state. According to eudaimonism, if the person is happy, he is faring well. Therefore, Attitudinal Hedonistic Eudaimonism is a mental state theory of welfare. AHE implies that a person's welfare depends entirely on certain facts about his or her mental states.

Views relevantly like this have been criticized on a variety of different grounds. One especially interesting line of attack is based on the fact that there are psychological maneuvers that we can use to defend ourselves against suffering when in bad situations. A person may find himself in a situation that seems pretty rotten; yet he may blind himself to the rottenness of the situation; he may deceive himself; he may engage in rationalizations; he may adopt a policy of trying to find something to enjoy though the circumstances seem bleak. In a case in which such maneuvers succeed, AHE may declare that the person is faring well—yet well-informed observers may feel that there is something amiss. The happiness seems to be dependent upon some sort of defense mechanism. So either the theory of happiness is wrong, or else there is more to welfare than mere happiness. Wayne Sumner takes this to be 'the main reason for questioning the adequacy of any subjective theory of welfare.'[7]

---

[7] Sumner (1996: 162).

One of the classic statements of this objection was presented by Amartya Sen in this passage:

A person who has had a life of misfortune, with very little opportunities, and rather little hope, may be more easily reconciled to deprivations than others reared in more fortunate and affluent circumstances. The metric of happiness may, therefore, distort the extent of deprivation, in a specific and biased way. The hopeless beggar, the precarious landless labourer, the dominated housewife, the hardened unemployed or the over-exhausted coolie may all take pleasures in small mercies, and manage to suppress intense suffering for the necessity of continuing survival, but it would be ethically deeply mistaken to attach a correspondingly small value to the loss of their well-being because of this survival strategy.[8]

While, of course, Sen was not thinking precisely of the form of eudaimonism presented here, it seems to me that his objection bears directly on the theory I mean to defend. Thus, it seems appropriate to consider a version of his objection directed against AHE. I want to discuss this objection in part because I think doing so may help to clarify both the concept of happiness and the concept of welfare.

Imagine a "precarious landless labourer." He has a very hard life and is constantly worried about how he will be able to provide for his family. His "precariousness" is fundamentally a matter of uncertainty about the future. Will he be able to find work? Will his health hold out? Will there be enough money to feed his children? Suppose that one morning when this laborer arrives at his worksite, the boss tells him that there is no work for him today. This is more bad news for the laborer, since if he doesn't work, he will earn no money that day. His family will fall even deeper into poverty. But the worker shrugs off this disappointment. He doesn't allow it to get to him. He determines to make the best of the situation. He will return home to attend to some chores and to get some needed rest. Thus, he 'suppresses intense suffering for the necessity of continued survival.' He has adopted this attitude as a "survival strategy." He finds that it makes it easier for him to carry on.

Sen says that 'it is ethically deeply mistaken to attach a correspondingly small value to the loss of [the laborer's] well-being because of this survival strategy.' The formulation is not entirely perspicuous. Perhaps we can understand Sen to be pointing out that eudaimonism gives an incorrect evaluation of the magnitude of the laborer's misfortune.[9] In order to investigate this, we will have to add some further

---

[8] Sen (1987: 45–6), as quoted in Sumner (1996: 162).
[9] I am grateful to Alex Sarch for some illuminating discussions concerning the interpretation of Sen's argument.

detail to the story. Let us suppose that the lack of work is really quite bad news for the laborer. He knows this. But as a result of his survival strategy, he takes only 5 units of intrinsic attitudinal displeasure in the fact that he has no work today. Were it not for the survival strategy, he would have taken 10 units of displeasure in that fact.

AHE now entails that the welfare of the laborer is reduced by 5 units. His already unfortunate life is made 5 units worse by the displeasure he takes in his involuntary layoff. As I understand him here, Sen is saying that this calculation underestimates the magnitude of the laborer's misfortune. He says it is 'ethically deeply mistaken to attach a correspondingly small value to the loss of their well-being because of this survival strategy.' Perhaps Sen would say that the actual magnitude of the misfortune is −10.

If this is the objection, it can be stated as a little argument:

1. If AHE is true, then the welfare of the laborer is diminished by only 5 units by the displeasure taken in the involuntary layoff.
2. But the welfare of the laborer is diminished by more than 5 units by the displeasure taken in the involuntary layoff.
3. Therefore, AHE is not true.

Since happiness, on my view, is entirely a matter of attitudinal pleasure and displeasure, and since the laborer takes 5 units of displeasure in the fact that he has been laid off, it follows that the laborer is 5 units less happy as a result of his displeasure. AHE then implies that the laborer is 5 units worse off as a result of being laid off. So it seems that (1) is true.

As I have interpreted him, Sen would claim that the displeasure of the laborer has been misevaluated. It has been given a disvalue of only −5. But the misfortune of the laborer is really worse than this. That displeasure should be given greater weight *because it is the product of a desperate survival strategy.* Thus we have (2).

I think this is the argument that Sen means to be advancing in the passage.[10] But I think it is unpersuasive. I see no reason to accept (2). The survival strategy seems to me to be effective. By steeling himself against disappointment, the laborer manages to make his life a bit less bad for him than it otherwise would have been. Surely the laborer would have been even worse off if he had allowed the bad news to make him miserable; surely his unfortunate life would have been even more unfortunate if he had broken down in despair when he heard that there was no work for the day. Though, of course, his survival

---

[10] Others, including Sumner, have interpreted the passage in other ways.

strategy is not sufficient to make the laborer's life on balance a good one for him, it may help to make it a little less miserable. So I reject (2).

Note that I have been focusing here only on the component of unhappiness that is contributed by the news about the loss of work for the day. I have not said that the overall welfare level of the "precarious landless laborer" is just −5. Surely it is reasonable to suppose that this laborer has plenty of other things to be unhappy about. Maybe he is unhappy about the fact that he has no land of his own; maybe he is unhappy about the fact that he cannot provide adequate food for his children; maybe he is unhappy about the fact that he earns such a small amount of money for his hard work. Attitudinal Hedonism about Happiness implies that each of these (and any other episodes of displeasure that he may experience) adds to the laborer's unhappiness. If there are no compensating pleasures, the laborer's overall happiness level will be negative. Attitudinal Hedonistic Eudaimonism then yields the result that the laborer has negative welfare. His life is going poorly for him. Given the natural assumptions about the case, this seems like the right evaluation. The case, therefore, poses no real threat to the form of eudaimonism that I am advocating.

8.4 *The Fragmentation of Happiness*

Scattered through the literature on happiness, we find remarks suggesting that there is an essentially *global* or *life-holistic* element in happiness. These remarks suggest that a person's lifetime happiness cannot simply be the sum of the momentary bits of happiness that he enjoys. According to this view, we cannot calculate lifetime happiness by adding up the contributions of atoms of momentary happiness. Perhaps it works the other way around: first we look at the life as a whole; we determine the amount of happiness in the life in some holistic way; then we can look back at the momentary bits to see what contribution each of them makes to the whole. The greater the contribution of some moment, the happier we declare the subject to have been at that time.[11] If any such holistic claim is true, then Attitudinal

---

[11] Some philosophers go further. They claim (or at least seem to claim) that it makes no sense to speak of a person's happiness level *at a moment*. Richard Taylor is a case in point. In a discussion of the differences between pleasure and happiness, he says 'Again, pleasures, like pains, come and go, and can be momentary; but one cannot momentarily be a happy person. One can momentarily exult or rejoice, to be sure, and while such states are typically ingredients of a happy existence, they are certainly not the same thing' (*Virtue Ethics*, 2002); quoted in Cahn and Vitrano (2008: 225). My hunch is that Taylor was not talking about happiness as a

Hedonistic Eudaimonism is false; for one of the essential components of AHE is precisely this atomistic principle: the welfare-value of a life for a person is the sum of the welfare-values for that person of the various episodes of attitudinal pleasure and displeasure that the person experiences during the life.

Julia Annas is a good example of a philosopher who has been explicit in her commitment to the idea that there is something holistic about happiness.[12] She sketches two conceptions of happiness according to which happiness in life as a whole is understood to be the aggregate of elements of a kind of happiness that fundamentally comes in *episodes*. According to one conception, the episodes are those in which the subject has a "smiley-face feeling." Presumably Annas is thinking of sensory hedonism. According to the other conception, the episodes are ones in which the subject's desires are being satisfied. This suggests a preferentist conception of happiness. In either case, the subject's lifetime level of happiness would be determined by adding up the bits of happiness he enjoys in those little episodes.

Annas rejects these approaches. She says that if you try to measure a subject's lifetime happiness by adding up the bits of happiness enjoyed in "smiley-face episodes" 'the results will be grotesque.'[13] She also rejects the preferentist account, in part because it would count as happy even for a person who has desires based on addiction or obsession.[14]

In opposition to these atomistic views, Annas defends a kind of holism about happiness. She says that 'happiness has an essential

---

psychological state. Rather, he may have been thinking of happiness as an evaluative state—the state of having a good life. But, even if he was talking about this sort of evaluative happiness, it seems to me that his claim is false. It seems to me to make perfectly good sense to speak of a person's welfare level at a moment. Jeffrie Murphy is another example. In his essay on 'The Unhappy Immoralist' (also in the Cahn and Vitrano (2008) anthology), Murphy rejects the idea that "happiness is simply a matter of *now*." He says, 'happiness is better understood as an attribute, not of a present moment of one's life, but of a whole life—the wisdom in the ancient Greek saying that we should call no man happy until he is dead' (Cahn and Vitrano 2008: 264).

[12]   Julia Annas, 'Happiness as Achievement,' in Cahn and Vitrano (2008: 238–45). Originally published in *Dialogue* (spring, 2004).

[13]   Annas, in Cahn and Vitrano (2008: 239). Annas does not explain precisely why she thinks the results of this calculation would be "grotesque." One possibility is that the results would be grotesque not because they involve summation, but rather because they involve summation of the values of *the wrong atoms*. I tried to explain in Chapter 2 that sensory hedonism about happiness is unacceptable. Thus, I accept the conclusion that we won't come up with the right numbers if we sum the amounts of sensory pleasure and pain in a person's life. But my objections do not turn on the fact that we used summation. My objections turned on my claim that there is more to happiness than mere "smiley face feelings."

[14]   Annas, in Cahn and Vitrano (2008: 240).

connection with my life as a whole.'[15] We cannot properly understand our experience if we think of it in a linear way, simply as a series of episodes. Rather, in order to understand what happens to a person, we must see her experiences globally. We must see that her aims are nested—she wants to achieve one thing because she wants to achieve another larger thing.

So thinking about the way one action is done for the sake of another leads seamlessly into thinking about my life in a nonlinear way, one we can call *global*... I have to move to thinking of my life as a whole—a whole given in terms of my goals and the way they fit together overall—rather than as mere duration through time.[16]

When she made these comments, Annas was not thinking of a conception of happiness relevantly like the one I have presented here. Thus, she did not present any argument specifically designed to refute the kind of attitudinal hedonism about happiness that I mean to defend. Nevertheless, it seems to me that it would be fairly easy to construct an argument against my view based on her remarks.

On my view, a person's level of happiness during an extended period of time, or during life as a whole, is determined by adding up his levels of happiness during the moments within the interval or life. If a life contains a suitable preponderance of happy moments, it is declared to be a happy life. Thus, my view has precisely the feature that Annas means to reject. So let us see if we can imagine a life that does contain such a preponderance of happy moments, but one that lacks the holistic element that Annas emphasizes. We are looking for a life in which the episodes of attitudinal pleasure are not "nested;" they do not "fit together overall;" the subject does not perform one action for the sake of another.

The natural place to look for a description of a fragmented life such as this is in the pages of *The Man Who Mistook His Wife for a Hat*. Within that book, we in fact do find descriptions of several lives that are extreme examples of the sort Annas mentions. These are the lives of unfortunate individuals who have suffered brain injury leading to severe memory impairment. One of them is described in 'The Lost Mariner.' This is Jimmie G., who apparently has Korsakov's Syndrome. Jimmie (about 49 years old at the time Sacks describes) can recall almost nothing that has happened to him since the mid-1940s, when he was about 18 years old. He cannot keep anything in mind for more than a minute or two. As Sacks describes him, Jimmie is a

---

[15] Ibid. 241.   [16] Ibid.

"Humean being"—a man whose mental life is nothing more than an incoherent sequence of fleeting and unrelated episodes.[17]

Let us then use an enhanced and perhaps distorted Jimmie as the basis for a test case for eudaimonism. Let us suppose that our Jimmie takes pleasure in many things each day. He enjoys seeing some children playing baseball in the playground; he enjoys playing a game of checkers; he enjoys attending church services. But these experiences are quickly forgotten. They do not fall into any meaningful pattern. On the next day, he may enjoy a different game; seeing some children doing some other thing in the playground; having a meal. By then, of course, he has no recollection of the pleasures he enjoyed on the previous day. And, on the following day, he will have no recollection of the second day's pleasures. Let us assume that Jimmie's life goes on like this for many years. He has no long-term aims; his pleasures are not "nested." The activities of each day are unconnected with the activities of the previous day and the subsequent day. Jimmie's mental life is just a chaotic hodge-podge of experiences. Jimmie takes pleasure in many of these experiences as they are occurring and then forgets them and his brief enjoyment. He cannot make any plans; he has no aims; he lives entirely in the present.

The problem, then, is this: it may appear that Attitudinal Hedonistic Eudaimonism (AHE) implies that Jimmie has a life high in personal welfare. Yet we would all agree that Jimmie's case is pathetic. As Sacks says, Jimmie seems to be in a 'hopeless state of neurological devastation.'[18] If this assessment is right, and Jimmie has negative welfare, this would refute AHE. Jimmie's life is not good in itself for him.

The objection, as I see it, is not successful. One problem is empirical; the other is axiological. The empirical problem is that we have paid very little attention to Jimmie's displeasures. Though we have mentioned some of the things he enjoys, we have not said much about the things that pain him. Sacks mentions some of these in passing: Jimmie seems vaguely aware of the fact that there is something wrong with his memory. When he sees his own face in a mirror, he is confused and dismayed.[19] What he sees in the mirror makes no sense to him. (He thinks he is still 19 years old; the face in the mirror seems to be the face of an old man.) Sacks reports that Jimmie screams in fear, 'Is this a nightmare? Am I crazy?' From time to time Jimmie is deeply troubled by unintelligible signs of illness. When asked if he enjoys life, he says

---

[17] The case of Jimmie is described in Sacks (1987: 23–42).
[18] Sacks (1987: 39).   [19] Ibid. 25.

'I can't say that I do.'[20] So it appears that there are plenty of moments in Jimmie's fragmented life that have to get negative or neutral ratings with respect to intrinsic attitudinal pleasure. As a result, his happiness level for these moments and for his life as a whole may be negative, or at least not very high. So we should not be too quick to say that AHE implies that Jimmie has a life high in welfare.

If we are willing to engage in possibly unrealistic thought experiments, we may be able to construct a case that will illustrate a purer form of "fragmented happiness." Suppose Jamie is another patient in Jimmie's institution. Suppose Jamie suffers from a disorder similar to Jimmie's. But suppose that Jamie is not shocked, dismayed, or confused. He doesn't recognize that there is anything wrong with him. He isn't pained by his loss of memory. Suppose that Jamie just goes about his fragmented business each day. He takes pleasure in one trivial thing after another, but with no pattern or structure. Since Jamie is not engaged in any temporally extended projects, none of his pleasures is pleasure taken in the completion of a step in such a project. Nor can Jamie take pleasure in things he has done, since he cannot recall anything he has done. But still we can suppose that he takes a fair amount of pleasure in his experiences as they happen. Beyond that, his emotional life is empty. We may assume that Jamie goes on like this for a long time. He eventually dies, never realizing what has happened to him.

In this case, AHE in fact does imply that Jamie has positive welfare. Since he took attitudinal pleasure in many things, and attitudinal displeasure in few, his life is rated by AHE as being fairly good in itself for him. But now we must confront the question whether this evaluation is wrong.

It must be acknowledged that Jamie has a serious disability. He is unable to engage in many activities that most of us enjoy. As a result of this, he will not have the opportunity to take pleasure in many things that ordinary people enjoy. Indeed, it seems likely that he will be unable to take pleasure in many things that he would have enjoyed were it not for his disability. So it is likely that he is much worse off than he would have been if he had the blessing of an intact memory. But, on the other hand, he is not in any pain; nothing is actually bothering him; he takes pleasure in many things. How can we be sure of Jamie's welfare?

The question before us is deceptively simple: does Jamie have positive welfare? I say that the question is deceptively simple because,

---

[20] Ibid. 36.

in spite of its straightforward five-word formulation, it is not an easy question to answer. Perhaps in the end we will just have to contemplate Jamie's life and see if we can "intuit" its value. Earlier, I mentioned that some philosophers have proposed some suggestive (though not quite decisive) tests for welfare.

Recall the "Crib Test." We are supposed to imagine a loving parent looking into the crib where her newborn baby is sleeping. We are supposed to imagine that the parent is filled with affection for her child. Something is welfare-good for the child if and only if the parent would hope for it for the child. We can apply the test to the present case. Would a loving parent want her child to end up living the life of Jamie?

I suspect that there would be very few loving parents who would hope that their child would end up with a life like Jamie's. We assume that Korsakov's Syndrome is a kind of "neurological devastation." This suggests that his life is low in welfare. However, it is not clear that we can rely on the Crib Test. The problem is that it is possible that the parents' preferences for their children might be based on something other than considerations of pure welfare alone. Maybe a loving parent would recognize that it would take huge amounts of support from health-care providers for a child like Jamie to manage. Maybe a loving parent would recognize that anyone in Jamie's situation would be wholly dependent upon others for support. Thus, if the support were to be withdrawn, the child would be unable to cope. In that case, he might be miserable. And in any case there is no guarantee that the child would not end up more like Jimmie. We have already seen that (according to Sacks) Jimmie does not have high welfare.

In his *Virtue Ethics*, Richard Taylor suggests a different test for welfare. Taylor maintains that "lesser beings" such as "children, idiots, barbarians, and even animals" can have pleasurable sensations, and even something Taylor is willing to call "the feeling of happiness." But Taylor claims that they are not enjoying high welfare. Their lives are not good in themselves for them. In this context, Taylor introduces a test that is apparently intended to help us appreciate his evaluation of these lives. He asks us to consider whether we would be willing to "be just like" such a contented moron, if we could thereby get to enjoy the same pleasurable sensations that the moron enjoys. 'Of course, the answer for any normal person is a resounding negative. This shows,' Taylor says, that the state enjoyed by the moron is not the state that 'a philosopher holds up as the highest good.'[21]

---

[21]   Taylor, quoted in Cahn and Vitrano (2008: 226–7).

Taylor's Swap Test seems to be something like this:

TST: If normal people would not be willing to swap lives with person M, then person M is not leading a welfare-good life.

I suppose that many normal people would not want to swap lives with Jamie. I consider myself to be fairly normal, and I would not want to swap lives with him. The Swap Test then implies that Jamie's life does not have positive welfare value.

However, I am not convinced that Taylor's Swap Test is a reliable test of welfare. It seems to me that there could be many explanations for the fact (if it is a fact) that normal people would not want to swap lives with Jamie. One especially important reason involves certain moral considerations. In virtue of his disability, Jamie is unable to do much good for others. He cannot teach anyone anything; he has no wisdom to impart. It's hard to see how he can even provide comfort to others who are suffering. Since I think it's important to do things that are helpful to others—especially to others who are suffering—I would not want to find myself in Jamie's condition.

Even if it were guaranteed that I would be happier living a life like Jamie's, I would still prefer not to swap lives with him. I have some projects that I would like to complete. I have commitments to fulfill. I would be unable to complete my projects and fulfill my commitments if I were locked up in a mental institution.

A third proposed test for welfare (also mentioned earlier) is Brad Hooker's Sympathy Test. The test suggests that if we would pity a person for failing to have a certain feature, X, then having X would contribute to the person's welfare. It seems reasonable to suppose that most sympathetic observers would pity Jamie for failing to have an intact memory. Most of us, I assume, would think this is a terrible loss. I certainly would.

Yet it does not follow that Jamie's life has negative welfare. Even if we conclude that the Sympathy Test works flawlessly here, the only conclusion we are entitled to derive is that Jamie's welfare is adversely affected by his disability. In other words, assuming that we pity Jamie for his lost memory, the test implies that the loss of his memory makes him worse off than he otherwise would have been. It is consistent with this to maintain that he nevertheless enjoys positive or even fairly high welfare.

So in the end I am inclined to say that there is no surefire way to determine the welfare value of Jamie's life. We have stipulated that he takes pleasure in many things and displeasure in few. My theory of happiness then implies that he is happy. That suggests that he has positive welfare. But we have also stipulated that his happiness is utterly fragmented. This suggests, but does not entail, that he has low welfare—or perhaps just that he has much lower welfare than he would have had if he had a properly functioning memory. As a result, it seems to me that examples involving fragmented happiness do not provide the basis for a completely convincing refutation of eudaimonism.

Two further thoughts may be worth mentioning here. The first concerns a sort of naive identification of happiness with welfare. An extreme example of this can be seen in Easterlin's remark—quoted earlier—to the effect that the terms 'happiness' and 'well-being' are "interchangeable."[22] It seems perfectly clear to me that Jamie is fairly happy. My theory of happiness has that implication. Given natural assumptions to fill out the case, several other theories of happiness would yield the same assessment. However, it is not clear to me that Jamie is enjoying a correspondingly high level of well-being. I am inclined to think that he is; but I recognize that this is a much harder question. The example thus drives home the fact that happiness and well-being are two different things; and they would continue to be two different things even if it should turn out that the amount of one that a person has is always equivalent to the amount of the other that he has. The terms are clearly not interchangeable.

Second, it seems to me that there are ways in which Attitudinal Hedonistic Eudaimonism can be revised so as to accord better with the intuitions of those who say that Jamie is not enjoying high welfare. We can claim that his happiness yields relatively lower welfare in virtue of the fact that he is taking pleasure in objects that are less worthy of having pleasure taken in them. I discuss this "desert-adjusted" form of AHE later in 10.2.

---

[22] Easterlin (2005: 29).

Five Grades of Demonic Possession

I have used the term 'eudaimonism' to refer to the family of views according to which welfare tracks happiness. Although my use of the term is consistent with current conventions, it nevertheless may lead to some confusion. Some philosophers use the term in other ways. In this Appendix, I try to sort out this terminological situation.

In what we may identify as its "garden variety" sense, 'eudaimonism' refers to theories according to which welfare tracks garden variety happiness. When I speak of "garden variety happiness" here, I have in mind the ordinary sort of happiness that non-philosophers mean to indicate when they speak of happiness. Happiness, thus understood, seems to be some sort of psychological phenomenon, though its precise nature is a matter of debate. I have discussed a bunch of philosophical and psychological theories about its nature. According to some of these theories, to be happy is to enjoy a positive hedono-doloric balance. According to others, to be happy is to have your desires satisfied. According to yet others, to be happy is to be satisfied with your life as a whole. I have defended my own view, according to which to be happy is to have a positive balance of attitudinal pleasure over attitudinal displeasure. For each different theory about the nature of happiness, we get a different variant of Garden Variety Eudaimonism. All of these different forms of eudaimonism are alike in this central respect: they all maintain that garden variety happiness (understood in one way or another) is the ultimate determinant of individual welfare.

Some philosophers might object to my use of the term 'eudaimonism' for the family of theories thus indicated. They might insist that it would be better to use some other name ("happiness-ism"?) for these theories. They might claim that the term 'eudaimonism' should be reserved for a different family of theories. The theories that deserve the name, they might say, are theories according to which welfare is determined not by "happiness," but rather by a different thing—*eudaimonia*. Advocates of this approach may claim to draw their inspiration from Aristotle. They may claim that Aristotelian Eudaimonism is *not* the view that welfare tracks some sort of garden variety happiness; instead, they claim that Aristotelian Eudaimonism is the view that welfare tracks *eudaimonia*, where a person may be said to have eudaimonia if he is flourishing, or living the life of virtue, or fulfilling his distinctively human essence. Different Aristotle scholars explain eudaimonia differently. In any case, some philosophers say that we should be more respectful of Aristotle. We should use 'eudaimonism' to refer to something akin to Aristotelian Eudaimonism, and thus not to Garden Variety Eudaimonism.

Let us distinguish this usage by saying that these philosophers are fans of "Aristotelian Eudaimonism." According to Aristotelian Eudaimonism, welfare tracks whatever Aristotle had in mind when he spoke of eudaimonia. It should be clear that Aristotelian Eudaimonism is distinct from any form of Garden Variety Eudaimonism.

At least one philosopher—Jeffrie Murphy—appears to advocate an even more extreme position. Murphy seems to be aware of the fact that the word 'happy' in ordinary English is in fact used to express what I am calling garden variety happiness—some sort of enjoyable but not necessarily exalted psychological state. But Murphy maintains that we should stop using 'happy' in the way we currently use it. He seems to claim that we should start using 'happy' to mean something else. He suggests (and in this claims to be following Plato and Philippa Foot) that we should reserve the word 'happy' for people who take satisfaction in the fact that they have personalities 'wherein all elements required for a fully realized human life are harmoniously integrated.'[1] Murphy acknowledges that his suggestion involves 'some conceptual or linguistic revision.' But he claims that in some cases this sort of revision has the capacity to "enrich our civilization." While he does not suggest that we rebuild the English language from the ground up, nevertheless he says 'conceptual or linguistic revision can sometimes enlarge and deepen our moral understanding—perhaps bringing to consciousness something that was latent all along.'[2]

This seems to me to be a strange recommendation. We have the (admittedly vague) concept of garden variety happiness; we have the concept of satisfaction taken in the harmoniously integrated personality. As a matter of empirical fact, English speakers currently use the word 'happy' to express the former concept. We use the phrase 'is satisfied in the fact that he has a harmoniously integrated personality' to express the latter concept. I see no reason to suppose that our civilization would be enriched if we somehow managed to alter our linguistic practice so that we used the word 'happy' to express the concept of being satisfied in having a harmoniously integrated personality. On the other hand, it seems pretty obvious that there would be practical costs involved in trying to get such a revision implemented. Surely confusion and misunderstanding would arise if some people were to continue to use 'happy' to express happiness

---

[1] Murphy, 'The Unhappy Immoralist', in Cahn and Vitrano (2008: 263).
[2] Ibid. 264.

and others were to begin to use it to express the concept of being satisfied in having a harmoniously integrated personality. Suppose, for example, that Murphy's proposed linguistic revision were under way. Suppose, in these circumstances, that someone were to wish you a happy birthday. You might at first think that he meant to express the hope that you would be cheerful, or satisfied, or pleased with things on your birthday. But then you might wonder whether he had been influenced by Murphy. You might think perhaps he was hoping that you would be satisfied in having a harmoniously integrated personality on your birthday. Of course, in the end, it wouldn't make much difference. Either way, it would be a nice thing to say on someone's birthday.

Suppose that after a transitional period during which some people use the word one way and others use it in the other, we arrive at a time when everyone settles on the novel usage. Suppose everyone uses the term 'happy' not to mean what we now call happiness, but rather to mean what Murphy seems to think we ought to mean by it—satisfaction in having a harmoniously integrated personality. I assume that we would have to settle on some other term to play the semantic role currently played by 'happy.' And then, when the linguistic dust had settled, everyone could manage to say all the things they currently say, though with a slightly revised vocabulary. I cannot imagine why going through this process of terminological revision would "enrich our civilization." So far as I can tell, it would leave us precisely where we started, except with some different words to describe the same old facts.

In any case, if Murphy's suggestion were implemented, we would face a further terminological difficulty. Suppose someone felt that welfare tracks satisfaction in having a harmoniously integrated personality. In keeping with the revised linguistic practice, he could express his view by saying 'welfare tracks happiness.' Readers who were not up to date with the linguistic revision might think the philosopher was endorsing some form of Garden Variety Eudaimonism. But, if the advocate of the new axiological theory were using 'happiness' to refer to the property of satisfaction in having a harmoniously integrated personality, he would not be talking about any sort of garden variety happiness and he would not be advocating any form of Garden Variety Eudaimonism. He would be advocating the view that (as we now put it) welfare tracks satisfaction in having a harmoniously integrated personality.

Other philosophers defend a more moderate position. They do not advocate a change in linguistic practice. Instead, they just maintain somewhat surprising views about the nature of happiness. They claim that ordinary people misunderstand what they are talking about when they talk about happiness. Ordinary people may think they are talking about a merely psychological state—some form of garden variety happiness. But these philosophers think that the state in question is quite different from what ordinary people imagine it to be. We may think of this as "the error theory" of happiness.

Richard Taylor maintains that happiness is not to be identified with any sort of garden variety psychological state. He emphatically denies that happiness can be identified with any mere feeling. It is not simply a matter of feeling pleasure, or any feeling that one gets as a result of having possessions, or being famous or loved. Rather, according to Taylor, to understand what happiness is, we must start over from scratch. We discover the nature of happiness by determining first the proper and distinctive function of people. Just as we say that a person is healthy when he fulfills the proper functioning of his body, so we may say that a person is happy when he fulfills the proper and distinctive functioning of the whole person. Thus, we must determine the proper function of people. He says:

> Human beings, in a word, think, reflect, and *create*. It is no wonder that we are referred to in Scripture as having been created "in the image of God," for this has traditionally been thought of as the primary attribute of God, namely, that God is the *creator*. . . .
> If we think of happiness as fulfillment, then it must consist of the fulfillment of ourselves as human beings, which means the [proper] exercise of our creative powers.[3]

Thus, according to Taylor, to be happy is to engage in the proper exercise of our creative powers.

Taylor, of course, recognizes that there are people who fail to exercise their creative powers properly, but who nevertheless feel quite happy. A person like this might be content, or satisfied with his life as a whole. He might consider himself to be happy. But Taylor claims that this is mere "specious happiness." It is not "the genuine thing."[4]

Suppose a person does not properly exercise his creative powers. Suppose, however, that his friends and colleagues think he's a wonderful person and accordingly shower him with undeserved respect and affection. Suppose he has power, fame, glory, wealth, and possessions. Suppose he is very pleased by all this and as a result always has a smile on his face, and cheery feelings in his heart. Suppose everyone thinks he is a very happy person. Taylor would claim that they are

---

[3] Richard Taylor, from *Virtue Ethics*, quoted in Cahn and Vitrano (2008: 231–2).
[4] Ibid. 232.

all mistaken. Taylor insists that 'we must not be misled by this. What such people have are certain feelings of happiness—feelings only.'[5] They are not really happy. Thus Taylor can say that such a person enjoys only "specious happiness."

Taylor's use of the terms 'specious happiness' and 'the genuine thing' gives us a hint of what may be going on here. It appears that Taylor may be engaged in what Charles Stevenson would have characterized as "persuasive high redefinition." As Stevenson described it, this is the process of taking a word (e.g., 'freedom') that already has a strong favorable emotive meaning but a somewhat vague cognitive meaning, and then attempting to attach a new cognitive meaning to the term ("real freedom is the capacity to obey the moral law"). Stevenson remarks that 'persuasive definitions are often recognizable from the words "real" or "true."' It is tempting to see Taylor's remarks about "genuine happiness" in this light. A Stevensonian might say that Taylor is trying to attach a new cognitive meaning to the term 'happiness' while retaining the term's acknowledged strong favorable emotive meaning.[6]

Suppose a politician is running for office. Suppose he has been accused of not being sufficiently "conservative." But suppose he needs the support of voters who are committed to conservative values. His campaign manager might dream up a campaign according to which "true conservatism" is identified with such policies as higher taxes, better health care for the needy, and no support for faith-based social programs. 'Let's say that this is what *true conservatives* believe, and then let's say that you are the *truest conservative* in the race.'

In this case, the campaign manager would be engaging in persuasive high redefinition. There are many voters who are inclined to vote only for "conservatives." They like "conservatives." But our candidate does not satisfy the familiar definition of this term. So, in order to get these voters to look more favorably on his candidate, the campaign manager is suggesting that we quietly substitute a new cognitive meaning for this term, while allowing it to retain its favorable connotations for these voters. The voters will have to see that our candidate is a positive instance of "conservatism" (under its new definition) and they will like him (because the term still carries favorable-for-them connotations).

It's easy to understand why a campaign manager would do such a thing. It's also easy to see why salesmen would do it. They want to get people to do certain things; hoodwinking them with linguistic sleight-of-hand may help. So they do it. But it is not easy to see why a philosopher would do it. As far as I can tell, this sort of thing increases

---

[5] Ibid. 235.   [6] Stevenson (1938: 331–50).

the risk of misunderstanding. It may lead readers to accept doctrines that they would reject if they were presented in familiar terminology.

In any case, let us use the term 'Stevensonian Eudaimonism' to indicate the view that welfare tracks happiness—but only when combined with the attempt to substitute some new and controversial cognitive meaning for the garden variety meaning associated with the word 'happy.'

So we have five different kinds of theory about welfare that might be indicated by 'eudaimonism.'

First, there are all the forms of Garden Variety Eudaimonism, according to which welfare tracks garden variety happiness. Most of the theories discussed in Part I of this book are forms of Garden Variety Eudaimonism.

Second, there is Aristotelian Eudaimonism, according to which welfare tracks whatever Aristotle meant by 'eudaimonia.' The details of Aristotle's view are all matters of somewhat technical controversy among Aristotle scholars. I have very little to say about it, aside from the fact that it appears to be a mistake to identify eudaimonia with any sort of garden variety happiness.

Third, there is Murphyesque Eudaimonism. This is a view suggested by Jeffrie Murphy. According to this view, it would be a good thing first to use 'happiness' to refer not to happiness, but to the property of being satisfied about having a harmoniously integrated personality. Then we could go on to say that welfare tracks happiness; but, if we say that, we must be sure to use 'happiness' in the proposed new sense. Hence, Murphyesque Eudaimonism is not equivalent to any form of Garden Variety Eudaimonism. So far as I can tell, it is not equivalent to any form of Aristotelian Eudaimonism either, but I would leave it to interested Aristotle scholars to determine that.

There is also Stevensonian Eudaimonism. Those who endorse forms of Stevensonian Eudaimonism introduce persuasive high redefinitions of 'happy.' They then go on to say 'welfare tracks happiness,' but they use 'happiness' in a manner consistent with their redefinition. Presumably, no form of Stevensonian Eudaimonism is equivalent to any form of Garden Variety Eudaimonism.

In this book I mean to be defending a specific form of the theory that welfare tracks garden variety happiness. When I speak here of 'happiness,' I mean the ordinary, somewhat obscure thing that the unperverted English-speaking person in the street means when he or she says that someone is 'happy.' Thus, my form of eudaimonism is a form of Garden Variety Eudaimonism. Since I think that Attitudinal Hedonism about Happiness provides the best account of the nature of garden variety happiness, my specific form of eudaimonism may be called 'Attitudinal Hedonistic Eudaimonism.' Attitudinal Hedonistic Eudaimonism is not equivalent to other forms of Garden Variety Eudaimonism; it is not equivalent to any form of Aristotelian Eudaimonism; it is certainly not equivalent to Murphyesque Eudaimonism.

I do not mean to use the word 'happy' in such a way that it expresses some novel concept while retaining its favorable connotations. I am trying to use the word in its ordinary vague sense, in which it expresses some familiar but perhaps hard to pin down psychological state. Attitudinal Hedonism about Happiness is my theory about the nature of the psychological state that a person must be in if the term is to apply correctly to him.

I should emphasize that I am not advocating any sort of linguistic revision. I am not proposing that we stop using the word 'happy' in the way we have been brought up to use it. Like so many other familiar words, it is vague. We use it in a variety of ritualized phrases wherein it seems to convey very little hard information. But it's not clear to me that this is problematic.

CHAPTER 9

The Problem of Inauthentic Happiness

9.1 *The Objection from Non-autonomous Values*

According to standard forms of eudaimonism, happiness is The Good. The happier you are, the better off you are. Assuming that levels of happiness and levels of welfare can be represented numerically, we can put the central elements of this form of eudaimonism simply: a person's level of welfare at a time is directly proportional to his or her level of happiness at that time; a person's welfare in life as a whole is directly proportional to the total amount of happiness he or she experiences in life as a whole. The welfare-good life is the happy life. I sometimes abbreviate all this by saying 'welfare tracks happiness.'

One persistent line of objection to eudaimonism concerns the possibility of "non-autonomous values." Suppose a person is leading what seems to be a pathetic life. But suppose he has been brainwashed or socialized into thinking that such a life is perfectly acceptable. Since the brainwashing has succeeded so well, he is satisfied with his life as a whole. Many popular theories of happiness then entail that he is happy. But it may seem doubtful that such a person is faring well. His welfare level seems to be lower than his happiness level. If the effects of the brainwashing were eliminated, and this fellow could evaluate his life with values that are more legitimately "his own," he would be far less happy about the kind of life he is living. This may seem to show that happiness based on non-autonomous values does not enhance welfare.

Perhaps the most well-known examples of non-autonomous value emerge in the discussion of a collection of cases mentioned by Amartya Sen and then later discussed by Wayne Sumner, Jennifer Hawkins, and others.[1] One of these cases involves a "dominated housewife"—we

---

[1] Sen's discussion can be found in Sen (1987: 45–6); Sumner's is in Sumner (1996: section 6.2); and Hawkins talks about it at length in Hawkins (2008).

can call her 'Bertha'—who has been socialized in such a way as to be unable to recognize that her life is demeaning and dehumanizing. Let's suppose that Bertha has been brought up in a traditional community where girls are taught that a woman's place is in the home. She has only the most rudimentary education. She is now married and has some children. She works long hours tending to the children and the home. Her husband is cold and demanding. Bertha is unaware of other possibilities. She doesn't realize that women in other countries have interesting careers, have the opportunity to travel and to have friends outside the home. When Bertha reflects on her situation, she doesn't see anything wrong. She thinks this is the way it's supposed to be. She is satisfied. Some theories of happiness—most obviously certain forms of Whole Life Satisfactionism—entail that Bertha is happy. If happiness directly translates into welfare, she counts as a person of relatively high welfare. Sumner remarks, 'The insidious aspect of social conditioning is precisely that the more thorough it is the less its victims are able to discern its influence on their judgements about their lives.'[2] Bertha is a case in point: in virtue of having these non-autonomous values, she thinks all is well with her life and so she is happy. This seems to illustrate a way in which welfare may fail to track happiness. Bertha is somewhat happy, but her welfare is low.

We can put the objection in this way:

1. If eudaimonism is true, then Bertha has high welfare.
2. But Bertha does not have high welfare.
3. Therefore, eudaimonism is not true.

In premise (1) 'eudaimonism' refers to the generalized form of eudaimonism that has already been introduced. It encompasses various theories according to which raw levels of happiness are assumed to translate directly into corresponding levels of well-being. Since Bertha is reasonably well satisfied with her life, she may be said to be reasonably happy.[3] Eudaimonism then implies that she has reasonably high welfare.

Since Bertha's values have been imposed upon her by a pernicious system of social indoctrination, and since she is leading a constrained, dominated, and exhausting life, she in fact does not have high welfare. Things are not going as well for Bertha as she thinks they are. So we have premise (2) and a serious problem for eudaimonism.

---

[2] Sumner (1996: 163).

[3] At least this is the case according to Sumner's theory of happiness. Later, in section 9.4, I will discuss the implications of the objection for the theory about the nature of happiness that I have been defending, Attitudinal Hedonism about Happiness.

9.2 *Sumner on Authenticity*

In *Welfare, Happiness, and Ethics,* Wayne Sumner describes an objection like this as 'surely the main reason for questioning the adequacy of any subjective theory of welfare, whatever its constituent ingredients.'[4] The fact that there are cases in which a person's happiness depends essentially on values that have been adopted as a result of brainwashing or other social conditioning shows, he suggests, that we cannot simply equate happiness with welfare.

In order to deal with this objection, Sumner introduces the idea of autonomous happiness. He goes on to suggest that, if we understand autonomous happiness correctly, we can maintain a revised form of eudaimonism according to which welfare tracks *autonomous happiness.*[5] On the revised theory, a person's happiness counts fully toward her welfare only if that happiness is autonomous. Since Bertha's happiness is not autonomous, the revised theory is not committed to the conclusion that she has high welfare. Thus, it is possible to reject the first premise in the objection as formulated here. But then we must provide a characterization of autonomous happiness.

It is not easy to say precisely what conditions must be satisfied for someone's happiness to be autonomous. One idea invokes second-order satisfaction with first-order satisfactions. So, if I am satisfied with my life, and I am satisfied with the fact that I am thus satisfied, then my satisfaction is deemed to be autonomous.[6] According to another idea, we determine if someone's satisfaction is autonomous by tracing its history. If it emerged in a natural way—without meddling by brainwashers, pernicious systems of socialization, and so on—then it is autonomous.[7] Sumner points out some difficulties with each of these approaches, but in the end seems to maintain that we have a sufficiently firm grasp on the concept of autonomy. The fundamental thing, as he sees it, is this:

Roughly speaking, an autonomy-preserving socialization process will be one which does not erode the individual's capacity for critical assessment of his values, including the very values promoted by that process itself.[8]

---

[4] Sumner (1996: 162).

[5] I am simplifying here. In fact, Sumner adds two conditions. One is the autonomy condition that I focus on in this chapter. The other is an information condition that I will not be discussing here. When both of these conditions are satisfied, the subject is said to have authentic happiness.

[6] Sumner (1996: 168).   [7] Ibid. 169–70.   [8] Ibid. 170.

My satisfaction with my life counts full credit toward my welfare only when it is "genuinely mine" rather than something that has been imposed upon me.

When someone's happiness is based on values that are not autonomously her own, then that happiness is deemed "inauthentic." And when happiness is inauthentic, its value is "discounted."[9] Sumner does not state a principle explaining the rate of discount. According to a reasonable extension of the theory, however, we can say that each subject's happiness can be evaluated for its degree of authenticity. To the extent that it is based on non-autonomously accepted values, it is inauthentic. This yields the discount rate. As a result, if a person is very happy (e.g., to degree +100) but her happiness is significantly inauthentic (e.g., 50 percent), this happiness will enhance welfare by only +50 points. If the happiness is totally inauthentic, it will yield no increase in welfare.

This suggests a way in which the case involving Bertha can be solved. We can grant that Bertha is quite happy. But now we can maintain, appealing to the revised theory, that her welfare is low or even zero. The precise welfare value of Bertha's life will depend upon the details of the case. If her values are largely non-autonomous, then the welfare-value of her happiness will have to be correspondingly discounted. Perhaps the theory will imply that Bertha has a welfare level of zero. So the revised theory yields results consistent with our evaluative intuitions about the case.

9.3   *Problems for Sumner's Solution*

Sumner's idea is imaginative, but his presentation is in several ways obscure and incomplete.[10] One problem concerns unhappiness. Sumner discusses this only briefly. He says:

In explicating the happiness theory we have focused almost exclusively on welfare rather than illfare, happiness rather than unhappiness. But the analogous treatment of these latter notions is straightforward, resting as it does on the negative counterparts of personal satisfaction and endorsement. A life is therefore going badly for someone when she (authentically) experiences its conditions as unsatisfying or unfulfilling, or disclaims or disowns them.[11]

---

[9] The precise details of Sumner's view remain somewhat obscure. He mentions discounting in a related context on p. 166.

[10] For a detailed discussion and a different line of objection to Sumner's view, see Hawkins (2008).   [11] Sumner (1996: 177).

It appears, then, that just as inauthentic happiness has a discounted effect on positive welfare, inauthentic unhappiness has a discounted effect on negative welfare. Let us look more closely into this.

Suppose Clarence has the misfortune of being sent to a fanatical religious school. Suppose he is subjected to long-term brainwashing that eventually instills some rigid values. Unfortunately, the values are so demanding that no one would ever be able to behave in such a way as to satisfy them. At the end of this process, when he contemplates his life, Clarence is seriously dissatisfied. He is dissatisfied because he recognizes that his own life does not match up to the impossibly stringent values that he now accepts. Since Clarence is seriously dissatisfied with his life, he is unhappy according to Sumner's theory of happiness. What shall we say about his welfare?

Presumably, the extended version of Sumner's theory of welfare says that we should discount the evaluative effect of Clarence's unhappiness. Since his values are not autonomous, Clarence's unhappiness is not authentic. If Clarence had not been subjected to the brainwashing, he would not have had those values. He would have been satisfied with his life. Therefore, we can conclude that his welfare is not seriously affected. He's not as badly off as he thinks he is.

But this assessment seems to me to be exactly wrong. As I see it, Clarence's welfare level is very low. In the first place, he is dissatisfied with his life. He seems to be an unhappy person. What makes his situation especially regrettable is that he is dissatisfied with his life largely because he sees that it fails to match up with some values; but the values in question are not even his own autonomously chosen values. Clarence seems to be a victim of two misfortunes. First, his fanatical religious training imposed some foreign values on him. Second, after he bought into those values, he became dissatisfied with his own life, which would (absent the meddling) have seemed OK to him. Clarence seems therefore to have suffered a serious loss of welfare. So I think that it's a mistake to *discount* the effect of non-autonomous values on unhappiness. If anything, the fact that the values were implanted in him by something akin to brainwashing seems to make things even worse.

Another problem with Sumner's theory arises in the case of a person who is fully satisfied with his life and thus counts as happy on Sumner's theory of happiness. Suppose a child, Aldo, is born with an innate predisposition to have values that would be impossible to satisfy.[12] Left to his own devices, Aldo would always see the glass as

---

[12] Empirical evidence strongly supports the idea that this supposition is plausible. A person with a certain sort of obsessive-compulsive disorder might be relevantly like Aldo.

half empty. Nothing would be good enough for him. If he were to get an A− on a test, he would consider it an unacceptable failure. If he were to take third place in an athletic contest, he would be dismayed. Suppose his parents are made aware of all this and take steps to ensure that their child develops a somewhat more serene outlook. Aldo is sent to happiness classes where he is trained to be more accepting of things as they are. Day after day he is forced to recite the Serenity Prayer:

God grant me the serenity to accept the things I cannot change; the courage to change the things I can; and the wisdom to know the difference. (Reinhold Niebuhr)

Suppose the training succeeds and Aldo becomes more satisfied with things as they are. When he reflects on his life, he no longer has any complaint about what he sees. The glass now seems to be half full. When he gets an A− or a third place finish, he is satisfied. Aldo judges that things are going well in all domains. Sumner's theory implies that he is happy. In this case, unless there are some important unstated other factors, I would agree. Aldo does seem to be happy.[13]

Yet, since Aldo's satisfaction with his life is based upon non-autonomously accepted values, and this satisfaction would extinguish if he were to assess his life in light of his own "natural" values, the happiness is declared to be non-authentic. The discount principle that I have suggested for Sumner then implies that the welfare value of Aldo's happiness must be discounted. Aldo is smiling and happy; he judges that his life is going well; he bases his judgment on a set of reasonable values; but the theory implies that he is not as well-off as he thinks he is. Aldo's welfare is lower because his values have been imposed upon him by a system of socialization.

This result seems to me to be implausible. I think Aldo is happy and that his welfare is high. I cannot see why the welfare value of his happiness should be discounted at all. The fact that the operative values in this case are inauthentic seems to me to make no difference. The inauthentic values seem to me to be in some ways better than the natural, authentic values that Aldo was born with. I would give Aldo's happiness full credit toward his welfare.

The examples of Aldo and Clarence may seem to be somewhat frivolous, but I think each of them illustrates an important sort of real-life case. The example of Aldo generalizes straightforwardly. Consider

---

[13] My explanation of Aldo's happiness would be different from Sumner's. I would explain it by appeal to Attitudinal Hedonism about Happiness rather than by appeal to Sumner's theory. More about this later.

any person who by nature has some self-destructive values. We may think here of the natural-born bully, or masochist, or irresponsible risk-taker. Any such person might be better off as a result of a well-conceived course of reprogramming. After undergoing such a course, the subject might have values that are not autonomously his own. But the new and non-autonomous values might be much better in prudential terms for the subject. The subject may gain in happiness when things happen that are in accord with the new values. It seems clear that we do *not* want to discount the welfare value of the happiness enjoyed by such a person.

The example of Clarence generalizes in a similar way. We may think of any youngster who is coercively brainwashed into accepting values that are not authentically his own. Where those values are overly stringent, having them may contribute to the child's unhappiness. I see no plausibility to the notion that such unhappiness has only a discounted impact on the subject's welfare. If anything, the impact seems multiplied.

9.4 *Relevance to My Form of Eudaimonism*

These considerations seem to show that the adjustment for non-autonomously chosen values does not help the imagined extended version of Sumner's theory to generate plausible welfare rankings. While it may seem to offer some improvement in the evaluation of the case involving Bertha, it generates unacceptable results in the cases involving Clarence and Aldo.

The patient reader may be wondering why I am bothering to go into such detail about this, since the whole discussion is framed in terms of Sumner's theory of happiness. As I made clear in Chapter 5, I don't think Sumner's theory—or any other form of Whole Life Satisfactionism—is a plausible theory of happiness. So it may be hard to see what point there could be in showing that an extended version of that theory does not provide the basis for a plausible theory of welfare.

I think, however, that considerations analogous to the ones that originally drove Sumner to reject the idea that welfare tracks raw happiness as he conceived it may also be thought to provide me with good reason to reject the idea that welfare tracks raw happiness as I conceive it. In other words, reflection on the same set of cases might be thought to show that there is something wrong with identifying a person's welfare level with her level of happiness as determined by Attitudinal Hedonism about Happiness. If that were the case, then my form of eudaimonism—Attitudinal Hedonistic Eudaimonism —would also stand in need of some modification. Let us look into this possibility.

Suppose that happiness is fundamentally a matter of taking attitudinal pleasure in things. Suppose that a person's momentary happiness level at a time is determined by summing the extent to which she takes intrinsic occurrent attitudinal pleasure and displeasure in things at that time, as explained in Chapter 6. According to my form of eudaimonism, a person's welfare level is directly determined by the amount of happiness (thus calculated) that the person enjoys. What then shall we say about the person who takes pleasure in things but only because of non-autonomous values?

Recall the dominated housewife, Bertha. She was satisfied with her life, but only because a lengthy course of socialization had induced her to accept some values that she otherwise would not have accepted. Let us agree on some further stipulations about Bertha's pleasures and displeasures. Suppose that she has managed to find some things to enjoy. Under the circumstances, these will be limited and (to the outside observer) trivial. Perhaps Bertha takes pleasure in the fact that she has done a good job of washing the dishes and ironing the children's clothing; perhaps she takes pleasure in the fact that she has prepared some acceptable meals in spite of her limited budget; perhaps she takes some small pleasure in the "fact" that she is performing her wifely duties.

Suppose that over the whole period of her marriage, Bertha continues to take pleasure in these "small mercies." Suppose also that she shrugs off the various indignities that befall her. She doesn't take much displeasure in these things. As a result of all this, she manages to have a positive balance of attitudinal pleasure over displeasure. That is, the total amount of intrinsic attitudinal pleasure that she takes in things during this period of time is greater than the total amount of intrinsic attitudinal displeasure that she takes in things. So my theory of happiness entails that Bertha is happy during her marriage. Attitudinal Hedonistic Eudaimonism (AHE) then entails that she has positive welfare during this stretch of time. This provides the basis for a revised version of the objection:

1. If AHE is true, then Bertha has positive welfare during her marriage.
2. But she doesn't.
3. Therefore, AHE is not true.

Bertha gets a positive score on my scale of happiness; but she seems to have a negative score on the welfare scale. So welfare apparently does not track happiness as I construe it.

Someone might at this point encourage me to consider a revision of Attitudinal Hedonistic Eudaimonism.[14] Note that Bertha's pleasures are in their own way inauthentic. She is pleased about such things as her success in washing, ironing, changing diapers, and cooking. But her pleasure in these things depends in large measure on the fact that she has been coercively socialized. If she had been given the freedom to develop her own tastes autonomously, she would not have taken the same amount of pleasure in these things. Thus, we can say that her pleasures are inauthentic. It might then seem a good idea to discount the value of Bertha's pleasures so as to reflect their inauthenticity. We might say that what really counts toward a person's welfare is pleasure taken in things, but only to the extent that that pleasure is authentic. In this way we could say that her case does not constitute a counterexample to a suitably revised form of Attitudinal Hedonistic Eudaimonism.

I think it would be a mistake to revise AHE in the suggested way. The problems are familiar. In some cases inauthentic pleasures seem just as welfare-enhancing as authentic ones. Recall the example involving Aldo, who was born with a natural tendency to have unattainable values. After several rounds of serenity training, he began to take pleasure in things that he would not otherwise have enjoyed. Thus, the pleasure that Aldo takes in things such as his A− and third-place finish is at least somewhat inauthentic. But I see no reason to discount the welfare value of Aldo's happiness. It seems to me that he is better off as a result of taking pleasure in such things as his pretty good grades and his pretty good athletic achievements. Though his happiness is inauthentic, it seems to me to yield a 100 percent enhancement of his welfare.

Similarly in the case of inauthentic unhappiness. Suppose that as a result of brainwashing Clarence now takes displeasure in lots of things that he otherwise would have found enjoyable. His displeasure is inauthentic. Yet it seems to me that there is no plausibility to the idea that we should discount the disvalue of his displeasure. Surely his welfare is adversely affected in full proportion to the magnitude of his displeasure. There is no need in this case to shave points.

So this leaves us with both the original form of Attitudinal Hedonistic Eudaimonism and our intuitions concerning the case involving Bertha. Something has to give. What will it be?

---

[14]   In fact, some friends, including Noah Lemos, actually did make this suggestion.

I want to pursue the idea that the welfare evaluation yielded by Attitudinal Hedonistic Eudaimonism in the case of Bertha may be acceptable after all. This may seem surprisingly counterintuitive. I'd like to make five comments that may help to make this judgment seem a bit less hard to swallow.

i. The first point is that the example of Bertha is psychologically implausible. It is doubtful that the socialization process that Bertha endured could have been so perfectly and painlessly successful. I suspect that any real-life Bertha would sometimes feel pangs of disappointment, worrying that something (though she may not be able to put her finger on it) is wrong. If her life is so hard, then surely there must be lots of things in which she takes displeasure. Isn't she sometimes displeased about feelings of exhaustion, or boredom, or meaninglessness? If her husband is abusive, then doesn't she sometimes take displeasure in his nasty behavior? Thus, even if she is convinced that she is living an excellent life, if the life is (as stipulated) demeaning and demoralizing, then there must be times when she feels demeaned and demoralized. Surely on these occasions there are things she finds unpleasant. And if there are things she finds unpleasant, her net balance of attitudinal pleasure over displeasure will not be high. It may even be negative. In this case, Attitudinal Hedonism about Happiness entails that she is not happy, or at least not very happy. Attitudinal Hedonistic Eudaimonism implies that her life is not very high in welfare.

These reflections point up an important difference between Sumner's theory of happiness and the theory I have been advocating. If we accept Sumner's theory, then there is fundamentally only one question that we need to answer in order to determine whether Bertha is happy: that is the question whether Bertha judges that her life is satisfactory. We have stipulated that Bertha does make this judgment and so Sumner is stuck with the conclusion that she is happy. But on my theory of happiness there are lots of things that bear on Bertha's level of happiness. These are all the various episodes of intrinsic attitudinal pleasure and displeasure that she takes in things. It is surely possible—even likely—that a person in Bertha's situation would take displeasure in lots of things. In that case, my theory of happiness could yield the result that she is not happy. Then my theory of welfare would yield the more intuitive judgment that things are not going well for Bertha. All of this is consistent with the stipulation that she steadfastly maintains that she is satisfied with her life.

On the other hand, the critic may simply insist that we stick to the example as originally stated. Let it be stipulated that, as a result of her indoctrination, Bertha actually has come to enjoy doing dishes, ironing clothes, and changing diapers. Let it be stipulated that she does not harbor deep-seated disappointment or regret. Let it be stipulated that the indoctrination has been so strangely successful that Bertha is genuinely pleased about the things that happen to her (things that a non-indoctrinated person would find unpleasant). Attitudinal Hedonistic Eudaimonism then really does imply that Bertha is faring well.

In this case, my intuitions about the example become unstable. I begin to think that it is no longer so clear that Bertha has a life of low or negative welfare. I acknowledge, of course, that there are things wrong with her life. (I discuss some of these below in point iii.) But if she really does take pleasure in the things that happen to her, and rarely takes displeasure in them, then it becomes less clear that her welfare is negative.

ii. Second, we must be sensitive to the possibility of a certain common error when reflecting on cases such as the case of Bertha. When someone tells us a story about a possible life, and asks us to estimate the welfare level of that life, we may be inclined to think about whether we would be willing to swap lives with the character in the story. Thus, when you heard the story of Bertha you may have felt an immediate repugnance. Perhaps you thought that you would never want to swap lives with her. You would not want to wake up some morning finding yourself in the demeaning and dehumanizing situation that Bertha endures. And so you may have concluded that her life is low in welfare.

However, the question here is not whether *you* would want to live her life; the question is whether her life is good in itself for *her*. The difference is important. You know lots of things about Bertha's life that she does not know. You know that her life is demeaning and dehumanizing; she does not know these things. In fact, she thinks it is a perfectly satisfactory life for a woman like her. Furthermore, you know that there are many women who live richer and more fulfilling lives. Bertha is in the dark about that too. Furthermore, you know that if Bertha had more relevant information, she would no longer take pleasure in her daily activities, whereas Bertha thinks she already has all the relevant information. Furthermore, your values may be different from Bertha's. There are many activities and experiences that

Bertha finds enjoyable; perhaps you would not find those activities and experiences enjoyable. For all these reasons, you might not want to live her life.

We may agree that if you were to find yourself embedded in Bertha's life, you would be dismayed. You would experience a lot of attitudinal displeasure and very little pleasure. You would be unhappy. As a result, your welfare would be low. However, it does not follow that Bertha's welfare is low. Keep in mind that her tastes are different from yours. She takes pleasure in lots of things that you would find boring. But she does not find them boring. She enjoys doing them. She is happy.

So my second point is simple: you mustn't allow your evaluation of Bertha's life to be contaminated by thoughts about how disappointed you would be if you were forced to swap lives with her. When you try to evaluate her life, you must not think of it as a possible continuation of your life—a life that is already full of a certain collection of beliefs and values; a life that incorporates *your* psychology, including facts about what you enjoy and what you don't enjoy. You must focus on the life of Bertha as stipulated. When you do this correctly, I think you will find it a bit easier to see why someone might want to say that the life is not really so bad *for her* after all.

iii. Third, I think it's important that we be clear on the sort of evaluation we are making. We are considering a theory about welfare. The theory is intended to regiment our thoughts about this one crucial sort of value—well-being, or prudential value for the person affected. We are not engaging here in reflections on other categories of value. So, if in the end the case is described in such a way that we have to say that Bertha is happy, then the theory of welfare will say that her life is going well for her in terms of welfare. It is consistent with this to say that Bertha is doing very badly with respect to other scales of evaluation. For example, it remains true that she is doing poorly with respect to such values as freedom, knowledge, creativity, and so forth. Her life is hardly a stand-out with respect to aesthetic value. If we are looking for an example of a human being who develops and manifests all of her distinctively human excellences, Bertha is not the ideal candidate. So there are many scales on which a life can be weighed, and Bertha makes a poor showing in most of them. But none of this directly affects welfare itself.

iv. In addition, I think it's important that we acknowledge certain comparative evaluations. Failure to recognize these may lead to another sort of confusion.

Given a collection of assumptions about the amounts of pleasure and displeasure that Bertha takes in things, Attitudinal Hedonism about Happiness may be forced to admit that Bertha is happy. But it is consistent with this to insist in addition that she would have been a lot happier if she had not been brainwashed and indoctrinated. Suppose it had been possible for Bertha to escape her traditional community as an infant. Suppose she could have moved to a different place where she could be raised in a community with more progressive values. Suppose she could have enjoyed freedom to choose her style of life, and the opportunity to develop her talents, and the chance to think for herself. It is reasonable to suppose that if she had taken advantage of such an opportunity, she would have taken pleasure in a much richer variety of interesting things. Surely such pleasures would have been deeper and more long-lasting than the pleasures she is stipulated to enjoy in her constrained life. Attitudinal Hedonism about Happiness then implies that she would have been much happier under these other circumstances. Attitudinal Hedonistic Eudaimonism then implies that she would have been much better off. This seems right. Thus, when I suggest that Bertha might have positive welfare, I am not saying that she is living the ideal life. My claim is consistent with the (plausible) notion that she would have been far better off if she had not been subjected to brainwashing, but had instead been permitted to grow and develop autonomously in a community where that sort of thing is the norm.

But suppose that Bertha was definitely stuck in her traditional community. Suppose there was no way out. Then another comparison becomes apt. Would she have been better off if she had not been socialized into the values of her community? Would it have been better for her if she had been permitted to develop her own values while embedded in her social context? I think it very well may be that she would have been much less happy as a rebel. This would be especially obvious if nonconformists are treated harshly in her community. Perhaps she would have been truly miserable if she had failed to blend in. It's better from the perspective of personal well-being to be a happy, well-adjusted member of a traditional community (in spite of the obvious drawbacks) than an unhappy, rebellious outcast stuck in that same community. (Of course, when we look at the comparison from another perspective, we may get a different ranking. It may be better for future generations of the traditional community for Bertha to be an iconoclast. Then maybe girls of the future will have happier lives. Unfortunately, this sort of rebellion against traditional values very likely will come at a cost in welfare to the rebel.)

v. Finally, I think it's important that we take proper account of any costs that may have been involved in the brainwashing itself. We are imagining that Bertha was raised in a traditional community where girls are taught that a woman's place is in the home. We are imagining that the community's values are not natural for Bertha. Were it not for the brainwashing, she would not have adopted them. So this raises a question about the displeasures that Bertha experienced during her period of indoctrination. Surely she must have found it difficult. Surely it must have been painful for her to have her natural inclinations suppressed. So we can assume that there were hedonic costs involved in getting Bertha to the point where she could be satisfied with her life as a whole.

Attitudinal Hedonism about Happiness does not ignore those costs. They must figure in the calculation of Bertha's happiness level for her life as a whole as well as for any interval of time that includes the period of her socialization. As a result, my theory will yield a somewhat reduced total happiness level for any such period. Bertha's life as a whole is less happy as a result of the fact that she endured some rough socialization in her childhood. And, as a result of that, her lifetime welfare level is proportionally reduced.

This may provide an answer to a further question about my view. I have claimed that, given some unlikely but conceivable assumptions about her case, Bertha might count on my view as a person who has positive welfare. The incredulous reader may be wondering whether I am advocating a return to a more traditional social arrangement in which girls are brought up to be happy with the things that Bertha enjoys. The answer, which should be obvious, is that I am not advocating any such thing. There are many reasons. First and foremost is the fact that on my view girls (and everyone else) would be a lot happier and lot better off if they are raised to value freedom, creativity, and respect. Second, as I have been suggesting, there would be substantial hedonic costs involved in trying to create or maintain a system like the one in which Bertha was raised. Third, there are many other values at stake. Even if it were possible to enhance welfare by brainwashing a lot of people, doing so would adversely affect them in many other ways. Just as a hint: the brainwashed girls would grow up to be women who make no significant contributions to welfare beyond the contributions they make in their homes. What a loss! Think of all the good these people could do if they were given the opportunities they deserve.

So, in the end, it seems to me that the example involving the "demeaned and dehumanized housewife" may constitute a difficulty for Sumner's theory of happiness when it is combined with the simple view that welfare tracks happiness. Perhaps he was right to seek adjustments to his theory in order to deal with it. However, as I tried to show, the adjustment he suggested seems not to work. The case of Bertha seems to me to be significantly less problematic for my theory of happiness. I see no problem in accepting the claim that a person can be happy in spite of socialized values. Whether such a person has positive welfare is another question. I am prepared to say that, given a lot of assumptions about the case (some of which seem to me to be unrealistic), a person can be happy and faring well even though their happiness is inauthentic. My motto is this: 'it's better to have inauthentic happiness than no happiness at all.'

CHAPTER 10

—————

Disgusting Happiness

10.1 *A Problem for Eudaimonism of all Forms*

Since ancient times, philosophers have been attracted to the idea that happiness is The Good. 'The good life is the happy life' has a sort of intuitive ring to it; it seems almost analytic. 'I wish you a Happy New Year' seems to say about the same thing as 'I hope things go well for you in the New Year.' Yet skeptics have been quick to raise troubling doubts based upon an assortment of happy but disgusting characters. 'What about the happy sadist? What about the happy hit man? What about the happy pedophile? Are you claiming that these people are leading the good life? Is this the life eudaimonists advocate and defend? If so, then so much the worse for eudaimonism.'

Steven Cahn reminds us of a happy but disgusting character from the Woody Allen movie, *Crimes and Misdemeanors*.[1] This is Judah Rosenthal, a prominent, wealthy, respected ophthalmologist in New York (played by Martin Landau). Judah seems to have it all: a beautiful loving wife and children; a successful and very lucrative career; good health; the admiration and respect of a large crowd of friends, relatives, colleagues, and patients. He also has a slightly deranged girlfriend (played by Anjelica Huston). The girlfriend is threatening to reveal their affair as well as some information about Judah's shady dealings with money that had been contributed to a fund for the creation of a new wing on the hospital. Judah is in a tight spot. He turns to his brother, who has mob connections. The brother arranges to have the problematic girlfriend "go away." She is efficiently murdered by a hit man brought up from New Orleans. At first, Judah feels pretty guilty about this. After all, he has conspired to have an innocent person killed; indeed, an innocent person who was creating problems only because she loved him too passionately. But after a while Judah

—————

[1] Cahn discusses this in 'A Challenge to Morality,' in Cahn and Vitrano (2008: 265).

manages to overcome his guilt. He returns to his life of health, wealth, achievement, respect, and—apparently—happiness.

Judah is presented as a kind of moral monster. He deceives his wife and children; he misleads his girlfriend, suggesting to her that he may someday leave his wife so that he and the girlfriend can be together; he engages in some sort of financial hanky-panky with the hospital money; he conspires with his brother to have the girlfriend murdered. At the end, after an apparently brief period during which he feels some remorse, he gets over it. The suggestion is that he lives happily ever after.

The problem for eudaimonism should be obvious. Judah is presented as an outstandingly happy person—at least outside of the brief period during which he feels some pangs of guilt. Eudaimonism then implies that he is leading the good life. Yet he is a moral monster. His life seems far from ideal. This is not the life we would want for a loved one, or for ourselves. So eudaimonism seems to evaluate the life incorrectly.

To facilitate discussion, it will be helpful to have a simplified version of the problem at hand:

1. If eudaimonism is true, then Judah led a good life.
2. Judah did not lead a good life.
3. Therefore, eudaimonism is not true.

Premise (1) is based on one of the fundamental themes of the movie: Judah Rosenthal was a very happy person. According to the story, Judah had a successful medical career, a lovely wife, the respect of his colleagues and children, and the loving gratitude of many patients and acquaintances. He is shown smiling and satisfied on many occasions, and only briefly troubled. In one scene he is shown jogging joyously on the beach with his girlfriend. He seems to exemplify our familiar, vague concept of happiness.

It may be worth mentioning that he also seems to be a positive instance of most of the popular philosophical and psychological concepts of happiness that have been discussed here. If sensory hedonism about happiness is true, then Judah is happy. This follows from the stipulated facts that he enjoys expensive and tasty food and drink every day; that he has a vigorous and apparently enjoyable sex life with two women; that he is fit and healthy; and so on. There is no evidence in the movie that Judah suffers from any painful condition. No psoriatic arthritis for him.

If Kahneman's theory of happiness is true, then Judah would seem to be very happy at many times, and at least moderately happy during most of the rest. According to Kahneman's theory, a person's momentary happiness level is equal to the strength of his desire for his present experience to continue. While he is eating a tasty dinner and drinking expensive wine, Judah presumably wants his experience to continue. While he is jogging on the beach with the Anjelica Huston character, he presumably wants his experience to continue. He says he could continue jogging for miles. While he is receiving the accolades of his adoring public at a dinner in his honor, he presumably wants his experience to continue. If he had a happiness-level recording device attached to his belt, and the buzzer sounded at various times through his typical day, he would probably be inclined to input some relatively high numbers. (Although, of course, if the buzzer went off while he was engaged in sexual intimacies with his girlfriend, he might not hear it; or, if he happened to hear it, he might be annoyed.)

If Wayne Davis's theory of happiness is true, then Judah would seem to be a very happy person. He has many desires: for wealth, respect, good food and drink, a vigorous sex life, health, and so on. He seems to get just about everything he wants. In one of the central components of the plot, he develops a strong desire to have the Anjelica Huston character murdered. This desire is quickly and efficiently satisfied. Thus, it seems that if we calculate happiness according to Davis's form of local preferentism, we must conclude that Judah is very happy. Very many of his strongest desires are satisfied; very few are frustrated for long.

Some of the more plausible Whole Life Satisfactionist theories of happiness seem to yield the same result, though in this case we are required to make some assumptions about Judah's psychology that are not explicitly mentioned. Judging from the things he says and does at the end of the movie, it appears that he is satisfied with his life as a whole. It is reasonable to assume that if he were to reflect on his life and his ideals, he would say that his life matched up quite well with his ideals. After all, his main ideals seem to involve large doses of health, wealth, fame, respect, good food and drink, and sex. He gets all of these.

Suppose that the testers from Eurobarometer were to interview Judah. Suppose they were to ask him the standard questions about his level of satisfaction with specified domains of his life. For example, suppose they were to ask him whether he is satisfied with his employment, income, housing, leisure-time activities, health, and marriage. It is reasonable to suppose that Judah would report a very high score in every category—although for a short period of time he might say that there is considerable disappointment in the "leisure-time activities" domain. So he would be categorized as "very happy" by those who make use of any such testing instrument.

The attitudinal hedonism about happiness that I presented in Chapter 6 has the same implication. It appears that Judah takes pleasure in many things—he seems to be pleased that he is so wealthy and famous; he seems to be pleased that he has such a rich and varied sex life; he seems to be pleased that his brother knows people who will be able to rub out his girlfriend. Although he is displeased about some things in the movie, his displeasure doesn't last long. So my theory of happiness, together with the stipulated facts of the story, entails that Judah is very happy.

Thus, it seems that our common-sense view about happiness, as well as virtually every popular philosophical or psychological theory of happiness, implies that Judah is happy. Since in its simplest form eudaimonism says that the good life is the happy life, it would follow that Judah is living the good life. Thus we have premise (1).

As I mentioned in Chapter 9, Wayne Sumner does not defend the simple view that welfare is determined by raw happiness levels. On his view, welfare is determined by *authentic* happiness. Someone's happiness counts as authentic only if it satisfies both an information condition and an autonomy condition. Suppose a person is satisfied with his life as a whole. He passes the information test provided that the provision of further relevant factual information about his life would not induce him to stop being satisfied. He passes the autonomy test if the values by appeal to which he evaluates his life are "genuinely his own." I see no reason to suppose that Judah's satisfaction would fail either of these tests. He seems to know what he is doing; he seems to be autonomously and by nature a thoroughly rotten person. Thus, Judah is not only happy, but *authentically* so. Unless I have misunderstood Sumner's theory, or the example involving Judah, Sumner's theory yields the result that Judah is authentically happy and therefore enjoying high welfare.[2] Thus, even on a more sophisticated form of eudaimonism, Judah's life is declared to be good in itself for him.

According to the second premise of the argument, the life evaluation generated in this case by eudaimonism is incorrect. In fact, it is claimed, Judah's life is not so good. But here we must be careful. As I tried to explain in 8.2, there are several different scales of value on which a life can be weighed. Two are especially important here. Sometimes when we speak of a "good life" we have in mind the life of moral excellence.

---

[2] Similar results follow for the version of Whole Life Satisfactionism defended by Brandt. I leave it to the interested reader to work out the details.

On other occasions, we have in mind the life of high prudential value, or high welfare. If we think of the good life in the first way, then to say that Judah did not lead a good life is to say that Judah was not a man of virtue, or moral rectitude. If we understand premise (2) in this way, it seems true.

But, of course, if we understand premise (2) in this way, the argument becomes equivocal. This can be made clear by making our two uses of 'good' more explicit.

1. If eudaimonism is true, then Judah led a *welfare-good* life.
2. Judah did not lead a *morally good* life.
3. Therefore, eudaimonism is not true.

So interpreted, the argument is not valid. Nor would it help to replace 'welfare-good' with 'morally good' in premise (1). This would yield a valid argument:

1. If eudaimonism is true, then Judah led a morally good life.
2. Judah did not lead a morally good life.
3. Therefore, eudaimonism is not true.

On this reading, premise (2) is true, but there is no basis for premise (1) so interpreted. Eudaimonism is not a theory about what makes a person's life *morally* good; it is a theory about what makes a person's life *welfare-good*, or *good in itself for that person*.

So, to make the point of the actual objection somewhat less ambiguous, we can restate the argument this way:

1. If eudaimonism is true, then Judah led a welfare-good life.
2. Judah did not lead a welfare-good life.
3. Therefore, eudaimonism is not true.

Thus, we use 'good life' in both premises to indicate the life of positive welfare, or prudential value. The relevant concept is the concept of the life good in itself for the one who leads it. Eudaimonism is the view that welfare tracks happiness; since Judah was happy, eudaimonism *does* entail that Judah's life was welfare-good. So premise (1) is true.

The defense of premise (2) is troublesome. It's difficult to think of any decisive reasoning that would show beyond question that Judah's life in fact does not have high welfare value for him. If we focus on Judah's satisfied smile in the final scenes of the movie, we may think that his life has high welfare value. If we focus on his disgusting behavior we may think that his life has much lower value. Perhaps in the end we will just have to contemplate Judah's life and see if we can "intuit" its welfare value. But there are some considerations that are at least suggestive.

Earlier I mentioned the "Crib Test." We are supposed to imagine a loving parent looking into the crib where her newborn baby is sleeping. We are supposed to imagine that the parent is filled with affection for her child. Something is welfare-good for the child if and only if the parent could hope for it for the child. We can apply the test to the present case. Would such a parent want her child to end up living the life of Judah Rosenthal? If the life is worthless (as premise (2) says) then no mother could want such a life for her child.

Unfortunately, I think I can imagine a mother who wants nothing more than that her child should get a life in which he enjoys large amounts of wealth, health, fame, loving personal relationships, and vigorous sex. If the mother were a morally bankrupt person, and she thought that getting these things would make her child very happy, I can't see why it would be impossible for her, motivated by love for the child, to want the child to have them. Indeed, if the mother were truly amoral, she might want the child to have these things even if she realized that he would have to conspire to have an inconvenient girlfriend rubbed out. If such a mother is possible, then an application of the Crib Test yields the result that Judah's life might be of high welfare value—it all depends upon who is looking into the crib. In this case, premise (2) is false and we have no refutation of eudaimonism.

Suppose it can be shown that no loving parent would want her child to have a life like Judah's. It is not clear that this would show that Judah's life is low in welfare value. The problem is that it is possible that the parents' preferences for their children might be based on moral considerations rather than strictly on considerations of welfare. Maybe loving parents would recognize that Judah's life is high in welfare, but they would think that the cost in immorality is just too great. Maybe they would think that it would take a *huge* amount of welfare to make it all things considered worthwhile to live such a morally despicable life.

As a result, it seems to me that the application of the Crib Test in this case is not helpful. Maybe a loving parent could want the life of Judah for her child; maybe not. In either case, it is not clear that this would establish anything about the welfare value of Judah's life. Appeal to the Crib Test does not help either to establish or to refute (2).

Recall the "Swap Test" that was suggested by Richard Taylor in his *Virtue Ethics*. Taylor suggested that this test would reveal whether some life has positive welfare value. In its application to the present case, we would be asked to consider whether we would be willing to "be just like" Judah, if we could thereby get to enjoy the same pleasurable experiences that Judah enjoys. If we would not be willing to swap lives with Judah, this allegedly shows that his life does not have high welfare value.

I suppose that many normal people would not want to swap lives with Judah Rosenthal. I consider myself to be fairly normal, and I would not want to swap lives with him. This suggests that premise (2) is true.

However, I am not convinced that Taylor's Swap Test is a reliable test of welfare. It seems to me that there could be many explanations for the fact (if it is a fact) that normal people would not want to swap lives with Judah Rosenthal. In my own case, there is a pretty simple explanation: I am already a pretty happy person. It's not clear that if I swapped lives with him, I would be any better off. Another perhaps deeper explanation is this: I would not want to swap lives with him because I think he is leading a morally repugnant life. Even if that life were higher in welfare than mine, still I would not want that life because I care about being a decent person. Yet another reason for preferring not to swap lives with Judah Rosenthal is this: I have bonded with my wife, daughter, friends, and dog. I like them. I want to stick with them. If I swapped lives with Judah Rosenthal, I would find myself enmeshed in a lot of intimate social relationships with people who in fact mean nothing to me, and I would lose my ties to my actual friends and family. Finally, I would not want to swap lives with Judah Rosenthal because I would rather be a philosopher than an ophthalmologist.

Perhaps it will be worthwhile to mention another consideration that is sometimes thought to bear on the welfare value of a life. We might feel very strongly that we have no moral obligation to create, or support, or facilitate a life like Judah's. And we might infer from this that his life cannot be high in welfare value, for we might think that if the life were a good one, then we would have an obligation to create it, or to create lives like Judah's. In a famous passage in *Principia Ethica*, Moore seems to say something like this. In a context in which he is talking about a disgusting but pleasant life, he exclaims that if such a life were of high value, then 'all human endeavours should be devoted to its realisation. I venture to think that this view is as false as it is paradoxical.'[3]

---

[3] Moore (1903: 95).

The line of reasoning, applied to the present case, is this: if Judah's life were outstandingly good, then we would have an obligation to devote "all human endeavors" to its realization; but of course we have no such obligation; so Judah's life is not so good regardless of the amount of happiness it contains. Thus, we would have a defense of premise (2) of the argument.

The reasoning is flawed. There is no valid inference from the assumption that Judah's life is high in welfare value to any conclusion about what we ought to do. Even if Judah's life is one of the best (in terms of welfare) that any human being could live, nothing follows about our obligations. Perhaps Judah's high welfare is purchased at the cost of lowered welfare for others (such as his wife and girlfriend); perhaps Judah's high welfare depends upon the imposition of huge injustices upon others; perhaps welfare is not the only thing that bears on our obligations. Thus, though we may agree wholeheartedly that no one has any obligation to create a monster like Judah Rosenthal, we may not infer from this that his life is not good in itself for him.

So, in the end, I am inclined to say that there is no solid proof that Judah's life is low in welfare value. The life is morally despicable, to be sure. But for all that it might be good in itself for Judah. Hence, the appeal to disgusting pleasures does not provide the basis for a completely convincing refutation of eudaimonism.

10.2   *Avoiding Controversy*

I can imagine someone insisting that, though he can't *prove* that Judah's life has low welfare value, it just seems obvious to him that this is the case. Perhaps such a person would appeal to "moral intuition." Perhaps he would just insist that it's too disgusting. Maybe he finds that he cannot accept the idea that Judah has a "good life" even when he pays careful attention to the distinction between moral goodness and welfare goodness and makes sure to focus exclusively on welfare goodness. Suppose this person is right. Is there anything that can be said in defense of eudaimonism?

I think the eudaimonist has further options here. I think there is a way to tweak the eudaimonist thesis so as to make it consistent with the idea that disgusting characters like Judah Rosenthal have lives of low welfare in spite of their great happiness. I think my own theory of happiness is especially well suited to this project. I must admit at the outset, however, that the "tweaking" makes use of a controversial concept.

According to my theory of happiness, the ultimate "atoms" of happiness are episodes in which a person takes intrinsic attitudinal pleasure in things. Every such atom of attitudinal pleasure makes a contribution to a person's happiness in direct proportion to the magnitude of the pleasure taken. According to my theory of welfare, every bit of happiness is supposed to translate directly into welfare. Thus, since a person like Judah takes pleasure in many things and pain in few, he ends up with a high level of happiness and a correspondingly high level of welfare.

Note, however, that in many cases when Judah takes pleasure in something, it appears that he is taking pleasure in something that is not a suitable object for his enjoyment. Consider, for example, the pleasure he takes in the fact that his girlfriend has been rubbed out. That's a wholly inappropriate object for him to be pleased about. It would be more fitting for Judah to be pained when he learns that someone who loved him has just been killed. Consider, for another example, the pleasure Judah takes in the fulsome praise showered on him at the reception in his honor. The speaker rambles on about what a wonderful person Judah is—how kind, how generous, how wise. All the while Judah knows he is an adulterous husband, a fraudulent bookkeeper, and a deceitful boyfriend. Again, Judah takes great pleasure in hearing the praise, but it appears that there is something profoundly improper about the objects in which he is taking pleasure. He's clearly not a "wonderful person;" hence it seems inappropriate for him to take pleasure in being praised as a wonderful person. It would be more fitting for him to be embarrassed or ashamed. Judah also enjoys getting an affectionate hug from his girlfriend. But he gets this hug only because he lied both to his girlfriend and to his wife. However pleasant the hug may be, it seems inappropriate that Judah should be enjoying it so much.

These objects of Judah's pleasure seem to share a common feature. Each of them is an object (or state of affairs) that is an inappropriate object for Judah to be taking pleasure in. Instead, he should be ashamed about them, or embarrassed. Let us say that none of these objects deserves to be something that Judah is pleased about. This gives us a way of locating the common thread that explains why (at least according to one way of seeing the situation) some of Judah's happiness does not contribute to his welfare. As a rough and approximate first step, we can say that welfare tracks happiness—but only to the extent that the happiness is based on episodes of *deserved pleasure*. When a person is pleased about some state of affairs that does not deserve to be an object of his pleasure, then that pleasure serves to enhance his happiness, but does not enhance his welfare.

This idea can be stated somewhat more precisely. In some cases, when a person takes pleasure in a state of affairs, there is nothing inappropriate about his taking pleasure in it. For example, suppose that someone innocently spends the morning working in her garden. She pulls up some weeds, prunes some shrubs, and plants a few new flowers. Suppose that after thus working in her garden, this gardener stands back and surveys the scene. It looks good. Let's suppose that she is pleased about the way her garden looks. Unless there is something decidedly odd about this gardener or her garden, it appears that she is taking pleasure in a perfectly appropriate fact. The fact that her garden looks pretty seems to be a fine object for a person to take pleasure in.

In general, we can say that when a person takes pleasure in something good or beautiful—and there is nothing odd about the circumstances—then the person is taking pleasure in something that deserves to have pleasure taken in it.

Suppose, on the other hand, that a sadistic person observes the suffering of some innocent victim. Suppose the sadist takes pleasure in this suffering. Then it seems that the sadist is taking pleasure in something that does not deserve to have pleasure taken in it. Under the circumstances, it would be more fitting for the observer to be pained by that object (the suffering of an innocent person). In general, and subject to the proviso that there is nothing odd about the circumstances, we can say that when someone takes pleasure in something evil or ugly, then the object does not deserve to be an object of the person's pleasure.

There are other factors that may affect the extent to which a certain object deserves to be an object of pleasure for a certain person. Some of these are relevant to the case of Judah Rosenthal. Suppose Judah takes pleasure in some sexual activities with his girlfriend. There may be nothing ugly or evil in these activities; nevertheless, we may want to say that there is something inappropriate about the fact that Judah is taking pleasure in them. Perhaps the inappropriateness arises because these pleasures occur in violation of some solemn promises; perhaps it arises because the pleasures are dependent upon deceit of several sorts; perhaps it arises because it involves a violation of seemingly reasonable moral standards. In any case, we may want to say that when Judah takes pleasure in precisely *those* activities, he is taking pleasure in things that do not deserve to be objects of his pleasure.

We can imagine a numerical score that represents the extent to which a certain object, O, deserves to be an object of pleasure for a certain person, S. When O fully deserves to be an object of S's pleasure, we can say that O deserves *to degree 1* to be an object of S's pleasure. In such cases, it would be entirely appropriate for S to take pleasure in O. O is a "good thing" for S to be pleased about. When O is totally unsuited to be an object of S's pleasure, we can say that O deserves *to degree zero* to be an object of S's pleasure. In that case, O is a completely inappropriate thing for S to be pleased about. Other objects would get scores between zero and 1, indicating various intermediate degrees to which they deserve to be objects of S's pleasure.

Suppose some person, S, takes intrinsic occurrent attitudinal pleasure in some object, O. Suppose the intensity of that pleasure is 10. Then the raw amount of attitudinal pleasure that S takes in O is 10. But we may in addition take account of the extent to which O deserves to be an object of S's pleasure. If O deserves to degree 1 to be an object of S's pleasure, then we can say that the *desert adjusted* amount of pleasure that S takes in O is 10×1, or $+10$; whereas if O deserves to degree .5 to be an object of S's pleasure, then the *desert adjusted* amount of pleasure that S takes in O is $10 \times .5$, or $+5$. In general, the desert adjusted amount of pleasure in an episode of intrinsic occurrent attitudinal pleasure is equal to the raw amount of that pleasure multiplied by the degree to which the object of that pleasure deserves to be an object of the subject's pleasure.

Earlier I defined momentary happiness levels by saying that a person, S's, momentary happiness level at a time, t, is the sum, for all propositions, p, of the extent to which S takes intrinsic attitudinal pleasure in p at t. So if you take more pleasure in things at t, or if you take pleasure in more things at t, then (holding displeasure constant) you are declared to be happier at t. A simple form of eudaimonism would then say that your welfare level at t would be equal to the amount of happiness you enjoy then.

Making use of the idea of desert adjusted amounts of pleasure, we can introduce a new concept of happiness. We can say that a person's *desert adjusted* momentary happiness level at a time is the sum, for all propositions, p, of the extent, *adjusted for desert*, to which the person takes intrinsic attitudinal pleasure in p. Correspondingly, we can define a person's desert adjusted happiness level for an interval, a domain of life, and life as a whole by appropriate aggregation of information about desert adjusted momentary happiness levels. And now we can introduce a different theory of welfare. Instead of saying that welfare tracks raw happiness, we can say that welfare tracks desert adjusted happiness. We can call this theory "Desert Adjusted Attitudinal Hedonic Eudaimonism."

I have not discussed a desert adjustment for displeasure. To preserve symmetry, we might expect that the theory would involve a corresponding adjustment for displeasure taken in things, depending upon the extent to which those things deserve to be objects of displeasure. However, it seems to me that displeasure makes you unhappy in equal measure, whether the object deserves displeasure or not. And it seems to me that displeasure decreases your welfare just as much in either case. Hence, there is no discount rate for displeasure taken in things that don't deserve it.

We are now ready to return to the case of Judah Rosenthal, the vicious ophthalmologist from *Crimes and Misdemeanors*. According to the story, Judah takes pleasure in lots of things and so is rated as being very happy by Attitudinal Hedonism about Happiness. Attitudinal Hedonistic Eudaimonism then implies that Judah is living the good life. Some find this hard to swallow. This is where Desert Adjusted Attitudinal Hedonic Eudaimonism comes in.

I already pointed out how plausible it is to say that, while Judah was taking pleasure in lots of things, many of those objects of his pleasure were things that did not deserve to be objects of his pleasure. Suppose he learns that his girlfriend has been killed. He is pleased about this. But the death of an innocent person is not the sort of thing that deserves to be an object of pleasure. So the desert adjusted amount of pleasure is much smaller than the raw amount of pleasure that Judah experiences. Suppose he enjoys a glass of fine wine. That seems good. But suppose in addition that he got the money for the wine by fraudulently removing it from the hospital fund. While the wine deserves to be enjoyed, it does not deserve to be enjoyed by Judah under these circumstances. If we see things in this way, we may want to say that the desert adjusted amount of pleasure is less than the raw amount of pleasure. As a result, we can say that Judah enjoyed lots of raw happiness, but not very much desert adjusted happiness—perhaps none at all, depending upon the details of the story. If welfare tracks desert adjusted happiness, then Judah's welfare is accordingly lower—perhaps zero. Thus, we have a form of eudaimonism that is consistent with the idea that Judah is not living the good life.[4]

---

[4] I leave it to the interested reader to determine whether similar considerations would yield the result that the abused housewife, Bertha (discussed above in Chapter 9), has a life of relatively low welfare.

Feldman's doubt

I am not entirely convinced that we need to move to the desert adjusted form of eudaimonism. I think that our sense that Judah's life is worthless may be the result of confusion. Perhaps it comes about as a result of confusing life evaluations in terms of *welfare* with life evaluations in terms of *moral excellence*. I think the term 'the good life' often serves to blur or blend these two forms of evaluation. Perhaps it would be acceptable just to say that Judah's life rates high in terms of welfare (just as Attitudinal Hedonic Eudaimonism says) and low in terms of moral excellence. I know that many philosophers don't share my view. They think a life like Judah's should get a low rating in terms of welfare. I invite them to make use of Desert Adjusted Attitudinal Hedonic Eudaimonism. It will get them the evaluation they want.

CHAPTER 11

Our Authority over Our Own Happiness

Writers on happiness often discuss a question about each person's authority with respect to her own happiness. Some maintain (perhaps with reservations) that we do have authority; others (also with reservations) seem to deny it. Others seem to be saying that we ought to have authority over our own happiness. There are often scattered remarks about the "liberal tradition."

This is a vexed topic, in part because talk of 'authority' is ambiguous. There is an epistemic concept of authority. We say, for example, that someone is "the authority" on Greek drama, meaning that he has definitive and broad knowledge on the topic. If a question about Greek drama should arise, we could turn to him for an answer. Whatever he says will settle it. There is also a concept of authority that seems to have nothing to do with knowledge; in this sense to say that someone "has authority" is to say that she is "in charge; is in a position to issue commands and directives." The police or security officers may sometimes be described as "the authorities."

So, if a writer on happiness says that each individual "has authority" with respect to her own happiness, there is a chance of misunderstanding. Does the writer mean to say that each individual *is knowledgeable* about her own happiness; or does the writer mean to say that each individual *has control over* her own happiness?

11.1 *Epistemic Authority* know best

Telfer gives an account of the nature of happiness. According to her, it is fundamentally a matter of being pleased with your life as a whole. She also says that a happy person has all the major things that he wants, and wants to keep (is pleased with) the major things that he has. Then she says this:

my analysis entails that, broadly speaking at least, a man is himself the authority on whether or not he is happy. Other people may say, 'You've got this and that—you *ought* to be happy'—meaning either 'We would expect you to be happy,' or 'A person of sound attitudes would in your position be happy'—but if he insists that he is not, they are in no position to refute him. Of course other people may be better judges than the man himself of what will make him happy or unhappy in the future.[1]

It appears that Telfer is thinking of some kind of epistemic authority. She says that if a man insists that he is not happy, then others are in no position to refute him. Presumably, her thought was that others cannot refute him *because he knows best about his own happiness*.

Telfer is careful to mention that she is not talking about a person's future happiness, or things that will make him happy in the future. Her caution seems justified. Empirical research has suggested that most of us are bad predictors and explainers of our own future happiness. Although she does not mention past happiness, it seems pretty clear that the same problems would arise. My memory might be playing tricks on me. I might think I was very happy last year when in fact I was not very happy at all. So if we are to formulate a principle of epistemic authority with respect to happiness, we must be careful to restrict it to current levels of happiness alone.

Telfer does not formulate her thesis of epistemic authority in any detail. In fact, her remarks are consistent with a variety of different interpretations. Surely this would be too strong:

EAH1: If a person, S, believes at a time, t, that his momentary happiness level at t = n, then S's momentary happiness level at t = n.

Surely there are plenty of ways in which a person's estimate of his own current happiness level could go wrong. Maybe I think I am happy to degree +87; but it is really only +86. We need to weaken the principle.

A very weak version of the epistemic authority principle can be formulated in this way:

EAH2: If a person, S, believes at a time, t, that his momentary happiness level at t is positive (negative), then S's momentary happiness level at t is positive (negative).

---

[1] Telfer (1980: 9).

Even this weak principle seems too strong. If I could make a 1 point mistake in the case where I think I am happy to degree +87 but it is really +86, then there seems to be no reason why I could not make a similar 1 point mistake in a case where I think I am happy to degree +1 but it is really zero.

Suppose that Telfer's theory of happiness is true. Then a person is happy only if she has all the major things that she wants. Suppose a person mistakenly believes that she has all the major things that she wants. Suppose that in fact she doesn't have some of these things (e.g., though she does not realize it, her car has just been stolen from the parking lot). Then she might think she is happy when (according to Telfer's theory) she is not. Suppose my theory of happiness is true. Then a person's happiness level at a time is determined by the extents to which he takes pleasure and displeasure in things at that time. Suppose I am taking pleasure in several things but at the same time taking displeasure in several other things. Suppose I mistakenly think that I am taking slightly more pleasure in one of these things than in fact I am. Then when I do the arithmetic, I might come out with a net balance of +1 when in fact the net balance is zero. So I think I am happy but in fact I am not.

We can weaken the principle still further:

EAH3: If a person, S, believes at a time, t, that his momentary happiness level at t is very high (low), then S's momentary happiness level at t must be at least positive (negative).

The point of EAH3 is to say that if you think you are *very happy*, then you must be at least somewhat happy; and if you think you are *very unhappy*, then you must be at least somewhat unhappy. Your epistemic authority goes this far: you can't be *wildly wrong* about your own current level of happiness.

But I am inclined to think that even this weakened principle is too strong. Suppose a person is suffering from depression. He is always glum and pessimistic. He goes to a charismatic psychiatrist who gets him to believe that in fact he is approximately as happy as some of the happiest people he knows. After a while, the patient is fooled. He comes to believe that he is very happy when in fact he is still just as unhappy as he was before.

Recall the case of Timmy (described in Chapter 5). Timmy is a happy-go-lucky party animal. Timmy is introduced to Richard Taylor at a party. They strike up a conversation. Taylor convinces Timmy that Timmy's happiness is entirely specious. He does not have "the genuine article." Timmy is at first dubious. He certainly feels happy. But Taylor explains that lots of people feel happy. This, he says, has nothing to do with genuine happiness. Genuine happiness has to do with developing your creative talents. 'To what extent have you done that?' 'Not at all.' says Timmy. 'I just sing and dance and go to parties.' 'Then you are in fact very unhappy.' 'I guess you are right. I thought I was happy, but I was wrong. I am unhappy.' Here Timmy has been hoodwinked. He has come to think that he is very unhappy when in fact he is not unhappy at all.

Sumner offers tentative approval to a considerably watered-down principle about epistemic authority about happiness.[2] He mentions the possibility that someone might give an irrelevant response when asked about happiness. Suppose that, after Timmy's encounter with Richard Taylor, a questioner asks Timmy if he is happy. Timmy says that he is not. But Timmy's response is irrelevant, since his interpretation of the question has been distorted by his interactions with Richard Taylor. Timmy is not really talking about *happiness*. Sumner also mentions the possibility that a response might be insincere. A respondent might overstate his level of happiness in order to represent himself as being very happy, when in fact he is only moderately happy.[3] Finally, a respondent's transitory mood might affect his judgment. On one occasion, he might give an inaccurate account of his level of happiness in virtue of the fact that he has been asked at a time when he is feeling gloomy. At another time, he might go wrong because he is feeling especially chipper.[4] Sumner concludes his discussion by saying, 'People's self-assessments tend to be reliable when they are relevant, sincere, and considered.'[5]

Sumner's discussion is throughout framed in terms of his own theory of happiness, which is a form of Whole Life Satisfactionism. In effect, Sumner seems to be saying that if a person says that he is satisfied with his life as a whole to some degree n, then if (a) he properly understands the concept of *whole life satisfaction*, and (b) he is sincere in his assessment, and (c) he makes this assessment after due consideration and in a cool moment, then it is very likely that he is in fact satisfied with his life as a whole to degree n.

Since I doubt that a person's happiness level is equal to his level of whole life satisfaction, I am inclined to think that Sumner's conclusion is not directly relevant to the question about our epistemic authority concerning *happiness*. Even if I am likely to be right about how much whole life satisfaction I have, it does not follow that I am likely to be right about how happy I am. Furthermore, it seems to me that Sumner

[2] Sumner (1996: 150–6). [3] Ibid. 154. [4] Ibid. 155. [5] Ibid.

overstates the likelihood that people will be right in their estimates of whole life satisfaction. This would depend on how fine-grained the assessments are supposed to be. Suppose the subject needs only to judge whether he is (a) very satisfied, or (b) somewhat satisfied, or (c) neither satisfied nor unsatisfied, or (d) somewhat dissatisfied, or (e) very dissatisfied with his life as a whole. Then (subject to Sumner's provisos about relevance, sincerity, and consideration) he may get it right. But if the subject is given a numerical scale with numbers from −100 (maximally dissatisfied) to +100 (maximally satisfied), and is required to pick the number that correctly represents his level of whole life satisfaction, then it seems to me that the subject's assessment would probably be wrong more often than it would be right. It would be difficult to construct an experiment that would resolve this definitively, since that would presumably require some independent procedure to determine the actual level of whole life satisfaction. It's not clear to me that we have any way of doing that—especially if the procedure has to be independent of the assessments offered by the subject.

I tried to make a case for the idea that a person's momentary happiness level at a time is equal to the sum, for all propositions, p, of the extent to which the person takes intrinsic occurrent attitudinal pleasure or displeasure in p at that time. A person may take pleasure and displeasure in many things at a time; estimates of the amounts may be off the mark; arithmetic mistakes are common in any case. I see no reason to suppose that a person is sure to be right in his assessment of his own momentary happiness level. Even if he understands the relevant concept quite well, and even if he tries to avoid overstatement and understatement, it seems to me that a person can easily get this wrong. A friend or a psychiatrist may sometimes be able to make a better assessment. Thus, I am inclined to doubt that we have any sort of special epistemic authority with respect to our own current happiness level.

I cannot imagine why anyone would think that we have special epistemic authority with respect to past or future happiness levels; nor with respect to whole life happiness levels.[6] These things, I fear, are subject at best to dicey recollections and chancy estimates.[7]

---

[6] For a detailed discussion of the extensive literature on empirical research concerning predictions of future happiness, see Loewenstein and Schkade, 'Wouldn't It Be Nice? Predicting Future Feelings' (1999: 85–105).

[7] Haybron discusses (and also rejects) a principle about epistemic authority. The principle he rejects, however, seems to be one according to which each individual has special insight into

11.2 *Controlling Authority over Happiness*

[handwritten margin notes: we decide + constituents, incl primary source of H]

Suppose some philosopher informs you that in fact happiness is a matter of health, wealth, knowledge, freedom, achievement, and loving personal relationships. He has an algorithm that takes information about a person's levels of health, wealth, and so on, and then calculates that person's level of happiness. Suppose this philosopher takes your measurements and applies his algorithm. He then informs you that you are happy to degree +47. 'The problem,' he says, 'is your poor showing in the category of wealth. You are not rich enough. That's why you have only a moderate degree of happiness.' This "information" might annoy you. Maybe you consider yourself to be very happy; maybe you don't care about your modest wealth. Maybe you think wealth doesn't matter all that much provided that you have enough to keep a roof over your head and a chicken in your pot (both of which you have).

Some philosophers have suggested that there is something paternalistic about a theory of happiness like the one employed by the imagined philosopher. When you hear his assessment of your happiness, you might feel like saying 'who is he to tell me what makes for my happiness? I prefer to make these judgments for myself. Maybe in the case of certain other people wealth is a constituent of happiness. But in my own case, wealth is not relevant.'

Wayne Sumner seems to have something like this in mind in several passages in *Welfare, Happiness, and Ethics*. In one place, while discussing the merits of a preferentist theory of happiness, Sumner mentions "the liberal spirit of the modern age."[8] He suggests that this "liberal spirit" likes to see each person as 'a shaper of his own destiny, a determiner of his own good.' He mentions 'self-direction and self-determination.' I am not entirely clear on Sumner's point here. But he uses the expression 'determiners of our own good.' This might be taken to mean that each person has, or should have, or is thought by liberals to have, the authority to determine what will constitute happiness in his or her own case. This sort of authority would be an extreme sort of "controlling authority." It would be the

what makes him happy. Haybron calls this the principle of *Personal Authority*. He says it is popular among modern liberals and he sketches it as follows: 'people are highly authoritative about their own well-being: while they sometimes make mistakes, they pretty well know what's good for them and how they are doing, and generally make prudent choices in pursuit of their interests.' See Haybron (2008b: 13).

[8] Sumner (1996: 123).

subject's authority to determine what will constitute happiness in his or her own case. We can state one possible principle of controlling authority in this way:

CAH1: Each person has the power to determine what will be the constituents of happiness in his or her own case.

This idea seems incoherent. Surely it makes no sense to suppose that any person could have the power to determine what happiness actually *is* in his own case. If happiness is a matter of being satisfied with your life as a whole, then no one has the power to make happiness be something else. Suppose some form of Whole Life Satisfactionism is true. Then even I would have to acquiesce; I would not have the power to make happiness be net intrinsic attitudinal pleasure no matter how much I might want my own theory of happiness to be true.

I suspect that loose talk may be responsible for the confusion here. Some people persist in saying things like 'happiness is health, wealth, and loving personal relationships' when what they really mean is that health, wealth, and loving personal relationships are primary causes of happiness. It is not too hard to imagine that a person who talks in this confusing way might go on to say that happiness might "be something else" for another person. Perhaps he would say that happiness might "be" solitude and reflection for you. From here it would be only a short step to the conclusion that happiness "is" different things for different people.

But, of course, all this talk of happiness being different things for different people just means that different things are the primary causes of happiness for different people, not that happiness itself is something different for different people. To paraphrase Moore paraphrasing Butler: happiness is what it is and not another thing. Nothing we can do will make it become another thing. Liberals cannot coherently advocate that each person should have the right to let happiness be whatever he wants it to be.

A different sort of controlling authority would not involve anything as extreme as the determination of what happiness will *be* in your own case. Rather, it involves only the capacity to determine what will be the *primary source* of happiness in your own case. If a person had this more modest sort of control over his own happiness he would have to be content to live with whatever happiness happens to be. Perhaps the liberal idea is that each person should have the right to decide about what will make him happy. Thus, if I choose to let health, wealth, and loving personal relationships be the primary sources of happiness for me, then that should be my decision. If you, on the other hand, decide to let solitude and reflection be the primary sources of happiness in your case, then that should be up to you. But this presupposes that happiness itself *is* one thing, and the same thing for both us.

We can formulate a thesis that says that people have this sort of controlling authority:

CAH2: Each person has the power to determine what will be the primary sources of happiness in his or her own case.

It seems doubtful that we have the sort of controlling authority described by CAH2. Suppose that, in fact, as a matter of long-standing temperament, a certain person would be happy if she had a multitude of loving personal relationships. Nothing else could make her happy. Suppose, however, that as a result of some misfortunes she is living alone. She is lonely and unhappy. Surely it is unreasonable to suppose that she could simply decide to let solitude and meditation become the primary sources of her happiness. Merely willing won't make it so. Since she has no power to choose another primary source for her happiness, it would be pointless for a liberal to insist that this person should have the right to choose what shall be the primary source of her happiness. It would be a right that she could not exercise.

I acknowledge that, in some cases, a person might have the power to do things that would, in the long term, alter the primary sources of his happiness. If a person recognized that the primary sources of his happiness were things that would destroy his health, or if he recognized that they were morally indefensible, or if he could see that they were ruining his marriage, he might want to take steps to alter them. Maybe a psychiatrist could help him to develop new tastes or preferences. Maybe after a course of hypnosis or other suitable treatment, he could develop new values, so that different things would become the primary sources of his happiness. So when I say that people do not have the power to determine what will be the primary sources of their own happiness, I mean to say only that no one has the power to do this *directly*. I acknowledge that someone could take steps that would, after a while and indirectly, lead to some revision in the primary sources of his or her happiness.

Another sort of controlling authority might be worth considering. Though you do not have the power to decide what happiness in your case will be, and you don't have much power to decide directly what will be the primary source of this happiness, you may have some slight control over the amount of happiness you will get. This is the authority to determine how happy you will be. A liberal might think that each of us should have the right to do that. The relevant principle of controlling authority might be this:

CAH4: Each person has the power to determine how happy he or she will be.

It is a commonplace in the empirical happiness literature to point out that research tells us that in fact we don't have much of this sort of control over our level of happiness. I am inclined to think that the significance of this research has been exaggerated. Part of my reason should be clear: quite a lot of the research is based upon the assumption that a person's level of happiness is equal to his level of whole life satisfaction. In many cases the research actually shows that people tend to revert to their former level of whole life satisfaction after having especially good or bad experiences. If I thought that happiness were whole life satisfaction, then I might find this research to be a bit more interesting. However, as I tried to show in Chapter 5 and Appendices A and B, these theories about happiness are all false. Insofar as the research depends upon the assumption that happiness is whole life satisfaction, it is inconclusive.

I think it is interesting to note that different theories about the nature of happiness may have different implications for the question whether we have controlling authority over our own happiness. Suppose that some form of Whole Life Satisfactionism is true. According to this theory, a person's momentary level of happiness is determined by the evaluative judgment he makes about his standing in several domains of his life as a whole. Let these domains be work, marriage, housing, leisure-time activities, and health. Suppose a person is well aware of the fact that his standing in these domains is not very good. Suppose he has very limited power to alter his standing in these domains. Suppose he has no power to deceive himself into making exaggerated judgments about his standing in those domains. Then he is more-or-less doomed to being unhappy, according to the theory.

A similar thing happens in the case of Kahneman's theory. According to this theory, a person's momentary level of happiness is determined by the strength of his desire for his present experience to continue. Suppose that on most occasions a certain person does not like her present experience. Suppose that on most occasions she has little power to change those experiences. Most of the time she just goes on wishing that it would be different. According to Kahneman's theory, so long as this person goes on wishing that her present experiences would cease, she goes on being unhappy and there is not much she can do about it.

A typical form of local preferentism about happiness seems to have the same feature. According to theories of this sort, a person's level of happiness is determined by his level of subjective desire satisfaction. If a person wants a bunch of things to be true, but believes they are not true, then (according to this sort of theory) the person is unhappy. Suppose a person wants to be healthy, wealthy, and wise. Suppose he thinks he is sickly, poor, and stupid. What can he do? Surely he cannot just choose to stop having those desires. Surely he cannot just choose to start thinking that he is healthy, wealthy, and wise. He seems to be stuck in his unhappiness so long as he continues to have these beliefs and desires. That may be a long time.

My own theory of happiness seems to have different implications. Suppose that my theory of happiness is correct. That is, suppose that a person's momentary happiness level is determined by the extent to which he takes attitudinal pleasure and displeasure in things. Now it begins to seem that there may be a strategy that will enable a person to increase (or decrease) his level of happiness.

Of course, I recognize that some things simply *demand* our attention. If you have a toothache, it's hard to ignore it. It intrudes upon your consciousness. When you notice it, you are forced to take occurrent attitudinal displeasure in the way it feels. As a result, you are less happy (according to my theory). You can't do much about it. Suppose a loved one shows up and gives you a big, affectionate hug. It feels wonderful. You simply have to take occurrent attitudinal pleasure in that. And, as a result of that, your level of happiness increases (according to my theory). There's not much you can do about that, either. But there are many other objects over which you may have some control. These are things that have this combination of features: you are not *forced* to focus your attention on them; you have the power to focus your attention on them; if you focus your attention on them, then you will take pleasure in them. We can call these things "voluntary happifying objects." Contrariwise, we can say that a "voluntary unhappifying object" is an object that you are not forced to focus upon; but that you can focus upon; and such that if you focus upon it, you will take displeasure in it.

This indicates some steps you can take in an effort to increase your level of happiness. If you think about voluntary happifying objects, you will take pleasure in them. And if you take pleasure in them, you will be happier (according to my theory). And if you avoid thinking about voluntary unhappifying objects, you will avoid taking displeasure in them. Thus, you will avoid sources of unhappiness.

So, if my theory of happiness is true, then there is a happiness-enhancing strategy available to us. The first step is to *identify the things that are voluntary happifying and unhappifying objects for you*. This should be pretty easy for most of us. We just need to engage in a bit of reflection. We need to find the items that we enjoy thinking about as well as the items that we disenjoy thinking about. We need to consider what we can do to bring the happifying objects into consciousness; we need to consider what we can do to keep the unhappifying objects out of consciousness.

The second step may be a bit harder. We need to *stop thinking about things in which we take displeasure*. Suppose, for example, that Bruce (discussed above in Appendix A) has a bad job, a bad marital situation, bad living conditions, bad leisure-time activities, and some health trouble. The advocate of certain forms of Whole Life Satisfactionism is required to say that so long as Bruce judges these things to be bad (which he knows they are) he will be unhappy. Indeed, hypothetical forms of Whole Life Satisfactionism say that so long as Bruce is such that, if he were to think about them, he would judge these things to be bad, he is unhappy. Be that as it may, I would encourage Bruce to stop thinking about those things.

The third step in my procedure is to start thinking about voluntary happifying objects. Maybe you can follow the example of Bruce. Bruce was doing poorly in all domains of life. If he were to think about his job (he was unemployed), or his marriage (he was divorced), or his health (he was sickly) he would be unhappy. But Bruce found a way to concentrate all of his attention on other topics. He thought about his "glory days." After a few beers, he would think exclusively about his youthful exploits. He took pleasure in a variety of facts about his past. If we assume that this strategy actually succeeded in Bruce's case, then we must conclude that it helped to make Bruce happier. So the third step is to *start focusing on some happifying objects*.

It may seem that I am advocating a program of self-conscious repression—as if I am suggesting that you put the bad stuff out of mind and just think about the good stuff. That is precisely right. My philosophy is "count your blessings; repress thoughts about your burdens." If you can succeed in doing this (and avoid alcoholism at the same time) you will be happier (according to my theory of happiness).

The reader may suspect that there is an argument lurking here. It may appear that I am claiming that my own theory of happiness is somehow preferable in virtue of the fact that if it were true, we would have a certain limited sort of controlling authority over our own happiness. The argument might go like this:

1. If Attitudinal Hedonism about Happiness is true, then there is a strategy we can use that may well help us to become happier.
2. If some competing theory of happiness were true, there would not be any strategy we could use to help us become happier.
3. It would be a good thing if there were a strategy we can use that may well help us to become happier; it would be a bad thing if there were no strategy that we can use to help make us happier.
4. Therefore, Attitudinal Hedonism about Happiness is true and each competing theory is false.

There are some good things to be said about this argument. I think the premises are true. I also think that the conclusion is true. Alas, there is no logical connection between the premises and the conclusion. The conclusion follows by the non-logical principle generally known as "wishful thinking." Wouldn't it be nice?

PART III

IMPLICATIONS FOR THE EMPIRICAL STUDY OF HAPPINESS

CHAPTER 12

Measuring Happiness

12.1 *Why Measure?*

In many situations, we would like to choose a course of behavior that will make people better off. In a wide range of typical cases, it is reasonable to suppose that they will be better off if they are happier. Since a person's level of happiness seems more directly open to observation and measurement than his level of well-being itself, we focus on happiness. We aim for the course of behavior that will make people happier, assuming that if they are happier, they are better off. In order to determine whether our efforts have been successful, we'd like to have a way to assess their impact on levels of happiness. This provides one rationale for developing a systematic way of measuring amounts of happiness.

In the simplest sort of case, we are hoping that our choice of behavior will have a direct impact on happiness. Recall the case involving Tristan and Dr. Goldberg (discussed above, after Chapter 5, in Appendix A). Tristan was suffering from depression. He was unhappy. He consulted Dr. Goldberg because he hoped that Dr. Goldberg would be able to help. Dr. Goldberg prescribed a medication that had the desired effect. Tristan's depression lifted; he became happier. It was a success for everyone involved.

There are many ways in which the medical intervention could have failed. For example, imagine a different outcome. Suppose that after taking the medication Tristan started to smile a lot more. Suppose he began to laugh and joke with his friends. Suppose he no longer sulked or cried. But suppose (and this may seem a bit paradoxical but it is surely possible) that when asked, Tristan said that in fact he was no happier. Suppose he expressed some perplexity about his behavior. Suppose he said, 'I know that I am *acting* as if I were happier; I realize that my behavior suggests happiness. But I am just as miserable as I was before. I still *feel rotten*. From my perspective, I guess I would say that the medication has been a total failure.'

In a case such as this, we might like to have some way to measure the happiness itself. The measurement must not be thrown out of kilter by the misleading behavior. Tristan would surely prefer a medication that would make him happier, even if it did not make him laugh and smile. I assume that Dr. Goldberg would agree.

There are many cases involving comparisons of large-scale public policies. Health care is a good example. We might be interested in the implications of nationalized health care. We might wonder how a nationalized system stacks up against our current system, in which individual patients (if they can afford it and can find a practitioner willing to take on their case) are free to engage the services of for-profit medical providers. One way to proceed is to select another country where they have nationalized health care and compare the effects of their system with the effects of ours. But there are many differences. The people in the other country may pay higher taxes, doctors there may get lower salaries, poor people may get better health care, wealthy people (it is sometimes alleged) may have to come to the US to get really superb health care. Confronting this thicket of apparent pluses and minuses, we may look for a bottom line. 'Are the citizens of Canada better off with their systems of universal health care? Or are we better off under our system?' That's somewhat amorphous. What would make them "better off"? If we assume that people are better off under one system rather than another when they are happier under that system, then we may feel that we have a handle on the questions. Now we can ask whether Canadians are happier with their systems than US citizens are with ours. Our question then becomes 'Which system leads to the greater happiness of the citizenry?' That seems to sum up the focus of our interest.[1] And it makes us confront the question about the measurement of happiness.

How do we measure happiness?

---

[1] Dan Doviak reminded me that the impact on happiness would not necessarily be our only criterion. We might also consider such things as the fairness of the resulting distribution of happiness, or the constitutionality of the proposed system. I mean only to suggest that we might be especially interested in how the proposed health-care system would affect the welfare of citizens; and thus we might want to know how it would affect their happiness.

12.2 *Satisfaction with Life and Its Domains*

Some researchers have adopted a very straightforward approach: they simply ask subjects to tell them how happy they are.[2] The test instrument may have only one question:

QH: On a scale of −10 to +10, where −10 indicates extreme unhappiness and +10 indicates extreme happiness, how happy are you right now?

While this sort of test instrument is obviously simple enough, it is not clear that the results are meaningful. In his review of measurement instruments, Ed Diener discussed "single-item measures." He pointed out that such instruments have been criticized on several different grounds.

Despite the evidence for moderate reliability and validity, these measures suffer from several faults. Scores tend to be skewed . . . Acquiescence is a potential problem . . . Finally, the scales cannot hope to cover all aspects of [subjective well being], but must rely on subjects' integration of these in arriving at a single response. The single-item scales do not offer a finely differentiated view of a person's subjective well-being.[3]

While each of these may be a genuine problem, it seems to me that the most worrisome problem with such scales is the likelihood that respondents will misinterpret the question, or will interpret it in different ways. If a bunch of different subjects, perhaps of different ages and in different countries, are simply asked to estimate how "happy" they are, they may understand the question in different ways. One person's "+8" may indicate a level of happiness that is very different from another person's "+8." It's not clear that their answers provide the basis for any meaningful comparisons. Since there are no other questions on the test, there will be no further evidence to shed light on the significance of the single answer concerning "happiness." As Diener says, 'With reliance on a single item, the variance due to the specific wording cannot be averaged out.'

Perhaps because of this problem, and also in the hope of achieving a "more finely differentiated view," many researchers are attracted to test instruments that attempt to direct respondents' attention to various *domains of life*.[4] For each domain, they ask the respondent to

---

[2] For a discussion of these "single item measures," see Diener (1984: 544), or Larsen and Fredrickson (1999: 44–5). [3] Diener (1984: 544).

[4] A good example might be the British Household Panel Survey (BHPS), or the German Socio-Economic Panel (GSOEP).

report the extent to which he or she is satisfied with how things are going in that domain in his or her own life. Respondents may also be asked to answer a question about satisfaction with life as a whole. The working assumption, presumably, is that scores on the test give some insight into levels of happiness, and this is taken to be worthy of study because happiness (so construed) is taken to have some important bearing on welfare. A typical test instrument[5] might contain a series of questions like these:

Q1: As you reflect on your marriage, would you say that you are: (a) very satisfied; (b) somewhat satisfied; (c) neutral; (d) somewhat dissatisfied; or (e) very dissatisfied with the way things are currently going in your marriage?

Q2: As you reflect on your job, would you say that you are: (a) very satisfied; (b) somewhat satisfied; (c) neutral; (d) somewhat dissatisfied; or (e) very dissatisfied with the way things are currently going in your job?

Q3: As you reflect on the conditions of your health and the health care available to you, would you say that you are: (a) very satisfied; (b) somewhat satisfied; (c) neutral; (d) somewhat dissatisfied; or (e) very dissatisfied with the way things are currently going with respect to your health and health care?

There might be a collection of further questions like these. Each one would ask for an expression of satisfaction with some domain of the respondent's life. In one series of tests, the domains are: job, financial situation, health, housing, amount of leisure time, use of leisure time, social life, and marriage.[6] In a similar study, the list of domains added 'environment' and deleted 'social life' and 'marriage.'[7]

There might in addition be a question that calls for some sort of summary judgment:

Q4: As you reflect on your life as a whole, would you say that you are: (a) very satisfied; (b) somewhat satisfied; (c) neutral; (d) somewhat dissatisfied; or (e) very dissatisfied with the way things are currently going in your life as a whole?

In some instances, respondents are given a numerical scale instead of a set of five options. Thus, the questions might look more like this:

---

[5] In fact, these questions are simplified versions of the questions asked in the BHPS (Wave 10).

[6] Van Praag and Ferrer-i-Carbonel (2004: 45). This is from BHSP.

[7] This is from GSOEP; also cited in van Praag and Ferrer-i-Carbonel (2004).

Q5: On a scale of −10 to +10, where −10 means totally dissatisfied and +10 means totally satisfied, how satisfied are you with your job?

Researchers have pointed out all sorts of problems with test instruments such as these. Some have emphasized the fact that the answers respondents give to these questions are too easily affected by seemingly irrelevant features of the context in which the questions are asked. For example, respondents give different responses if the questions are asked on a sunny day rather than on a rainy day. Others have pointed out that answers to these questions can be affected by the order in which the questions are asked. But it's hard to believe that a person is really less happy if he is asked Q4 *before* Q1 rather than the other way around.

While I recognize that all of these are genuine sources of worry concerning these "Satisfaction with Life Domain" test instruments, I think the problem runs far deeper. I think the problem is that, even if all the wrinkles could be ironed out, any such instrument would still be measuring the wrong thing.[8] That is, the test instrument would not be measuring *happiness*. Let's consider some examples that may help to illustrate this point.

Case 1. Suppose two subjects are taking a happiness text on a certain day. Suppose that as they walk into the test facility, Subject A is smiling and Subject B is frowning. Suppose that A is smiling because he is beginning to think that he is getting better at racquet ball. He optimistically hopes that he soon will be able to beat some other players to whom he previously lost. He has also lost some weight and has been feeling more energetic. These are matters of real significance to him and he has been thinking about them a lot. At the same time, A has a somewhat boring job that does not pay well. He lives in a cramped apartment and often squabbles with his wife. Fortunately for him, these matters are not important to him. He really doesn't care one way or the other and he rarely worries about them. In fact, so long as nobody mentions these things to him, he does not think about them at all.

On the other hand, B is frowning because he is troubled by some recent developments at his job. He has been forced to take a cut in

---

[8] Earlier, in Chapter 5, I tried to show that we cannot identify happiness with whole life satisfaction. My argument there turned on the fact that most people do not participate in happiness tests. Some of them may never have any occasion to form a judgment about whole life satisfaction. Yet it would be absurd to conclude that those people are not happy; or that they do not have *any* level of happiness or unhappiness. My point here is different. Here I am focusing on people who do take the test. I am considering the question whether the scores they get on the test reflect their actual levels of happiness.

pay and is worried about the impact on his finances. He also lives in a cramped apartment; he also squabbles with his wife from time to time. These things have been on his mind constantly over the past several days. He is uneasy about each of them and his worries have colored his whole emotional outlook. He has no problems on the racquet-ball court or with his health, but these things are not important to him. In fact, so long as nobody mentions these things, he would not have thought of them as things that could bear on his happiness.

Suppose now that A and B take the test. Their results are as follows:

	Subject A	Subject B
Job	Somewhat dissatisfied	Somewhat dissatisfied
Finances	Somewhat dissatisfied	Somewhat dissatisfied
Housing	Somewhat dissatisfied	Somewhat dissatisfied
Social life	Somewhat dissatisfied	Somewhat dissatisfied
Marriage	Somewhat dissatisfied	Somewhat dissatisfied
Health	Somewhat satisfied	Somewhat satisfied
Leisure	Somewhat satisfied	Somewhat satisfied

These test results suggest that A and B are equally happy, but this suggestion is clearly wrong. When he focuses his attention on these matters, A is reminded that he has a somewhat unsatisfactory job and that his finances are a bit shaky. However, he is ordinarily not concerned about these matters. A takes his job and finances to be relatively unimportant; he does not worry about them. His poor finances do not trouble him. He is more focused on his leisure activities. He thinks about racquet ball nearly all the time. Since his skills are still not fully developed, he is not exactly thrilled about recent developments in racquet ball. But he is somewhat optimistic. He is thinking he will get better. So his attitude toward racquet ball shows up as a 'Somewhat satisfied' in his answer to the leisure question. Since he really cares a lot about racquet ball, his modest success there has a substantial impact on his happiness. That's why he is happy in spite of his bad job. He spends more time thinking about his success in racquet ball than he does worrying about his financial situation.

B, on the other hand, is much more concerned about his job and finances. So he is unhappy largely as a result of his mild worries about his job. When his attention is drawn to his leisure activities, he recognizes that he is doing well in racquet ball, and is somewhat satisfied with his performance in racquet ball, but this satisfaction does not affect his happiness since he does not care much about games and devotes almost no time to thinking about this. If the question had not appeared on the test, the topic would not have come to mind.

This example shows that satisfaction levels, by themselves, may not be good guides to happiness. If a person cares a lot about a certain domain, then satisfaction in that domain may have a big impact on his happiness. If he does not care about that domain, then that same level of satisfaction may have no impact on his happiness. Perhaps it would be better to adjust the significance of a report of satisfaction within a domain. Perhaps it would be better to take these reports more seriously when they are reports about domains about which the respondent cares more. Perhaps this could be done if the respondents were asked to estimate the proportion of time that they spend thinking about the topic.

Case 2. Suppose two subjects are taking a happiness test on a certain day. Suppose that as they walk into the test facility, Subject A is smiling and Subject B is frowning. Suppose that Subject A is smiling because he just heard some news about Richard Dixon—a political figure he hates. He heard that Dixon has been indicted, charged with taking bribes. 'Good,' says A to himself with a grin. 'I hope he is found guilty and sent to jail.' Subject B is frowning largely because he just heard the same news. The difference is that B has been a long-time supporter of Dixon. B thinks that the indictment must be a politically motivated fraud, and that the whole business just shows that the system is completely corrupt. He is unhappy about this.

Suppose now that the two subjects are asked to give satisfaction ratings for some domains of their lives. Suppose the two subjects respond as follows:

	Subject A	Subject B
Job	Satisfied	Satisfied
Finances	Satisfied	Satisfied
Health	Satisfied	Satisfied
Housing	Satisfied	Satisfied
Leisure	Satisfied	Satisfied
Social life	Satisfied	Satisfied
Marriage	Satisfied	Satisfied

Neither of them has any complaints about his experiences in any of the domains mentioned in the test. In light of this information, the tester might conclude that Subjects A and B are equally happy at the time of the testing. But they are not. A is very happy and B is very unhappy. The problem is that the object of A's happiness is not something about his standing in any of the proposed domains. A is happy because he heard some "good news" about Dixon. This is not something that is involved in A's job, or marriage, or housing, or leisure-time activities. It is not something that is involved in any of the indicated domains.

A similar thing is true in the case of Subject B. B is unhappy at the time of the test, but his unhappiness does not concern his own life. It has nothing to do with his marriage, or social life, or job, etc. His emotional state is affected by something "external." Like A, his emotional state is primarily affected by the news of the indictment of the political figure. Unlike A, however, B is unhappy about what he has heard in the news.

It's important to see that this emotional difference between A and B very well might not show up in their responses to a question about "whole life satisfaction" either. Each of them might be reasonably well satisfied with his own life, as reflected in the unbroken string of 'satisfactory's that they gave in their responses to the questions about the domains. The emotional difference is founded upon a fact that is not internal to any of the listed domains; nor is it founded upon a fact that bears on their satisfaction with the subjects' own "whole lives."

I am inclined to suspect that there are many people who are like A and B in this example. Their happiness does not depend so directly on things that are going on in their own lives. Consider people who are most deeply concerned about such things as the political situation in the Middle East, or global warming, or the treatment of women in certain third world countries. Such a person might be in a particularly gloomy mood because of developments concerning those issues. His unhappiness, in that case, would not show up in his response to the test items concerning domains of his own life. The test results might suggest that he is happy.

This thought experiment suggests that if the test instrument is to measure *happiness*, then it should not require subjects to give their ratings of satisfaction levels in a pre-selected set of domains. Someone's happiness might be affected by a factor that is not incorporated in any of the domains in the list. The same experiment also suggests that the test instrument should not require subjects to give their ratings of satisfaction levels in domains *associated with their own lives*. A person might be happier, or less happy, because of an emotional reaction to something that does not fall into any domain of his life. Thus, a better question might be:

Q6: As you reflect on *things that are going on*, would you say that you are: (a) very satisfied; (b) somewhat satisfied; (c) neutral; (d) somewhat dissatisfied; or (e) very dissatisfied with the way *these things* are currently going?

In other words, instead of asking about satisfaction within some specified list of domains of the respondent's life, or about the respondent's life as a whole, the question might be phrased in such a way as to elicit levels of satisfaction "with things"—whatever they may be. If a person were satisfied with something in his job or marriage, of course he could mention that. But if his satisfaction were primarily in some other area, and not related to any domain of his life, he would have the option of mentioning it.

Case 3. Suppose two subjects are taking a happiness test on a certain day. Suppose that as they walk into the test facility, Subject A is smiling and Subject B has a sort of "blank" look on his face. He shows no evidence of joy, bliss, happiness, pleasure, or any other "positive" emotion. They then take the test with these results:

	Subject A	Subject B
Job	Satisfied	Satisfied
Finances	Satisfied	Satisfied
Health	Satisfied	Satisfied
Housing	Satisfied	Satisfied
Leisure	Satisfied	Satisfied
Social life	Satisfied	Satisfied
Marriage	Satisfied	Satisfied
Life as a whole	Satisfied	Satisfied

When the test is completed, and the results recorded, the tester is puzzled. It seems to him that B is much less happy than A, yet he sees that they have answered the test questions in exactly the same way. Either their affect is misleading, or the test has failed to measure happiness. He is not puzzled by the responses of Subject A. Subject A looks happy and says he is satisfied in all domains and with life as a whole. So his response seems to fit his affect. That's not puzzling. But B's responses are harder to understand. He turns to Subject B. 'When you responded to the questions, you said you were satisfied in all the listed domains and that you were satisfied with your life as a whole. Yet you don't look happy. What gives?' Imagine that B responds as follows: 'This world is full of pitfalls and snares. Human life is precarious. So long as we live, we can be afflicted with all sorts of pain and suffering. We can become sick or destitute; we can be enslaved; we can lose our friends and family. But in my case, due to sheer good luck, I have managed to avoid all these disasters. I don't exactly *enjoy* my job, but at the same time I am not suffering. I get a regular paycheck. I don't *enjoy* my marriage, but I recognize that my wife is a satisfactory companion. I am not happy, but neither am I unhappy. So I have nothing to complain about. I am satisfied. I only hope that my luck will continue so that I will continue to avoid disaster up until I die.'

This example illustrates one way in which *satisfaction* differs from *happiness*. The two subjects were equally satisfied with their lives, but they were not equally happy. It is important to notice that this problem is independent of the problem about *domains*. If we were to ask B to report on his level of satisfaction with "things in general" as opposed to domains in his own life, or his own life as a whole, he still might report that he is satisfied. He focuses on the potential for disaster, which he takes to be enormous; he sees that there is in fact not much disaster; he declares himself to be satisfied even though he is not exactly *enjoying* anything.

Another example may help to make the point even clearer. Suppose a certain individual has a wonderful job, and has plenty of money, and is in excellent physical shape. He fully appreciates everything he has got. He knows he is in the top 1 percent in every category and he is delighted. Yet in addition to this he is tremendously ambitious. He always aims high. He is a millionaire, and aims to be a multi-millionaire; he is in very good physical shape, but he aims to be in *fabulous* physical shape. Similarly for the other categories. His motto is 'aim for the stars.' Though he is very happy where he is, he is never content to remain there. He always strives for even greater achievements.

This person may report that he is never satisfied with his current situation in any domain. If he takes the "Satisfaction with Domains of Life" test he may say that he is *dissatisfied* in every domain. The inference would be that he is unhappy, but again this would be wrong. He is very happy; it's just that he wants always to be rising. 'I'm happy where I am, but never satisfied. I would be even happier with more!'

These examples taken together suggest to me that if we want to measure something that could reasonably be called 'happiness,' and if we want the thing we are measuring to be plausibly linked with well-being, then we should not focus on levels of satisfaction with domains of one's own life. A person can be happy—and things can be going well for him—whether he is satisfied with his standing in those domains or not. The tests seem to be measuring the wrong thing.

12.3 *A Better Way to Measure Happiness*

In Chapter 6, I presented a theory of happiness. According to that theory, an atom of happiness is an episode in which a person takes intrinsic attitudinal pleasure in something. A person's momentary happiness level for a moment, t, is defined as the sum, for all propositional objects, P, of the amount of intrinsic attitudinal pleasure that the person takes in P at t. A person's happiness for an interval is the integral of his momentary happiness levels for all the moments in the interval. I went on to argue, in Chapter 7, that there is at least a fairly close connection between a person's level of happiness so construed and his welfare. In other words, the happier we are, the better off we are. If this is right, or even nearly right, then those who are interested in measuring happiness ought to be working with test instruments that yield measurements of this thing I have called happiness.

Consider a single-item test instrument on which the sole question is this:

Q7: Using the word 'happy' in precisely the sense that Feldman explicates in Chapter 6 of his book *What is This Thing Called Happiness?*, would you say you are: (a) very happy; (b) somewhat happy; (c) neutral; (d) somewhat unhappy; or (e) very unhappy?

It will not be necessary to say much about the imagined test instrument. The question would be almost meaningless to nearly every person on earth.

I think a more practical test instrument would aim to measure the thing that I call happiness, but would do it in a more accessible way. It would have a couple of features: first, it would not direct the respondent's attention to any pre-selected set of domains of his life. As we have seen, a person's level of happiness may not be dependent upon his attitude toward happenings in those domains. Maybe he is happy or unhappy mainly about things that are not in those domains. Furthermore, mentioning specific domains may encourage the respondent to think about things that he normally does not think about. It could yield results that do not reflect the subject's actual happiness level, or the happiness level he would have been at if he had not taken the test. Thus, there would be *no pre-selected domains*.

Second, it would not insist that the respondent focus on *his own life*. As I tried to show, in some cases happiness depends upon a person's attitude toward things happening in the lives of others, or in states of affairs that do not involve lives. Thus, it would not focus on *the personal affairs of the respondent*.

Third, if there are domains, or if the respondent is given the opportunity to choose his own list of domains, it may be a good idea to allow the respondent to indicate the centrality of those domains in his emotional life. A favorable attitude toward recent developments in a domain that is a constant focus of attention should weigh more heavily than a similarly favorable attitude toward recent developments in a domain that the respondent rarely considers. There must be some way to record *levels of centrality* of items mentioned in the test.

Finally, the test instrument would not ask the respondent to record levels of *satisfaction*. A person can be satisfied without being happy and can be happy without being satisfied. Instead, it would give him the opportunity to record his level of *attitudinal pleasure or displeasure* with things.

Ideally, then, the test instrument would offer the respondent the opportunity to list the main things he has been thinking about recently. 'What topics have been on your mind during the past few days?' might be a good way to start. Perhaps with an eye toward eventual interpersonal comparisons, the question might direct the respondent to list a specific number of things: 'What would you say are the eight things that have been on your mind most during the past few days?' Then, if in fact he had been thinking about these things, the respondent could list job, finances, housing, amount of leisure time, leisure-time activities, marriage, health, and "my life as a whole." In this case, he would end up focusing on the domains listed in the German study mentioned above. On the other hand, if he had been thinking about other things instead of these, he could list those other things. Perhaps he would list 'political situation in Middle East,' or 'global warming,' or 'the decline of morality among young people today,' and some other things.

Suppose the subject has been thinking of only seven things recently and the test asked for a list of eight. What then? The person administering the test might encourage the subject to think of some minor topic that is of little importance. As I will explain in a moment, listing an extra topic will not affect the outcome of the test.

Then the test instrument could offer the respondent the opportunity to indicate how central these things are to him. This might be done merely by allowing the respondent to place them in order of centrality, but that would yield only a weak ordering. Perhaps a better procedure would be to give each item a score on "centrality in your thoughts recently." The question might be:

Q8: Using 0 to indicate a topic that you have thought about very rarely if at all, and +10 to indicate a topic that has been on your mind constantly recently, please assign a number to each of the eight topics that you have listed.

If the subject has listed some topics that he never thought about, or that just flitted through his consciousness on a few occasions recently, these will get a centrality score of zero. As a result, they will have no impact on the calculations to follow.

Next, we want to know whether the respondent is taking pleasure in these things or taking displeasure in them. Furthermore, we want to know, for each thing, how much pleasure or displeasure he is taking in it. It will be difficult to formulate a simple question that will be guaranteed to elicit precisely the right information, but perhaps something like this will work:

Q9: Using −10 to indicate that you have been very displeased as you thought about the topic, 0 to indicate that you have been neither pleased nor displeased, and +10 to indicate that you have been very pleased about the topic, please assign a number to each of the ten topics you have listed.

The interpretation of the test would be straightforward: for each topic, there will be two numbers, one representing "centrality" and the other representing "pleasure taken in it." These should be multiplied together to yield a weighted pleasure ranking for the item. Then the products should be summed. The result is the respondent's current happiness level.

There are a couple of features of the test that make it very likely that a respondent's score on the proposed test would not be precisely the same as his actual happiness level. For one thing, results on the proposed test will have to fall within certain finite boundaries. The highest possible score would be achieved by a person who has been thinking about eight things (if eight is the maximum number of topics allowed on the test), who considers each to be maximally central, and who is maximally pleased about each of them. His score on the test would be $(8 \times 10 \times 10 = 800)$. But the theory of happiness developed in Chapter 6 does not have this feature. According to that theory, there is no upper bound on amounts of happiness. No matter how happy someone is, it is always possible on that theory for someone to be happier. The test concept of happiness has this feature in part because it requires the respondent to list just eight items that he has been thinking about and it assigns a score of +10 to things about which the respondent is maximally pleased. The Chapter 6 theory imposes no such limits.

A second difference concerns intrinsicality. Largely in an effort to avoid conceptual complexity, the proposed test simply asks the respondent to indicate how pleased he is about the items he has mentioned. It does not ask him to distinguish between intrinsic pleasure and extrinsic pleasure. It is possible that this will allow some cases of double counting to slip through. Careful questioning of respondents might make it possible for such double counting to be eliminated.

A third difference concerns time. According to the theory presented in Chapter 6, the atoms of happiness are momentary states in which a person is taking intrinsic attitudinal pleasure in something *at an instant*. The person's momentary happiness level is the sum of the values of these atoms for a moment. Happiness during an interval is the integral of momentary happiness levels. But the proposed test does not ask the subject to report on the things he is pleased or displeased about *at the very moment of the test*. Instead, it asks him to report on the things he has been thinking about *recently*. In this way the test yields results about a vague interval—"the last week or so."

The subject's recollections may be wrong. He may report that a certain item had a low level of centrality during the past week or so, when in fact it had a higher level of centrality. He may neglect to report a certain item even though he in fact did think about it, and his level of happiness in fact was affected by it. These are weaknesses in the proposed test. Unfortunately, I do not see any practical way of eliminating them.

12.4 *Review of Cases*

Earlier, I discussed some cases. The cases were constructed in such a way as to highlight what I take to be deficiencies in a typical "Satisfaction with Domains of My Life" test instrument. Now I'd like to return to those cases. I'd like to explain why I think my proposed test would yield more meaningful scores.

Recall Case 1. This case involved two subjects. I stipulated that Subject A is smiling because he is pleased about his progress in racquet ball. I also stipulated that racquet ball is a matter of real significance to him. He thinks about it all the time. At the same time, A is aware of the fact that he has a marginal job that does not pay well. Fortunately for him, financial matters are not important to him. He ignores this most of the time. I also stipulated that B is frowning because he is troubled by some recent developments at his job.

They were asked to record their levels of satisfaction with seven pre-selected domains of life. Their results were as follows:

	Subject A	Subject B
Job	Somewhat dissatisfied	Somewhat dissatisfied
Finances	Somewhat dissatisfied	Somewhat dissatisfied
Housing	Somewhat dissatisfied	Somewhat dissatisfied
Social life	Somewhat dissatisfied	Somewhat dissatisfied
Marriage	Somewhat dissatisfied	Somewhat dissatisfied

Health	Somewhat satisfied	Somewhat satisfied
Leisure	Somewhat satisfied	Somewhat satisfied

These test results suggest that A and B are equally happy, but that would be a mistake. Behavior, affect, mood, and statements made by the subjects, all suggest that A is much happier than B; indeed, that B is actually unhappy at the time of the test.

Now suppose these same subjects are asked to take my proposed test. Each is asked to list the topics about which he has been thinking. For each topic, the subject is to record a level of centrality and a level of pleasure or displeasure. Perhaps the results of A's test would look like this:

	centrality	pleasure taken in	weighted pleasure
Job	2	−2	−4
Finances	2	−2	−4
Housing	2	−2	−4
Social life	2	−2	−4
Marriage	2	−2	−4
Health	8	+8	+64
Racquetball	8	+8	+64
Total Happiness:			+108

When B takes the test, he mentions the same topics, but he ranks them differently for centrality as well as for pleasure. His test sheet looks like this:

	centrality	pleasure taken in	weighted pleasure
Job	8	−4	−32
Finances	8	−4	−32
Housing	8	−4	−32
Social life	8	−4	−32
Marriage	8	−4	−32
Health	2	+2	+4
Racquetball	2	+2	+4
Total Happiness:			−152

We see, then, that my proposed test indicates in this (imaginary) example, that Subject B is much less happy than Subject A. The explanation is simple: B is displeased about several things that he is obsessing about; A is pleased about two things that are always on his mind. This disparity in happiness levels was not revealed by the "Satisfaction with Life Domains" test.

It also seems to me that my proposed test is designed to measure something that is of axiological significance. It seems to me that happiness as measured by my proposed test is conceptually linked to happiness as understood by the theory developed in Chapter 6—Intrinsic Attitudinal Hedonism about Happiness. As I tried to show in

Chapter 7, it is reasonable to suppose that happiness (so construed) provides a good estimate of a subject's welfare (at least in a wide variety of typical cases). If all this is right, then the proposed test gives at least a rough guide to welfare, whereas the "Satisfaction with Life Domains" does not. My axiological intuition tells me that in the imagined case (unless there are other important factors that have been left out) Subject A is in fact enjoying higher welfare than Subject B. My test confirms this; the "Satisfaction with Domains of Life" test does not.

Recall now Case 2. This case also involved two subjects. Subject A is smiling because he just heard that a hated political figure ("Dixon") has been indicted, charged with taking bribes. Subject B is frowning because he admires Dixon, and he just heard the same news. He is unhappy about this. The case is intended to highlight the fact that in some cases a person's happiness depends upon something that is not a domain of his own life. Sometimes it is something "external." This focus of happiness would not be reflected in the "Satisfaction with Life Domains" test. Neither subject would be given an opportunity to record his attitude toward the news about Dixon, yet that news is clearly affecting their emotional lives.

But now consider the results of my proposed test. When A takes the test, he comes up with a list of topics that includes the political news; and his happiness score is dramatically affected by his attitude toward that topic:

	centrality	pleasure taken in	weighted pleasure
Job	2	+5	+10
Finances	2	+5	+10
Health	2	+5	+10
Housing	2	+5	+10
Social life	2	+5	+10
Marriage	2	+5	+10
Dixon Indictment	10	+10	+100
Total Happiness:			+160

Earlier, I stipulated that Subject B really likes Dixon, and is dismayed by the news of his indictment. Assume that B is relevantly like A in other areas. Then his test results might look like this:

	centrality	pleasure taken in	weighted pleasure
Job	2	+5	+10
Finances	2	+5	+10
Health	2	+5	+10
Housing	2	+5	+10
Social life	2	+5	+10
Marriage	2	+5	+10
Dixon Indictment	10	−10	−100
Total Happiness:			−40

Previously, I described two cases that were intended to show that there is a difference between *satisfaction* and *happiness*. I'd like to focus on the second of these. It involved an individual whose motto is 'Aim for the stars!' He has a wonderful job, financial situation, and marriage. He is in excellent health and enjoys his leisure activities. He is vibrant, optimistic, and cheerful. He seems to be very happy. Yet he claims that he is not satisfied with his standing in any domain; he always looks forward to even greater achievements. I suggested that a "satisfaction with domains of life" test would declare this individual to be unhappy, whereas in fact he seems to be extraordinarily happy.

The problem, as I see it, is that the test measures the wrong thing. It asks the subject whether he is satisfied with his standing in the domains. This subject says that he is not satisfied. He derives a lot of pleasure from his activities in each domain; but he always wants more. Thus, if we are interested in the subject's current level of happiness, we should not ask about *satisfaction*. We should ask about the pleasure (or displeasure) he is taking in the domains and in life in general. If this individual were to take my proposed test, he would first be asked to list things that he has been thinking about. Let's assume that he would mention his job, financial situation, health, leisure activities, marriage, and social life. But, instead of asking about *satisfaction*, my test would ask the subject to indicate how much *pleasure or displeasure* he takes in these things, as well as the level of centrality for each. If he answers the questions as I think he might, his results would be:

	centrality	pleasure taken in	weighted pleasure
Job	8	+8	+64
Finances	8	+8	+64
Health	8	+8	+64
Leisure	8	+8	+64
Housing	8	+8	+64
Social life	8	+8	+64
Marriage	8	+8	+64
Total Happiness:			+448

Note that this subject did not take maximal pleasure in any domain. That's because he is always striving for more. He recognizes that while his achievements are wonderful, there is still room for improvement. He would be more pleased if he had reached the highest possible level of achievement. Thus, he does not record +10 in any domain.

I think that if we are interested in how happy this subject is, it would make more sense to use my proposed test rather than a test that asks respondents to indicate levels of satisfaction with pre-selected domains of his own life.

12.5 *Methodological Comments*

I am inclined to think that my proposed test would provide a good measure of happiness. I hypothesize that it would provide a better measure of happiness than a typical "satisfaction with domains of life" test. How can my hypothesis be tested?

Ideally, we might like to proceed by working up an actual test instrument like the one I have sketched. We could then administer the test to a suitably large number of subjects. Then we could compare their scores on the test with their actual levels of happiness. We could also compare their scores with their actual levels of welfare, or well-being. Then we could calculate the validity of the test both as a measure of happiness and as a measure of welfare. If the test had high validity on both counts, we could declare that my hypotheses have been confirmed: the proposed test is a good measure of happiness and welfare.

Obviously, however, it is impossible to do the imagined evaluation. There is no independent way to determine actual levels of happiness or welfare. Thus, there are no independent scores to be compared with the scores on the imagined test. We must remain content with something less.

Empirical researchers confront this problem with any test designed to measure an elusive and controversial quantity. (Think of the controversies about proposed measures of intelligence.) In some cases, researchers have claimed that their tests have "desirable psychometric properties."[9] It may be alleged that high test-retest reliability is one of these properties.

To say that an instrument has high test-retest reliability is to say that subjects tend to get the same score on that instrument when they take the test again later. When the instrument is intended to measure something that remains relatively constant, a high test-retest correlation would seem to be a good thing. Thus, for example, suppose we have a device that is intended to measure the weight of steel ingots. Suppose we place an ingot on the device and it records '10 pounds.' Suppose the ingot is then placed in a cool, dark closet for 24 hours and then placed on the measuring device again. Suppose the device records '14 pounds.' We would have good reason to be worried about the device. But if the device recorded '10 pounds' every time we put the

---

[9] Diener et al. made this claim about their "Satisfaction with Life Scale," in Diener et al. (1984: 72).

ingot on it, we would assume that it is doing a good job of weighing the ingot. We could say that the device has very high test-retest reliability.

Our confidence in this case depends entirely on an important feature of the example. The steel ingot sits unmolested in a cool, dark closet between weighings. We assume that its weight remains constant. But the corresponding assumption would be unrealistic in the case of a test designed to measure happiness. Subjects do not sit in cool, dark closets between test sessions. They undergo all sorts of experiences. Clearly, their experiences may affect their levels of happiness. Furthermore, even if they have a relatively steady stream of unchanging experiences, their emotional state can change. The job, salary, housing situation, etc., that I found pleasant last year might by now seem tedious and unpleasant. Whereas I was happy last year, this year I am unhappy. It does not seem reasonable to look for high test-retest reliability in a test for a feature—like happiness—that is assumed to fluctuate. Thus, we cannot appeal to this allegedly desirable psychometric feature to evaluate my proposed test.

Some researchers evaluate proposed test instruments by comparing the results given by the proposed test with the results of other test instruments already in circulation. This might yield interesting information in some cases. For example, suppose someone comes up with a new design for a scale for weighing steel ingots. Suppose he tests the new scale by comparing its results to the results given by several of the most accurate scales currently in use. The results generated by the new scale may be different from the results generated by any of the old scales, but still the comparison may tend to show that the new scale is doing a good job of measuring the weight of the ingots. This could happen, for example, if the weights recorded by the new scale are consistently lower than those recorded by the old scale that always gave the highest weights of all tested scales. Similarly if the weights recorded by the new scale are consistently higher than the weights recorded by the old scale that always gave the lowest weights.

This sort of comparison might be useful in the evaluation of many sorts of test instruments, but I think it would be much less useful in the evaluation of a proposed test for happiness. Part of the trouble, as I see it, is that some of the old tests were intentionally designed to measure satisfaction with domains of life. I have given reasons for thinking that happiness does not vary in accord with this sort of satisfaction. I would take it as a cause for concern if my proposed test for happiness always yielded results coincident with the results yielded by a test such as the BHPS. Similarly, I would take it as a cause for concern if my proposed test always yielded results coincident with the results yielded by a test that measured amounts of sensory pleasure and pain. In earlier chapters of this book I have tried to show that there is something wrong with the theories of happiness upon which such tests are apparently based. I have attempted to sketch a possible test with the conscious intention that it should measure something that those tests are not designed to measure. I would prefer to have a test that measures the thing that I take to be happiness—that is, the net amount of intrinsic attitudinal pleasure that a subject is experiencing. Since those other tests are not designed to measure this thing, I would take it as no problem at all if my test were to yield results inconsistent with the results yielded by those tests.

Thus, many of the techniques that are used to evaluate happiness tests are not suitable for the evaluation of my proposed test. Nevertheless, it seems to me that there are things that can be said for or against the proposed test. I want to focus on three of these.

First, we are looking for a test that will measure something that corresponds fairly closely to some pre-theoretical concept of happiness. A mark of success here would be that people who score higher on the test should be, by and large, people who would naturally be described by themselves and by those who know them well as "happier." I have described several cases in which (as it seems to me) happier people would score higher on the proposed test. I have also explained how the item measured by the proposed test relates to the concept of happiness that I explicated in Chapter 6. If my claims on behalf of the Chapter 6 analysis of happiness are plausible, and if the proposed test yields measurements of something quite like that concept, then the test does well on the first criterion.

I recognize that this is largely a matter of linguistic intuition. I described some cases. I tried to give sufficient detail. I ask the fair-minded reader to consider whether he or she would describe the individuals in question as 'happy.' I tried to show that it is reasonable to suppose that if such individuals were to take the test, they would have scores that would reflect what we take to be their levels of happiness. The ones we would describe as 'happier' would probably have higher scores. I have informally discussed these cases with friends and colleagues. They seem to share my linguistic intuitions. I recognize that this is far from conclusive. Perhaps someone will want to develop a scheme for more rigorous testing. I would welcome the opportunity to have someone construct and administer a test such as the one I described; I would welcome the opportunity to have it evaluated.

There is a widespread notion that the word 'happy' in English is ambiguous, and (in the relevant sense) vague. So it might be thought that there simply is no such thing as "the concept of happiness." Nevertheless, it might be reasonable to suppose that among the various senses of 'happy,' or within the vague blur of possible meanings for the term, there is one precisification that is of special interest. That would be the precise sense of the term in which it expresses something that tracks welfare. In other words, there might be some explication of the concept of happiness that has this feature: the happier (in this sense) a person is, the higher his welfare. This gives rise to a second criterion that can be applied to my proposed test.

I have described several imaginary cases. I have attempted to provide sufficient detail so that the reader can visualize the individuals involved. I have indicated my view about the level of welfare enjoyed (or suffered) by the imaginary subjects. I have asked the reader to consider whether he or she would agree with my assessments. Thus, in Case 1 I said that, in spite of equal satisfaction levels, Subject A was actually happier than Subject B. I based this assessment on the stipulated fact that A was taking considerable pleasure in a matter (racquet ball) that was deeply important to him, while Subject B was displeased about matters (his job and financial situation) that were deeply important to him. I would say that things are "going better" for A than they are for B. I ask the reader to reflect on the case dispassionately; see if you also would say that A's welfare is higher than B's.

The second criterion, then, is this: we seek a test not just for any random concept of happiness, but for a concept of happiness that serves as an explication or precisification of the concept of happiness that figures in the formulation of a fairly attractive form of eudaimonism. We want a test for a concept of happiness that (at least in the typical run of cases) tracks welfare. My hope is that the proposed test has this feature too. I have attempted to explain how the proposed test would measure the extent to which subjects are taking attitudinal pleasure in things; and I have claimed that we can call this a form of happiness; and I have argued (in Chapter 7) that one's happiness level (so understood) tracks one's level of welfare. I leave it to the interested reader to reflect on the cases, and to see whether he or she agrees with my evaluation of the welfare levels of the characters depicted.

The third criterion is more practical. We want a test that will provide a measure of a concept of happiness that is reasonably clear, precise, open to some sort of observation, and at least in principle measurable. The test I have proposed is designed to measure (approximately) the concept of happiness that I explicated in Chapter 6. That concept of happiness seems to me to be pretty clear and precise. To be happy, in that sense, is to take intrinsic attitudinal pleasure in things. In a wide range of typical cases, a thoughtful subject will be able to tell what he is pleased about. If you see a broad smile on someone's face and you ask him what he's so pleased about, he will be able to give a reasonable answer—at least in the typical case. If you carefully explain the significance of the numbers on a numerical scale indicating degrees of attitudinal pleasure and displeasure, a subject may be able to understand the meaning of the scale and he may be able to indicate, for each main thing he has been thinking about, how pleased or displeased he is about it.

Obviously, it will be difficult to be sure that different subjects interpret the scale in the same way. Interpersonal comparisons may be open to some doubt. It would be silly to deny this. Nevertheless, I think the proposed test does at least as well on the practicality criterion as other tests currently in use.

I am not a psychologist. I have no experience in the construction or testing of psychological tests. Thus, I am not qualified to pursue my proposal much further. But if others with the relevant expertise were to attempt to construct a proper test relevantly like the one I have described, I would be delighted. And if they could administer the test to a suitable collection of victims, I would be very eager to see their results. I have not done these things. I make no claims for my idea beyond these: it is intended to measure what I take to be the relevant sort of happiness; it is intended to yield results bearing on welfare; it is intended to be implementable.

CHAPTER 13

Empirical Research; Philosophical Conclusions

In recent years, there has been a tremendous surge of interest in happiness. It seems that just about every week there is an announcement of a new book on the nature of happiness, or the measurement of happiness, or the causes of happiness, or the history of happiness. Some of these books have been written by philosophers. Others have been written by psychologists, economists, sociologists, and other empirical scientists.

One feature of this burgeoning literature especially interests me. There are many instances in which it is alleged that some body of empirical research has important implications for some long-standing philosophical question. The suggestion seems to be that philosophers had better pay more attention to the work of their colleagues in psychology or economics, lest they embarrass themselves by being ignorant of important findings that bear directly on their philosophical work.[1] This suggestion meshes nicely with the current "science worship" prevalent among some philosophers.[2]

In this chapter, I focus on one particularly stark instance in which it is claimed—or at least it seems to be claimed—that empirical research yields philosophical conclusions concerning happiness.

---

[1] This attitude may be illustrated by this remark from Daniel Haybron: 'Philosophical reflection on the good life in coming decades will likely owe a tremendous debt to the burgeoning science of subjective well-being and the pioneers, like Ed Diener, who brought it to fruition. While the psychological dimensions of human welfare now occupy a prominent position in the social sciences, they have gotten surprisingly little attention in the recent philosophical literature. The situation appears to be changing, however, as philosophers begin to follow the lead of their peers in psychology and other disciplines and examine seriously the psychology of human flourishing' (Dan Haybron, 'Philosophy and the Science of Subjective Well-Being,' in Michael Eid and Randy J. Larsen, *The Science of Subjective Well-Being* (2008)).

[2] For a vigorous and amusing discussion of the pernicious effects of "scientism," see section 9.4.4 of Michael Huemer's *Ethical Intuitionism*.

13.1   *Layard on the Reality of Happiness*

In his Lionel Robbins Memorial Lecture,[3] as well as in his book on happiness,[4] the distinguished British economist Richard Layard provides a brief summary of some empirical research that was undertaken by Richard Davidson, a psychologist at the University of Wisconsin. According to Layard, Davidson had taken brain scans of various subjects while they were undergoing certain controlled experiences. After describing this research, Layard concludes by saying, 'I hope I have persuaded you that there is such a thing as happiness, as Bentham believed.'[5] Apparently, Layard is claiming that Davidson's empirical research provides reason for us to accept the conclusion that "there is such a thing as happiness" or, as he expresses it in his book, that "happiness exists."

Layard's remark is puzzling. He seems to be saying that Davidson's empirical research provides support for what appears to be a metaphysical or conceptual conclusion ("there is such a thing as happiness"). I wonder whether the metaphysical conclusion needs any sort of support; I wonder how it could be thought that Davidson's research provides that support. Let us look more closely into this.

Davidson and his colleagues at Wisconsin did a lot of studies involving brain-imaging technology. Among other things, they put people in MRI machines, or gave them PET scans, or EEGs. In some cases, they asked their subjects how they were feeling. They discovered that there is a high correlation between reports of "positive feelings" and 'brain activity in left side of the pre-frontal cortex, somewhat above and in front of the ear.' (For convenience in what follows, let us call this the 'LH area' of the brain—short for 'Left Happiness.') This finding emerged only in cases in which the subjects were right-handed. In left-handed people, Davidson discovered a correlation between "positive affect" and increased activity in the corresponding area on the other side of the brain. (Let us call this the 'RH area.') In another series of experiments, people were put into an MRI machine. They were shown pictures of babies. One of the pictures showed a cute smiling baby; another displayed a baby with a disturbing facial deformity. Davidson found that there is a high

---

[3] 'Happiness: Has Social Science A Clue?,' delivered at the London School of Economics on March 3, 4, and 5, 2003; Lecture One: 'What Is Happiness? Are We Getting Happier?'
[4] Richard Layard, *Happiness: Lessons from a New Science* (2005).
[5] Layard (2003: 11). In the corresponding passage in Layard (2005: 24), he says, 'I hope I have now persuaded you that happiness exists and is generally good for your physical health.'

correlation between seeing the cute baby and having increased activity in the LH area (whereas there is a high correlation between seeing the deformed baby and having increased activity in the RH area). Again, this held true for right-handed subjects, but the reverse was true for left-handed subjects. In yet another series of experiments, it was found that right-handed people who have a lot of activity in the LH area also tend to smile a lot and also are judged by their friends to be pretty happy, whereas right-handed people who have a lot of activity in the RH area tend to report "negative thoughts" and to smile less and to be reported as being less happy. It was also found that when babies suck on something nice, their LH area becomes active. And it was also found that 2.5-year-old toddlers with active LH areas are more exploratory, whereas other children who tend to cling to their mothers had lower amounts of activity in the LH area.[6]

In fact, Davidson and his colleagues have performed many more experiments. Their work has been described in great detail in an impressive series of publications.[7] It has also been discussed in a number of newspapers and magazines.[8] Though brief, Layard's summary seems fundamentally accurate and is certainly adequate for our purposes here.

Layard evidently thinks that, after learning about Davidson's work, we should be persuaded that 'there is such a thing as happiness.' How would the reasoning go?

On the most straightforward interpretation, the argument (admittedly somewhat compressed) would look like this:

Argument A

1. There is a high correlation between increased activity in the LH area and reported positive thoughts, being reported as happy, seeing cute babies, sucking on something nice, and exploring.
2. If (1), then there is such a thing as happiness.
3. Therefore, there is such a thing as happiness.

Premise (1) is intended to be a brief summary statement of some of Davidson's results. Premise (2) links these results to Layard's conclusion (3). But (2) seems to presuppose several contentious assumptions. It will be worthwhile to make these more explicit.

---

[6] This research is summarized in Layard (2005: 17–25) in a section entitled 'Brainwaves.'

[7] A list of publications can be found at: <http://psyphz.psych.wisc.edu/>.

[8] See, for example, Penelope Green 'This is Your Brain on Happiness' (2008: 233–5). For a list of popular newspaper and magazine articles, as well as TV interviews, see Davidson's website at: <http://psyphz.psych.wisc.edu/>.

So far as I have been able to determine, Davidson himself never explicitly said that the subjects in his experiments were all happy. Rather, he described them in a variety of other ways. Some were said to be crawling around energetically; others were said to be sucking on "something nice;" others were looking at pictures of cute babies. Perhaps the underlying assumption is that those subjects were all happy, whereas babies who were clinging to their mothers and sucking on things that were sour were unhappy. Let us consider what happens to the argument when this is made explicit.

Perhaps the argument would be expanded as follows:

Argument B

1. There is a high correlation between increased activity in the LH area and reported positive thoughts, being reported as happy, seeing cute babies, sucking on something nice, and exploring.
2. If (1), then there is a high correlation between increased activity in the LH area and happiness.
3. If there is a high correlation between increased activity in the LH area and happiness, then there is such a thing as happiness.
4. Therefore, there is such a thing as happiness.

When the argument is expanded in this way, some of its weaknesses become more obvious. Premise (2) is a focus of several different sorts of trouble; (2) is puzzling partly because nothing has been said to support the assumption that the subjects were actually happy when undergoing the listed experiences or engaging in the listed activities. There's no evidence that subjects who were seeing pictures of cute babies were happier than those seeing pictures of deformed babies. Or that infants clinging to their mothers or not sucking are less happy than those exploring or sucking. The pieces of information that have actually been given might bear not on happiness, but on pleasure, or curiosity, or feelings of security, or even thirst. In order to establish (2), one would first have to run an entirely different experiment. One would have to give the babies sweet things to suck on, etc., and then determine whether they were happy. If it could be shown that sucking and crawling babies, people looking at pictures of cute babies, and so on are all happy, then we would have some support for premise (2). So far as I know, Davidson never attempted any such experiment. It is hard to imagine how such an experiment could be constructed. It would require that we have some independent way of determining when all these subjects are happy. In the case of the adults, of course, the experimenter could just ask them if they are happy.[9] In the case of the babies, the determination would presumably be based on the idea that thoughtful researchers can tell when a baby is happy just by observing the baby's behavior and facial expression.

But these problems may seem to be relatively trivial. Perhaps we may be permitted to assume that the sucking and crawling babies were happy. Even granting this point, the argument would still be puzzling. The deeper problem with premise (2) is that it seems to presuppose precisely the thing that the argument is designed to establish. That is, premise (2) presupposes that the subjects in Davidson's experiments were happy when they were sucking on sweet things and crawling around, and so forth. But of course if there is no such thing as happiness, this could not be true. If there were no such thing as happiness, no one would ever be happy. Hence, the assumption that the subjects were happy during the experiments begs the question at issue. It assumes that there is such a thing as happiness. What could be the point in assuming that a certain bunch of subjects are all happy, and then finding that there are some physiological similarities among them, and then concluding that there is such a thing as happiness? The existence of the physiological similarity may be interesting, but it does nothing to establish that there is such a thing as happiness; the existence of happiness was already assumed when the subjects were assumed all to be happy.

In some passages in his papers, Davidson himself speaks more generally of "positive emotions." Maybe he was thinking that the crawling and sucking babies, the observers of pictures of cute babies, and the others in his experiments were all alike in this respect: they all were experiencing "positive emotions" while their brains were being scanned. While one might of course fuss about the painfully vague phrase 'positive emotions,' let us consider what happens to the argument if we understand it in this way.[10]

---

[9] As I attempted to show in Chapter 12, there is considerable doubt whether asking this "single measure" question would be entirely decisive.

[10] I said that 'positive emotions' is vague. I'd like to say a bit more about that. I tried to find a definitive account of positive emotions. I did not succeed. I found a list that is reproduced on many websites. It contains 310 allegedly positive emotions starting with 'absolved,' 'abundant,' and 'accelerated,' and going all the way to 'worthy,' 'yielding,' and 'zealous.' It seemed to me that most of the items on the list are not emotions at all, and hence could not be positive emotions. I saw no particular commonality among the items. I found another list that contained seven items listed as positive emotions. (The URL is: <http://www.worldtrans.org/TP/TP2/TP2A-35.HTML>.) These are: interest, enthusiasm, boredom [*sic*], laughter, empathy, action, and curiosity. The author of this list mentioned that "tears" and "pity" might be positive emotions and might be negative, depending upon the circumstances. I found many more lists, but with

Suppose we alter premise (2) so as to say (roughly) that there is a high correlation between increased activity in the LH area of the brain and "positive emotions." We could then adjust the conclusion so that it said merely that there really are such things as positive emotions. The argument as a whole would look like this:

Argument C

1. There is a high correlation between increased activity in the LH area and reported positive thoughts, being reported as happy, seeing cute babies, sucking on something nice, and exploring.
2. If (1), then there is a high correlation between increased activity in the LH area and positive emotions.
3. If there is a high correlation between increased activity in the LH area and positive emotions, then there are such things as positive emotions.
4. Therefore, there are such things as positive emotions.

There are two main comments to be made about this argument. First, and most obviously, it is no longer clear that the argument establishes any conclusion concerning happiness. There is no mention of happiness in the conclusion. Thus, it would not be relevant to the conclusion that Layard apparently meant to derive. Second, although the precise meaning of the conclusion is unclear, the central point seems to be presupposed in premise (2). Any advocate of this argument would have to assume that sucking and crawling babies, etc., are experiencing positive emotions. If there are no such things as positive emotions, the babies could not be experiencing them. And, if the babies were not experiencing them, the cited experimental evidence could not support the claim that these emotions are correlated with activity in the LH area of the brain. So it appears to me that the argument does nothing to establish that positive emotions exist; rather, it makes use of the assumption that they exist as part of the basis for affirming premise (2).

This whole line of thinking seems to me to be fundamentally confused. Nothing in Davidson's research gives us any new reason to suppose that there is such a thing as happiness. Understood in one way, one of the premises of the argument simply assumes that

little agreement about what justifies including anything on the list of positive emotions. Some listers explicitly say that positive emotions need not be "good" in any way; others say precisely the opposite. I was not able to find two lists that agreed on which emotions should be counted as positive, though there was some overlap. My hunch is that the term is too obscure to be of any value in the reporting of serious empirical research.

there is such a thing as happiness. Understood in another way, it has no relevance to the existence or non-existence of happiness. In any case, it is hard to see why we would need to resort to MRI machines to gain evidence that there is such a thing as happiness. Don't we all know this already simply in virtue of the fact that we have been happy?

13.2 *The "Objective Reality" of Happiness*

Layard actually says that he hopes he has persuaded us 'that there is such a thing as happiness.' However, it is possible that this is a loose and misleading expression of the thesis he meant to affirm. In earlier passages, Layard makes some remarks that suggest another interpretation of his thesis. There, he suggests that the real question is whether when people report being happy their reports 'correspond at all accurately to any kind of objective reality.'[11] He refines this by asking whether when they make those reports 'there is a corresponding event that can be objectively measured.'[12] He goes on to say that it is a 'cardinal variable' and that the 'correlation holds strongly across people, confirming our view that happiness can be compared between people.'[13]

All of this suggests that perhaps Layard was really trying to persuade us of a fundamentally different thesis about happiness. Perhaps his aim in citing Davidson's research was not to persuade us that happiness is real, or that it exists, but rather to persuade us that happiness corresponds to a not-merely-introspectable but externally-observable, intersubjectively measurable (possibly measurable on a cardinal scale) phenomenon. To say that it "corresponds" to this phenomenon is to say presumably that there are laws of nature according to which amounts of happiness are directly proportional to amounts of this intersubjectively measurable phenomenon. The intersubjectively measurable phenomenon is, presumably, electrical activity in the LH area of the brain.

Utilitarianism, hedonism, and other associated normative theories have from the outset been troubled by the difficulties involved in

---

[11] Layard (2003: 8).   [12] Ibid.

[13] Ibid. As a result of some editing and rewriting, these passages do not appear in the same form in Layard (2005). In the later work, he says, 'Brain science confirms the objective character of happiness' (p. 20). He also says, 'We can also use physical measures to compare the happiness of different people' (p. 19). So, though the words have been changed, the suggestion that Davidson's research bears on interpersonal utility comparisons remains.

establishing reliable interpersonal utility comparisons. Critics would allege that there is no empirical observation that can establish that your pleasure when you say '10 hedons' is just as intense as my pleasure when I say '10 hedons.' During the heyday of positivism, it would then be inferred that it makes no sense to say that your pleasure is equal in magnitude to mine (or that it is not equal in magnitude to mine). The whole utilitarian project was thus called into question. Nowadays the positivistic overkill has been discarded, but the problem remains: we worry about adding up numbers when there is no way to determine whether equal units represent quantities that are in fact equal in magnitude.

But, if it can be shown that happiness corresponds to an intersubjectively measurable phenomenon, then the objection can be answered. We can say that even if there is no *direct* way to compare amounts of happiness experienced by me with amounts of happiness experienced by you, still the amounts can be compared *indirectly*. We can in principle accomplish the comparison by noting that amounts of your happiness correspond to levels of electrical activity in the LH area of your brain; that amounts of my happiness correspond to levels of electrical activity in the LH area of my brain; and the levels of electrical activity in our brains can be compared using Davidsonian methods. In this way, it might be claimed, the problem of interpersonal utility comparisons is solved.

If this is really what Layard had in mind, then we get a new interpretation of the argument. As I see it, the argument would go like this:

Argument D

1. There is a high correlation between increased activity in the LH area and reported positive thoughts, being reported as happy, seeing cute babies, sucking on something nice, and exploring.
2. If (1), then there is a high correlation between increased activity in the LH area and increased levels of happiness.
3. If there is a high correlation between increased activity in the LH area and increased levels of happiness, then happiness corresponds to an intersubjectively measurable phenomenon.
4. If happiness corresponds to an intersubjectively measurable phenomenon, then the problem of interpersonal utility comparisons is solved.
5. Therefore, the problem of interpersonal utility comparisons is solved.

In summary, then, the point would be that Davidson's empirical research revealed that amounts of happiness correspond to amounts of electrical activity in the LH area of the brain. Since these amounts of electrical activity are in principle measurable and comparable on a cardinal scale, they make it possible to compare amounts of happiness being experienced by different people. And thus we have a solution to the old problem of interpersonal utility comparisons. I should emphasize that Layard did not present precisely this argument. He stated the claim that appears as the conclusion—'happiness can be compared between people'; he stated the claim that appears as the first premise. I have speculated that he may have intended to derive the conclusion from the premise; I have speculated that he may have been thinking of premises like the ones I have provided.

Whether this is Layard's argument or not, it should be clear that it is unsuccessful. Again we focus on premise (2). Notice that when the empirical researcher performs his experiments, he makes observations on his subjects, including some babies. Baby A is sucking on something sweet and has fairly great electrical activity in the LH area of its brain; similarly for Baby B. The researcher has his MRI machine to determine the levels of electrical activity. Perhaps the levels are observed to be equal. In order to establish a correlation between amounts of happiness and amounts of electrical activity, the researcher must first determine that the babies are enjoying equal amounts of happiness. But how does the researcher determine that Baby A is just as happy as Baby B? From the fact that they go on sucking, nothing follows about levels of happiness. Maybe Baby A sucks that much when he is very happy, while Baby B sucks that much when she is considerably less happy. Maybe she is not happy at all, just thirsty. From the fact that they smile while sucking, nothing follows about levels of happiness. Maybe Baby A smiles broadly when moderately happy, while Baby B smiles narrowly when very happy. The researcher must then just assume that if the babies are sucking equally vigorously and smiling equally broadly, they must be equally happy. Obviously, however, if the researcher does this he has simply assumed that he has the capacity to make interpersonal comparisons of happiness—which is precisely the thing that the argument in its present form is supposed to establish. One could not ask for a more blatant example of begging the question.

It is possible that Layard cited Davidson's research merely to support an even weaker conclusion. Assume first that there is such a thing as happiness; it exists. It is a psychological state that we can observe in ourselves by introspection. Assume next that when other people observe us, they are sometimes able to tell how happy we are. Perhaps they do this by observing our smiles; perhaps they do it by listening to our declarations of happiness. Assume finally that outside observers have the capacity to compare the amount of happiness experienced by one person with the amount of happiness experienced by another. Let us agree, for the time being, that none of these assumptions is in question.

Perhaps Layard cited Davidson's research merely to support the thesis that amounts of an observable, objectively measurable brain state correspond pretty closely to amounts of happiness. The brain state, of course, would be electrical activity in the LH area. The argument would not be relevant to the question whether happiness exists, because that would be a presupposition of the research. Nor would it be relevant to the question about interpersonal utility comparisons, because the research methodology presupposes that we can make these comparisons prior to the use of MRI machines. All it would show is that variations in one observable, measurable, interpersonally comparable phenomenon (happiness) correspond to variations in another observable, measurable, interpersonally comparable phenomenon (electrical activity in the LH area).

Of course, since I am a philosopher, I am interested in philosophical questions. When I read Layard's words, I thought he was claiming that Davidson's research was relevant to a familiar and important philosophical question. On the present interpretation, that would be a mistake. The claim here is not that Davidson's research has any relevance to any philosophical question. It's interesting, presumably, simply because it shows that there is a correlation between happiness and a certain kind of brain activity.

It's not clear to me why anyone would care about this. Surely no one would claim that it paves the way toward an easier way to measure happiness. Surely no one would think that it would be easier or more convenient to measure happiness indirectly by the use of a machine that weighs 13,000 pounds and costs more than a million dollars when it is possible to measure happiness more straightforwardly just by asking the subject how happy he is.[14] There is no need for a million-dollar machine to measure indirectly what can be measured more straightforwardly just by observing the behavior or listening to the reports of subjects.

---

[14] Information about the weight and cost of a Toshiba MRI recently purchased by Bellevue Hospital in New York can be found here: <http://www.bellevuehospital.com/new_mri_moves_in.htm>.

A somewhat deeper worry is that it is not clear that in fact the subjects studied by Davidson did have degrees of happiness that were proportional to their degrees of LH activity. As I noted above, some of them may have been experiencing some other "positive emotion" and not happiness at all. For all Davidson has shown, it remains possible that some subjects were experiencing more intense positive emotions than others even when they were found to have equal amounts of electrical activity in the LH area.

13.3 *Happiness as a Natural Kind*

There is yet another way to understand Layard's claim that 'there really is such a thing as happiness.' There is not much in Layard's lecture or book that would substantiate the claim that this is what he had in mind when he wrote those words; but I suspect that many philosophers will naturally assume that something like this provides an interesting and plausible reinterpretation or extension of his idea.

The thesis in question essentially involves the notions of "folk psychology," "mature psychology," and "natural kinds." Thus, I should begin by saying a few words about these things. I start with an analogy.

Consider a Just So story about "the sniffles." In an earlier era, and perhaps even today among the naive, there is the concept of "the sniffles." Naive people might say that a person had the sniffles if that person had a runny nose, some inflammation of the nasal passages, perhaps some irritation of the eyes, and so on. Associated with the concept of the sniffles, there might be some naive views about what would cause the sniffles (e.g., a cold, the flu) and some naive views about what could be done to relieve the sniffles (e.g., blow your nose, put on a warm sweater, take a shot of whiskey). As time went by, researchers discovered that some snifflers really had colds, while other snifflers had allergies. These have completely different causal histories and completely different methods are appropriate for their relief. What works for one will not work for the other.

As the insights of the researchers trickled down to the people in the street, they came to see that cases that they had lumped together under the title 'the sniffles' were really of two distinct kinds. In some cases people are suffering from a runny nose due to a cold, and in other cases they are suffering from a runny nose due to an allergy. Instead of speaking of "the sniffles," people began to speak instead of "infectious rhinitis" and "allergic rhinitis." People stopped talking about the sniffles. Eventually the word 'sniffles' will drop out of our vocabulary and the concept will fade into oblivion. It does not carve nature at a joint. It lumps together cases that are in fact of two different natural kinds.

In the earlier era, when people spoke confidently of "the sniffles," they had a whole collection of naive views about colds, runny noses, infections, cures for colds, and so on. This whole body of information, misinformation, superstition, urban legend, etc. may be understood to be a component of "folk medicine." Later, when serious researchers discovered the underlying biological facts, they replaced those naive views with a whole collection of sophisticated views about infectious rhinitis, allergic rhinitis, the causes of each, the remedies for each, and so forth. This whole body of information may be called "mature medicine." The concept of the sniffles is not a component of mature medicine. It has been discarded since it was discovered that nothing in nature corresponds properly to it.

All this suggests another way to interpret Layard's remarks about happiness. We can imagine that the concept of happiness might have turned out to be like the concept of the sniffles. Here's a way in which that could have happened: it might have turned out that when psychologists studied happiness closely, they discovered that there are really two importantly different phenomena currently lumped together under the name of 'happiness.' For example, they might have found that in some people happiness corresponds to increased activity in the LH area, whereas in others it corresponds to increased activity in the J area. They might also have found that LH-happiness has a certain causal history and functional role, and that it presents itself in consciousness in a previously not noticed distinctive way, whereas J-happiness is different in all these ways. Such discoveries, if they had happened, might suggest that in the future people will stop talking about happiness, and will instead talk about LH-happiness and J-happiness. The concept of just plain happiness will disappear.

Although Layard does not say anything quite like this, it is not too far-fetched to imagine that he may have thought that Davidson's research supported the notion that happiness is not a mere figment of some soon-to-be-abandoned folk psychology. Since he found that all instances of happiness have the same underlying neurophysiological basis, his research shows (or at least begins to show) that happiness is a natural kind. The moral of his research is that the concept of happiness will persist in a mature psychology. So the statement that 'there is such a thing as happiness' might be taken to mean that happiness is a natural kind—the concept of happiness will persist in mature psychology.

If this is the correct interpretation of what's going on here, then the argument should be revised as follows:

Argument E

1. There is a high correlation between increased activity in the LH area and reported positive thoughts, being reported as happy, seeing cute babies, sucking on something nice, and exploring.
2. If (1), then there is a high correlation between increased activity in the LH area and increased levels of happiness.
3. If there is a high correlation between increased activity in the LH area and increased levels of happiness, then happiness is a natural kind; the concept of happiness is not merely a component of naive folk psychology but will persist in mature psychology.
4. Therefore, happiness is a natural kind; the concept of happiness is not merely a component of naive folk psychology but will persist in mature psychology.

It is important to see that this line of thinking is confused.

One focus of difficulty can be seen in premise (2). Suppose that in fact Davidson's research had established that there is a certain kind of increased brain activity that can be found in all the sucking and crawling babies, all the subjects seeing pictures of cute babies, all the subjects reporting "positive thoughts," and so on. Still it would not follow that there is a correlation between that sort of increased brain activity and *happiness*. The problem, as I have already pointed out, is that it is not clear that all of these subjects are in fact happy.

Suppose we accept the currently most popular conception of happiness; we think that happiness is fundamentally a matter of being satisfied with one's life as a whole. Then it is very doubtful that all of Davidson's subjects were happy while undergoing their MRIs. Consider the sucking and crawling toddlers. One may reasonably doubt that those toddlers were satisfied with their lives as wholes (from beginning to end) as they sucked and crawled. One may reasonably doubt that those toddlers were judging that their lives as wholes matched up quite well with their ideals. (Do 2.5-year-old toddlers have life ideals? Do they think about their lives as wholes?)

Consider a toddler in Davidson's experiment who is clinging to his mother. It's possible—even likely—that this toddler would be dismayed if someone started to pull him away from his mother. So he very well may want his current experience to continue. So Kahneman's theory of objective happiness would rate this baby as happy; yet Davidson noted a correlation between clinging behavior and *decreased* activity in the LH area of the brain. He cited these toddlers as examples of *unhappy* subjects.

Possibly those sucking and crawling toddlers were taking intrinsic attitudinal pleasure in the taste of the nice things they were sucking, or were taking pleasure in the sights and sounds they were experiencing as they crawled. In this case, my own theory of happiness would imply that they were happy (given a bunch of other assumptions about their cases). But, of course, it's also possible that they were not happy while taking the test. Maybe they were just curious, or thirsty, or amused. Or maybe they were just crawling around without being in any particular emotional state.

So my point is simple: Davidson's research may have found a neurophysiological commonality among a bunch of people. They had increased activity in the LH area of the brain. It is conceivable that every one of those people was experiencing some sort of "positive emotion" (although it is also conceivable that some of them were not). But there is little evidence to support the notion that every one of them was actually *happy*. Some theories of happiness suggest that they were happy; others suggest that they were not happy. But since there is little agreement about which theory is correct, and there is not much solid evidence about how the subjects were feeling, there is little justification for any claim about their happiness. And, even if they were happy, there is not much evidence to support the notion that their degree of happiness is correlated with the intensity of the electrical activity in their brains.

We may speculate that further research along the lines described would lead us to think that the cluster of "positive emotions" has a uniform neurophysiological basis. In this case, we might also suspect that this cluster should be viewed as a natural kind. Perhaps as our folk psychology matures, we will stop talking about happiness and start to talk about this cluster of positive emotions instead. Under these circumstances, we would likely say that Davidsonian research had no relevance to the question whether happiness is a natural kind. For all he showed, happiness might be a mere folk psychological concept that will not persist. His research, it might be claimed, had relevance only to the question whether "the positive emotion cluster" is a natural kind.

Another important point would remain even if all of Davidson's subjects were happy while undergoing the tests, and even if the degree of their happiness was proportional to the amount of electrical activity in their brains. This point concerns the notion that if we have a single underlying neurological state for all these different instances of happiness, then we should view happiness as a natural kind. We must recall that Davidson's research did not discover a single underlying neurological state in all the cases he studied. In fact, he says that he discovered one underlying state in the case of right-handed subjects, and a different underlying state in left-handed subjects.

Suppose that happiness counts as a natural kind only if it has a single underlying neurological basis. Then (granting all the assumptions just mentioned) Davidson's evidence would suggest that happiness is not a natural kind. Rather, there would instead be two natural kinds—"right handed happiness" and "left handed happiness."

What may be the most troubling feature of the proposed line of argument concerns an apparent presupposition. To bring this out, I want to sketch an implausible scenario. Suppose that Davidson's research had uncovered a surprising fact: even in right-handed people, there are two different areas of the brain that may be correlated with happiness. When right-handed people are happy about things that have already happened, area HP ("happiness about the past") lights up. When right-handed people are happy about things that they think will soon happen, area HF ("happiness in the future") lights up. That would be an interesting and unexpected result.

But it seems to me that even if his research had this surprising finding, the concept of happiness would not go away. It would not be discarded in the trash-bin of naive concepts of mere folk psychology. I suspect that even if people were to come to accept this interesting fact, they would go on describing themselves and others as being "happy." They would continue to wish each other a happy birthday and a happy new year. No one (except as a joke) would say "happy future-oriented new year." Thus, it is hard to see how the actual findings bear on the question whether happiness is a soon-to-be-discarded remnant of mere folk psychology.

So my conclusion is this: in fact, it is not clear that Davidson's research is actually about happiness. Perhaps it was intended to be about a cluster of "positive emotions." But even if it were about happiness, it would not tend to show that happiness is a single natural kind. It would suggest that there are at least two different natural kinds of happiness (right-handed and left-handed). And, finally, even if the empirical research had yielded completely different findings about the neurological basis of happiness, our conviction that "there really is such a thing as happiness" would not have been shaken.

13.4 *Concluding Warnings, Clarifications, Disclaimers*

I want to say a few words about the main points I have tried to make in this chapter. I especially want to emphasize some things that I have not even attempted to establish.

Richard Davidson has been doing a lot of empirical research into what's going on in the brains of people who are in various emotional states. Some of his subjects were experiencing (or were reported to have been experiencing) "positive emotions." Richard Layard strongly suggested that Davidson's research supports some conclusions that are of philosophical interest. First, there is the ontological thesis that 'there is such a thing as happiness, as Bentham believed.'[15] Second, there are some methodological doctrines about the measurement of happiness. Layard suggests that this research provides evidence that happiness corresponds to an 'event that can be objectively measured.'[16] He goes on to say that this corresponding phenomenon is a 'cardinal variable' and the 'correlation [between it and happiness] holds strongly across people, confirming our view that happiness can be compared between people.'[17] This suggests that Layard thinks that Davidson's research has some bearing on the problem of interpersonal utility comparisons. Philosophically inclined readers may suppose that Layard thinks that Davidson's research supports the view that happiness is a natural kind.

I have attempted to show that none of these claims would be correct. In fact, rather than establishing that happiness is real, Davidson's research seems either to presuppose that happiness is real, or to be neutral on this point. Davidson's research may suggest that there is some correlation between levels of electrical activity in the brain and levels of emotions from some vaguely defined set, but the research methodology seems to presuppose that happiness (or positive affect) is measurable on an interpersonally valid cardinal scale. In this case, it would do nothing to *establish* that happiness is measurable. Finally, so far as I can tell, Davidson's research has no bearing on the question whether happiness is a natural kind.

My conclusions are limited to these relatively small points. I have not said that Davidson's research is confused or pointless or a waste of time. Some readers will surely find it interesting to learn that there is a

---

[15] Layard (2003: 11). In the corresponding passage, in Layard (2005: 24), he says, 'I hope I have now persuaded you that happiness exists and is generally good for your physical health.'
[16] Layard (2003: 8).   [17] Ibid.

correlation between levels of a certain kind of brain activity and levels of certain kinds of emotion. For all I know, Davidson's discoveries might have great value. At present, it is not clear to me what this value might be, aside from the fact that it is kind of interesting to know that there is a physiological commonality among cases of positive affect.

Furthermore, I have not said that Davidson's research is of no philosophical interest. For all I know, it might be relevant to some philosophical question. Again, at present, I cannot think of any philosophical question to which that research would be relevant.

Furthermore, I have not said that the empirical research of others in the "positive psychology" field is either pointless or irrelevant to philosophical questions about happiness. Maybe there is some other researcher who has discovered something that bears on some philosophical question.[18] In spite of the fact that I have looked, I have not found any such research. I doubt that it will be found. However, I have not argued for that thesis here.

My point is that the research described by Layard does not have any relevance to the three philosophical issues discussed (or suggested) by Layard (namely, the ontological question about the existence of happiness; the methodological questions about the measurement of happiness; and the metaphysical question about the status of happiness as a natural kind). My claim is that, insofar as those questions are concerned, Davidson's research is irrelevant.

---

[18] For another perspective, see Kesebir and Diener, 'In Pursuit of Happiness: Empirical Answers to Philosophical Questions' (2008: 117–25).

CHAPTER 14

The Central Points of the Project
as a Whole

In this final chapter I would like to try to summarize what I take to be the central points of this project. Some of these are fundamentally philosophical. In making them, I intend to be engaging primarily with other philosophers. In some cases, I am trying to show that certain philosophical views about the nature and value of happiness are wrong. In an important case, I try to show that a certain philosophical view about happiness is right—or at least preferable to others currently under consideration in the literature. Other points that I try to make are directed primarily to non-philosophers. I have in mind those who are interested in empirical research concerning happiness, welfare, well-being, "positive emotions," and so on. I try to show that there are legitimate reasons to be concerned about the conceptual underpinnings of their research.

I want to emphasize the way in which these different claims fit together so as to constitute a comprehensive view about the nature and value of happiness.

First of all, I pointed out that talk of "happiness" is open to misunderstanding. In some cases, we think of happiness as a matter of evaluation. To say that someone is happy is just to say that things are going well for him. But this evaluative concept of happiness must be distinguished from a purely factual concept of happiness. In Part I of this book, I considered some theories about happiness understood as a factual, empirical, probably psychological phenomenon. The aim of such theories is to give an account of the nature of that phenomenon. A variety of theories was considered: sensory hedonism, local preferentism, global preferentism, Whole Life Satisfactionism of many forms, Kahneman's theory, and so on. I assume that each of these theories can be construed as a theory about happiness as a matter of fact. They are not theories about what is likely to cause or increase happiness. Nor are they theories about welfare, or well-being.

I tried to show that every one of these theories is open to objection. None of them (I claimed) gives a plausible account of the nature of happiness. There are pretty clear cases in which the implications of the theory are inconsistent with our common-sense judgments of happiness. Aside from those in the grip of some theory, no one would classify as happy all and only those who are happy according to the theory.

After dealing in this way with the received views in Part I, I presented my own theory of happiness—intrinsic attitudinal hedonism—in Part II. I devoted quite a lot of space to an attempt to explicate the central concept—intrinsic occurrent attitudinal pleasure. Attitudinal pleasure is not a feeling, or sensation; it is a propositional attitude. It's the attitude we attribute to a person when we say that he is pleased about something, or takes pleasure in some fact. I claimed that a person's happiness level at a time is equivalent to the net amount of intrinsic attitudinal pleasure that he is experiencing at that time. I tried to show that my theory provides plausible accounts of all the hard cases, as well as the easy ones.

I then turned away from the descriptive question—'what is the nature of happiness?'—and to the evaluative question: 'does individual welfare track happiness?' I explained a form of eudaimonism that employs my theory of happiness, and I tried to make a case for its plausibility. I claimed, in effect, that the happier you are (understanding happiness in the way I have proposed), the better your life is going for you.

I tried to defend this theory of welfare against a variety of likely objections. One of my main points here was that it is essential that we make sure to understand the concept of welfare correctly. My claim is that welfare tracks happiness; I surely do not mean to defend the view that moral or other excellence tracks happiness. When I say that the good life is the happy life, I do not intend to commit myself to the view that the morally good life is the happy life. I just mean that the welfare-good life is the happy life.

So I have presented a theory about the nature of happiness and I have claimed that it is plausible to suppose that happiness so understood is The Good. We then come to what non-philosophers may take to be the central point of the whole project. In recent years, we have seen the development of a relatively new field of empirical research concerning happiness and other related "positive emotions." This is sometimes called 'Positive Psychology,' or 'Hedonic Psychology.'

Empirical researchers in this field suggest that they are engaged in the psychological, or neurophysiological, or sociological, or economic study of happiness. I tried to indicate (in a respectful, collegial way) that in many cases there is some unclarity about the nature of the item that the empirical researchers are studying. Different contributors seem to be focusing on different subjects. Some say they are studying "subjective well-being"; others say they are studying "whole life satisfaction"; still others indicate that they are looking into "positive emotions." One distinguished contributor says that he is studying a certain item that may be described as 'well-being,' 'utility,' 'happiness,' 'life satisfaction,' or 'welfare.' As far as he is concerned, these terms are interchangeable. I hope it is by now clear that these terms are not interchangeable. There is no single thing that answers to all of them. I think that this confusion at the conceptual foundations of hedonic psychology is a serious problem. This is the problem of obscurity in the "conceptual underpinnings" of hedonic psychology that troubles me.

Evidence of the problem emerges in several different ways. One obvious way is this: one researcher reports that he has discovered that the lifetime curve of happiness takes the shape of a smile; another researcher reports that he has discovered that the lifetime curve of happiness takes the shape of a frown; yet another reports that the curve is a steadily rising roughly straight line. Upon closer inspection it turns out that the researchers are measuring three different things. For all we know, each of the researchers reported correctly on the phenomenon he or she was studying. In some cases, it is not clear what phenomenon that was. Perhaps it was just the scores achieved by respondents on some test. But it is not clear that we should have any particular interest in the shape of the curve of those scores. Do the scores correlate with happiness? Do they correlate with welfare?

Insofar as these empirical researchers are concerned, the central point of the book can now be seen more clearly. I have claimed that there is need for some agreement about the nature of the item that is supposed to be the focus of attention for positive psychologists. It should be some single clearly delineated psychological state. It should be a state whose status as The Good is defensible. It should be something that can be identified and measured. Ideally, it should be something relevantly like the thing ordinary people have in mind when they speak of happiness. I am offering (somewhat boldly, I acknowledge) that the concept of happiness that I have explained and defended in this book is the required state.

I have articulated my concept of happiness with some care. I have explained how it differs from other proposed concepts of happiness. I have defended the idea that our welfare is determined by the amount of happiness (thus construed) that we have. I have suggested that it might be possible to construct a test instrument that would measure amounts of this sort of happiness. I have suggested that this concept of happiness is the best precisification of the rough-and-ready concept of happiness already embedded in common-sense psychology. I have gone further; I have even suggested that this concept of happiness constitutes the core of meaning for ordinary uses of 'happy.'

I have thus completed my part of the project. I have reviewed and criticized other accounts of the nature of happiness. I have offered a novel account of my own. I have argued for the relevance and value of this concept. That, as I see it, is where the philosophical project ends. If I were to go further, I would be overstepping my boundaries and engaging in projects for which I have neither training nor aptitude. So I offer my proposed concept of happiness to others. I hope they find it to be of interest. I hope they will be able to make good use of it in their empirical studies of happiness.

BIBLIOGRAPHY

American Psychiatric Association Task Force on DSM-IV (1994), *Diagnostic and Statistical Manual of Mental Disorders: DSM-IV*, 4th edn (Washington, DC: American Psychiatric Association).

Annas, J. (1993), *The Morality of Happiness* (New York: Oxford University Press).

——(2004), 'Happiness as Achievement', in S. M. Cahn and C. Vitrano, *Happiness: Classic and Contemporary Readings in Philosophy* (2008), pp. 238–45; originally published in *Dialogue* (spring, 2004).

Argyle, M. (1999), 'Causes and Correlates of Happiness', in D. Kahneman, E. Diener, and N. Schwarz, eds, *Well-Being: The Foundations of Hedonic Psychology* (New York: Russell Sage Foundation), pp. 353–73.

——(2001), *The Psychology of Happiness*, 2nd edn (New York: Routledge).

Aristotle (1999), *Nicomachean Ethics*, translated, with Introduction, Notes, and Glossary, by Terence Irwin, 2nd edn (Indianapolis, IN: Hackett).

Austin, D., ed. (1988), *Philosophical Analysis: A Defense by Example* (Dordrecht: Reidel).

Bentham, J. ([1789]1948), *An Introduction to the Principles of Morals and Legislation*, edited by Laurence Lafleur (New York: Hafner).

Blanchflower, D. G., and Oswald, A. J. (2007), *Is Well-Being U-shaped Over the Life Cycle?*, Available online at: <http://www.nber.org.silk.library.umass.edu:2048/papers/w12935>.

Brandt, R. B. (1967), 'Happiness', in P. Edwards, ed., *The Encyclopedia of Philosophy* (New York: Macmillan Publishing Co, Inc. and The Free Press), pp. 413–14.

——(1989), 'Fairness to Happiness'. *Social Theory and Practice: An International and Interdisciplinary Journal of Social Philosophy*, 15: 33–58.

Brännmark, J. (2003), 'Leading Lives: On Happiness and Narrative Meaning'. *Philosophical Papers*, 32, 3: 321–43.

Bruckner, D. W. (2008), 'Philosophical Lessons from Positive Psychology'. *ISUS-X, Tenth Conference of the International Society for Utilitarian Studies* (Berkeley, CA: Kadish Center for Morality, Law and Public Affairs). Available online at: <http://repositories.cdlib.org/kadish/isus_x/by_D_W_Bruckner>.

Bruni, L., and Porta, P. L. (2005), *Economics and Happiness: Framing the Analysis* (Oxford and New York: Oxford University Press).

Cahn, S. M. (2008), 'A Challenge to Morality', in D. Cahn and C. Vitrano, *Happiness: Classic and Contemporary Readings in Philosophy* (2008), p. 265.

—— and Vitrano, C. (2008), *Happiness: Classic and Contemporary Readings in Philosophy* (New York: Oxford University Press).

Crisp, R., ed. (1996), *How Should One Live? Essays on the Virtues* (Oxford: Clarendon Press).

—— (2006a), 'Review of *Pleasure and the Good Life: Concerning the Nature, Varieties, and Plausibility of Hedonism*'. *Philosophical Quarterly*, 56, 222: 152–4.

—— (2006b), 'Hedonism Reconsidered'. *Philosophy and Phenomenological Research*, 73, 3: 619–45.

—— and Hooker, B., eds (2000), *Well-being and Morality: Essays in Honour of James Griffin* (Oxford: Clarendon Press).

Csikszentmihalyi, M. (1990), *Flow: The Psychology of Optimal Experience*, 1st edn (New York: Harper and Row).

Darwall, S. L. (2002), *Welfare and Rational Care* (Princeton, NJ: Princeton University Press).

Davis, W. (1981a), 'Pleasure and Happiness'. *Philosophical Studies: An International Journal for Philosophy in the Analytic Tradition*, 39: 305–18.

—— (1981b), 'A Theory of Happiness'. *American Philosophical Quarterly*, 18, 2 (April): 111–20.

De Marneffe, P. (2003), 'An Objection to Attitudinal Hedonism'. *Philosophical Studies: An International Journal for Philosophy in the Analytic Tradition*, 115, 2: 197–200.

den Uyl, D., and Machan, T. R. (1983), 'Recent Work on the Concept of Happiness'. *American Philosophical Quarterly*, 20: 115–34.

Diener, E. (1984), 'Subjective Well-Being'. *Psychological Bulletin*, 95, 3: 542–75.

—— (2008), 'Myths in the Science of Happiness, and Directions for Future Research', in M. Eid and R. J. Larsen, eds, *The Science of Subjective Well-Being* (New York: Guilford Press), pp. 493–514.

——, Lucas, R. E., and Oishi, S. (2002), 'Subjective Well-Being: The Science of Happiness and Life Satisfaction', in C. R. Snyder and S. J. Lopez, eds, *Handbook of Positive Psychology* (New York: Oxford University Press), pp. 463–73.

——, Emmons, R. A., et al. (1985), 'The Satisfaction with Life Scale'. *Journal of Personality Assessment*, 49: 71–5.

——, Suh, E. M., Lucas, R. E., and Smith, H. L. (1999), 'Subjective Well-Being: Three Decades of Progress'. *Psychological Bulletin*, 125, 2: 276–302.

Easterlin, R. A. (2005), 'Building a Better Theory of Well-Being', in L. Bruni and P. L. Porta, eds, *Economics and Happiness: Framing the Analysis* (Oxford and New York: Oxford University Press), pp. 29–64.

—— (2006), 'Life Cycle Happiness and its Sources: Intersections of Psychology, Economics, and Demography'. *Journal of Economic Psychology*, 27, 4: 463–82.

Edwards, P., ed. (1967), *The Encyclopedia of Philosophy* (New York: Macmillan Publishing Co, Inc. and The Free Press),

Eid, M., and Diener, E. (2004), 'Global Judgments of Subjective Well-Being: Situational Variability and Long-Term Stability'. *Social Indicators Research*, 65, 3: 245–77.

—— and Larsen, R. J. (2008), *The Science of Subjective Well-Being* (New York: Guilford Press).

Eysenck, M. W. (1990), *Happiness: Facts and Myths* (Hove, East Sussex: Lawrence Erlbaum Associates).

Feldman, F. (1988), 'Two Questions about Pleasure', in D. Austin, ed., *Philosophical Analysis: A Defense by Example* (Dordrecht: Reidel), pp. 59–81.

—— (1997), 'On the Intrinsic Value of Pleasures'. *Ethics: An International Journal of Social, Political, and Legal Philosophy*, 107, 3: 448–66.

—— (2002), 'The Good Life: A Defense of Attitudinal Hedonism'. *Philosophy and Phenomenological Research*, 65, 3: 604–28.

—— (2004a), 'Cahn on Foot on Happiness'. *Journal of Social Philosophy*, 35: 1, 3–7.

—— (2004b), *Pleasure and the Good Life: Concerning the Nature, Varieties, and Plausibility of Hedonism* (Oxford: Clarendon Press).

—— (2006), Review of Kahneman, Diener, and Schwarz, *Well-Being: The Foundations of Hedonic Psychology*. In *Utilitas*, 18, 2: 192–6.

—— (2007), 'Happiness and Subjective Desire Satisfaction: Wayne Davis's Theory of Happiness', in T. Ronnow-Rasmussen, B. Petersson, J. Josefsson, and D. Egonsson, eds, *Hommage a Wlodek: Philosophical Papers Dedicated to Wlodek Rabinowicz*. Available online at: <www.fil.lu.se/hommageawlodek>.

—— (2008), 'Whole Life Satisfaction Concepts of Happiness'. *Theoria: A Swedish Journal of Philosophy*, 74, 3: 219–38.

Foot, P. (1979), 'Moral Relativism'. *The Lindley Lecture* (Kansas: University of Kansas); reprinted in Foot (2002).

—— (2001), *Natural Goodness* (Oxford: Clarendon Press; New York: Oxford University Press).

—— (2002), *Moral Dilemmas and Other Topics in Moral Philosophy* (Oxford: Clarendon Press).

Green, P. (2008), 'This is Your Brain on Happiness'. *The Oprah Magazine* (March): 233–5.

Hawkins, J. (2008), 'Well-Being, Autonomy, and the Horizon Problem'. *Utilitas: A Journal of Utilitarian Studies*, 20, 2: 143–68.

Haybron, D. (2001), 'Happiness and Pleasure'. *Philosophy and Phenomenological Research*, 62, 3: 501–28.

—— (2003), 'What Do We Want from a Theory of Happiness?' *Metaphilosophy*, 34, 3: 305–29.

—— (2008a), 'Philosophy and the Science of Subjective Well-Being', in M. Eid and R. Larsen, *The Science of Subjective Well-Being* (2008), 17–43.

—— (2008b), *The Pursuit of Unhappiness* (Oxford: Oxford University Press).

Hill, S. (2009), 'Haybron on Mood Propensity and Happiness'. *Journal of Happiness Studies*, 10, 2: 215–28.

Hooker, B. (1996), 'Does Moral Virtue Constitute a Benefit to the Agent?', in R. Crisp, ed., *How Should One Live? Essays on the Virtues* (New York: Clarendon Press), 141–56.

Huemer, M. (2005), *Ethical Intuitionism* (Basingstoke and New York: Palgrave Macmillan).

Jost, L. J., and Shiner, R. A., eds (2000), *Eudaimonia and Well-Being: Ancient and Modern Conceptions* (Edmonton, Alberta, Canada: Academic Printing and Publishing).

Kahneman, D. (1999), 'Objective Happiness', in D. Kahneman, E. Diener, and N. Schwarz, eds, *Well-Being: The Foundations of Hedonic Psychology* (New York: Russell Sage Foundation), pp. 3–25.

——and Tversky, A. (2000), *Choices, Values, and Frames* (New York and Cambridge, UK: Russell Sage Foundation and Cambridge University Press).

——, Diener, E., and Schwarz, N., eds (1999), *Well-Being: The Foundations of Hedonic Psychology* (New York: Russell Sage Foundation).

Kamman, R., Farry, M., and Herbison, P. (1984), 'The Analysis and Measurement of Happiness as a Sense of Well-Being'. *Social Indicators Research: An International and Interdisciplinary Journal for Quality-of-Life Measurement*, 15: 91–115.

Kekes, J. (1982), 'Happiness'. *Mind: A Quarterly Review of Philosophy*, 91: 358–76.

Kesebir, P., and Diener, E. (2008), 'In Pursuit of Happiness: Empirical Answers to Philosophical Questions'. *Perspectives on Psychological Science*, 3, 2: 117–25.

Kraut, R. (1979), 'Two Conceptions of Happiness'. *Philosophical Review*, 88: 167–97.

Larsen, R. J., and Fredrickson, B. L. (1999), 'Measurement Issues in Emotion Research', in D. Kahneman, E. Diener, and N. Schwarz, eds, *Well-Being: The Foundations of Hedonic Psychology* (New York: Russell Sage Foundation), pp. 40–60 .

Layard, P. R. G. (2003), 'Happiness: Has Social Science a Clue?' Lionel Robbins Memorial Lecture (London: London School of Economics, March, 2003); available online at: <http://cep.lse.ac.uk/events/lectures/layard/RL030303.pdf>.

——(2005), *Happiness: Lessons from a New Science* (New York: Penguin Press).

Loewenstein, G., and Schkade, D. (1999), 'Wouldn't it Be Nice? Predicting Future Feelings', in D. Kahneman, E. Diener, and N. Schwarz, eds, *Well-Being: The Foundations of Hedonic Psychology* (New York: Russell Sage Foundation), pp. 85–105.

McGill, V. J. (1967), *The Idea of Happiness* (New York: Praeger).

McNaughton, R. (1953), 'A Metrical Concept of Happiness'. *Philosophy and Phenomenological Research*, 14: 172–83.

Mason, E. (2007), 'The Nature of Pleasure: A Critique of Feldman'. *Utilitas: A Journal of Utilitarian Studies*, 19, 3: 379–87.

Mill, J. S. (1957), *Utilitarianism*, edited by Oscar Piest (Indianapolis, IN: Bobbs-Merrill).

Montague, R. (1966), 'Happiness'. *Proceedings of the Aristotelian Society*, 67: 87–102.

Moore, G. E. (1922; 1903), *Principia Ethica* (Cambridge: Cambridge University Press).

Murphy, J. (2008), 'The Unhappy Immoralist', in D. Cahn and C. Vitrano, *Happiness: Classic and Contemporary Readings in Philosophy* (2008), p. 263.

National Opinion Research Center, General Social Survey (Chicago, IL: University of Chicago); available online at: <http://www.norc.org/projects/General+Social+Survey.htm>.

Nettle, D. (2005), *Happiness: The Science Behind Your Smile* (Oxford and New York: Oxford University Press).

Norcross, A. (2007), 'Varieties of Hedonism in Feldman's *Pleasure and the Good Life'*. *Utilitas: A Journal of Utilitarian Studies*, 19, 3: 388–97.

Oishi, S., Schimmack, U., and Diener, E. (2001), 'Pleasures and Subjective Well-Being'. *European Journal of Personality*, 15, 2: 153–67.

Quine, W. V. O. (1960), *Word and Object* (Cambridge, MA: MIT Press).

Rawls, J. (1971), *A Theory of Justice* (Cambridge, MA: Belknap Press of Harvard University Press).

Resnick, L. B., ed. (1976), *The Nature of Intelligence* (Hillsdale, NJ, and New York: Lawrence Erlbaum Associates; distributed by Halsted Press Division of J. Wiley).

Ross, W. D. (1930), *The Right and the Good* (Oxford: Clarendon Press).

Sacks, O. W. (1985; 1987), *The Man Who Mistook His Wife for a Hat and Other Clinical Tales* (New York: Perennial Library).

Schwarz, N., and Strack, F. (1999), 'Reports of Subjective Well-Being: Judgmental Processes and Their Methodological Implications', in D. Kahneman, E. Diener and N. Schwarz, eds, *Well-Being: The Foundations of Hedonic Psychology* (1999), 61–84.

Sen, A. K. (1987), *On Ethics and Economics* (Oxford and New York: Blackwell).

Sidgwick, H. (1962), *The Methods of Ethics*, 7th reissued edn (London: Macmillan).

Snyder, C. R., and Lopez, S. J., eds (2002), *Handbook of Positive Psychology* (New York: Oxford University Press).

Stevenson, C. L. (1938), 'Persuasive Definition'. *Mind: A Quarterly Review of Philosophy*, NS 47, 187: 331–50.

Sumner, L. W. (1992) 'Welfare, Happiness, and Pleasure'. *Utilitas: A Journal of Utilitarian Studies*, 4, 2: 199–223.

——(1996), *Welfare, Happiness, and Ethics* (Oxford: Clarendon Press).

——(2000), 'Something in Between', in R. Crisp and B. Hooker, eds, *Well-being and Morality: Essays in Honour of James Griffin* (Oxford: Clarendon Press), pp. 1–20.

——(2003), 'Happiness Now and Then', in L. J. Jost and R. A. Shiner, eds, *Eudaimonia and Well-Being: Ancient and Modern Conceptions* (Edmonton, Alberta, Canada: Academic Printing and Publishing).

Tatarkiewicz, W. (1966), 'Happiness and Time'. *Philosophy and Phenomenological Research*, 27: 1–10.

——(1976), *Analysis of Happiness*, translated from the Polish by E. Rothert and D. Zielinskn, Vol. 3 in the Melbourne International Philosophy Series (Melbourne, Australia: University of Melbourne); originally published as *O szczęściu* (Warsaw: PWN / Polish Scientific Publishers, 1962).

Taylor, R. (2002), *Virtue Ethics: An Introduction* (Amherst, NY: Prometheus Books).

Telfer, E. (1980), *Happiness* (New York: St. Martin's Press).

Tiberius, V. (2003), 'How's it Going?: Judgments of Overall Life-Satisfaction and Philosophical Theories of Well-Being'. Presented at Minnesota Interdisciplinary Workshop on Well-being. Available online at: <http://www.tc.umn.edu/~tiberius/workshop_papers/Tiberius.pdf>.

van Praag, B. M. S., and Ferrer-i-Carbonell, A. (2004), *Happiness Quantified: A Satisfaction Calculus Approach* (Oxford and New York: Oxford University Press).

White, N. P. (2006), *A Brief History of Happiness* (Malden, MA, and Oxford: Blackwell).

Wilkinson, W. (2007), 'In Pursuit of Happiness Research: Is It Reliable? What Does It Imply for Policy?' *Policy Analysis*, 590 (April 11, 2007). Available online at: <http://www.cato.org/pub_display.php?pub_id=8179>.

Yang, Y. (2008), 'Social Inequalities in Happiness in the United States, 1972 to 2004: An Age-Period-Cohort Analysis'. *American Sociological Review*, 73, 2: 204–26. Available at: <http://news.uchicago.edu/news.php?asset_id=1336>.

Zimmerman, M. J. (2007), 'Feldman on the Nature and Value of Pleasure'. *Philosophical Studies: An International Journal for Philosophy in the Analytic Tradition*, 136, 3: 425–37.

INDEX

Made in the USA
San Bernardino, CA
20 January 2017